THE
CYCLING
BIBLE

THE CYCLING BIBLE

THE COMPLETE GUIDE FOR ALL
CYCLISTS FROM NOVICE TO EXPERT

ROBIN BARTON

FALCONGUIDES

GUILFORD, CONNECTICUT
HELENA, MONTANA

AN IMPRINT OF GLOBE PEQUOT PRESS

To buy books in quantity for corporate use
or incentives, call **(800) 962-0973**
or e-mail **premiums@GlobePequot.com.**

FALCONGUIDES®

Copyright A&C Black Publishers Ltd 2011
First FalconGuides edition 2011

FalconGuides is an imprint of Globe Pequot Press.
Falcon, FalconGuides, and Outfit Your Mind are registered
trademarks of Morris Book Publishing, LLC.

Photography: Gerard Brown
Illustrations: kja-artists.com

Library of Congress Cataloging-in-Publication Data is available on
file.

ISBN 978-0-7627-6999-5

Printed in China

10 9 8 7 6 5 4 3 2 1

NOTE:

The author and Globe Pequot Press assume no liability for
accidents happening to, or injuries sustained by, readers who
engage in the activities described in this book.

CONTENTS

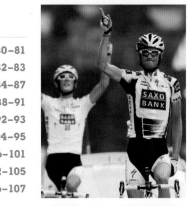

6. CYCLING DESTINATIONS

7. MAINTENANCE

INTRODUCTION

It is astonishing how far a couple of wheels, some metal tubing and a length of chain will take you. Some people have used a bicycle to travel around the world or become household names by racing on one. Others have used a bicycle to become fitter, healthier people, or simply to arrive at work on time without sitting in traffic for hours on end. But something all these different uses have in common is the simple pleasure of cycling.

Whether you're pedalling through Alpine scenery on a vacation or swishing along a city cycleway during your commute, the bicycle is a uniquely liberating and exciting way to travel.

In the 150 years since its invention, the bicycle has had its share of ups and downs. In some countries, such as China and India, it has, until recently, been an essential mode of mass transport. In Western countries, such as Britain, the bicycle has evolved into a piece of leisure or sporting equipment. These distinct views of how a bike can be used, however, are now merging, and a cycling renaissance is taking place across Europe, the USA and beyond.

In cities across the world, from London to Washington, DC, and from Toronto to Melbourne, bike-share schemes are sprouting. Computerized

Left
Beijing, China: Asian cities have depended on the bicycle for many years.

stations dispense sturdy bicycles for short trips around town. The bikes are returned to another kiosk ready for someone else to use. With so many people trying a bicycle again, perhaps for the first time since childhood, it's no surprise that cycling as transport is booming. Bike sales in Britain are predicted to increase to about four million per year in 2015, and miles of new bike paths are being laid. Even in fast-paced New York, hardly the most easy-going city for cyclists, the revolution has taken root, and streets are becoming car-free zones, as more than 1,200 miles of new bicycle lanes are planned to be in place by 2030. The result is an increase of 45 percent in cycle commuting in the three years to 2009: build it, and they will come.

People are turning to cycling for a number of reasons: a concern for the environment or as a way to cut down on vehicle fuel bills, for low-cost exercise or simply as a way of getting from A to B quicker than using a car or bus. And among these new cyclists there will be

some who will want to take their bicycle to new places or race it against other riders. This book charts that progression. Whether you're starting out, riding for fitness or becoming interested in racing, *The Cycling Bible* will share useful insights and information. It will explain how to buy the right bike, get in shape for the sport and teach you all the skills needed to ride farther faster. Road cycling and mountain biking are given equal prominence, and whether you ride on or off the road, you'll be guided through what to wear, the equipment you'll need and how to use it. Safety is a priority for any cyclist too, so expert advice is delivered on reducing all sorts of risk, whether you're commuting to work on busy roads or hitting the trails in your free time.

Top right
Mountain biking pioneers on Mt Tamalpais, California, took cycling to another level.

Right
Bike-sharing schemes are proliferating around the world.

INTRODUCTION

Right
Cycling in the mountains can be exhilarating.

Below
The World Bicycle Relief project in Africa gets school children cycling.

Throughout this book, the bicycle is celebrated. A functional machine it may be, but it inspires great devotion in its riders, whether they're schoolchildren or weekend racers. In part, this is thanks to what the bicycle enables. It's a means of getting together with friends, challenging yourself or simply getting away from daily stresses for a couple of hours to feel the wind in your hair and that sense of weightlessness.

rough-edged pothole, *The Cycling Bible* will explain how to repair a puncture in a matter of minutes.

Cycling's renaissance looks set to continue, attracting ever-greater interest, as a sport, recreation and transport solution. Whether you take up 24-hour mountain bike marathon racing or just take the children to school in a bike trailer, *The Cycling Bible* will be an essential companion.

'The bicycle is the most civilized conveyance known to man,' wrote author Iris Murdoch. 'Other forms of transport grow daily more nightmarish. Only the bicycle remains pure in heart.'

The bicycle opens minds, reveals cities and offers freedom. A cyclist becomes part of the whole scenery, absorbing sights, sounds and smells in an instant. Liberated from the confines of a train or car, the cyclist can take swooping detours through parks, stop to greet friends or freewheel down deliciously thrilling hills. And when the joy of cycling is rudely interrupted by a piece of broken glass or a

HOW TO USE THIS BOOK

Seven chapters introduce you to the key elements of owning a bicycle, from choosing the right bike, through learning how and where to ride it, to maintaining it at home and out on the road.

CHAPTER 1
THE BIKE

There are more types of bikes than ever, from town bikes to mountain bikes that are more expensive than a small car. New materials, technologies and features can seem confusing. But don't be daunted: this chapter looks at all the options, demystifies the jargon and gives practical advice on what to buy and how to get the best deal. It looks at the crucial topic of sizing and how to fine-tune the fit. The final section on security explains how to keep your pride and joy safe.

CHAPTER 2
THE GEAR

Staying warm and dry, whatever the weather, is key to enjoying cycling. This chapter explains what to wear, from top to toe. Cycle helmets and shoes each have a section, as does the rapidly growing range of cyclewear specifically designed for women. Mountain bikers have their own section on protective gear, while gadgets for all cyclists are covered together.

Right
The correct gear makes cycling more fun.

Above and above left
Cycling with friends and family is a great way of spending time together.

CHAPTER 3
TECHNIQUES
& SAFETY

This extensive chapter illustrates the most important skills a cyclist needs, from learning to ride safely on the street to advanced techniques for mountain biking. Clear, step-by-step instructions help wobbly riders improve and explain how best to introduce children to cycling. Diagrams break down complex techniques into simple-to-understand stages. But if you do fall off your bike, a section explains how to minimize the chance of injury.

INTRODUCTION

Above, top
The Tour de France epitomizes the excitement of bike racing.

Above
Fitness science helps the pros with training.

CHAPTER 4
FITNESS & NUTRITION

Riding a bike regularly will make you leaner, but this chapter illustrates how to maximize the health benefits of cycling, regardless of your starting point. Starting with a guide to the body, discover how to build on basic fitness. As you get stronger and faster, you might want to take up training for a goal, such as your first century (riding 100 miles). Fitness routines minimize aches and pains, while a healthy, balanced diet that meets a cyclist's specific nutritional requirements will help you make the most of your cycling experience.

CHAPTER 5
RACING

With training comes speed, and many cyclists will want to test themselves against others. This chapter deals with getting into racing for the first time. There is an introduction to the romance and extraordinary physical feats of the Tour de France. An insight into racing tactics and techniques will give competitors the edge, while an introduction to the world of amateur racing for every ability, on- or off-road, will help first-time racers prepare body and mind for competition. And the perennial question of why road riders shave their legs will be answered.

CHAPTER 6 DESTINATIONS

When you've cycled all possible routes from your doorstep, it's time to take your bike farther afield. From weekends away to week-long holidays, and even longer expeditions, the best of the world's must-ride destinations are described in this chapter. Avid cyclists may want to make a pilgrimage to the classic climbs of the Tour de France, while casual cyclists can follow the easygoing routes. You'll also find out what makes so many cities great for cyclists. Practical information includes how to pack panniers for a cycle touring trip and a guide to transporting your bike.

Below
See the world's most amazing scenery by bike.

CHAPTER 7 MAINTENANCE

Keep your bicycle running smoothly with this overview of the basic maintenance required. From changing a cable to repairing a puncture, step-by-step instructions simplify essential jobs. Tips and useful shortcuts from professional mechanics are there too, along with help for new cyclists on how to diagnose problems.

And finally, the glossary (*see* p. 338) defines some of the more obscure cycling words and phrases.

Below
Regular maintenance will keep your bike running smoothly.

CHAPTER 1
THE BIKE

THE BICYCLE: A HISTORY

Of the world's greatest inventions, few have had such a contested conception as the bicycle. The French, Germans and Scottish can all claim parentage, although the authenticity of a sketch of a bicycle by the Italian Leonardo da Vinci, dating from 1493, is much disputed. Perhaps it is best to think of the bicycle as a work in progress, with today's machines just the latest step in its evolution.

Above
The penny-farthing, so named because of the different diameter of its wheels, was a familiar sight in London.

The first recognizable bicycle was developed in 1817 by Baron Karl von Drais, from Baden in Germany. Known at the time as a 'Draisine', the design had a steerable front wheel, a saddle and a rear wheel. The rider would walk (or scoot), then coast along in the saddle when possible – think balance bike (*see* p. 38). By 1818, the idea was being copied in Britain, where it was christened the 'hobby-horse'.

But it was several more decades, during which these early bicycles gained one and then two wheels as tricycles and quadracycles, before someone had the bright idea of attaching pedals to create a genuinely human-powered, two-wheeled machine. Who that person was is still the source of fierce debate. Many, particularly the British, believe Kirkpatrick Macmillan, from Dumfriesshire, connected rods and cranks to the rear wheel in 1839.

Right
A wooden bicycle based on Leonardo da Vinci's 1493 sketch.

Far right
The Scottish Cycle Museum at Drumlanrig.

PROGRESS

The first confirmed example of a pedal-powered bicycle going into production, however, is usually credited to the French Michaux family, backed by Aimé and René Olivier. They used a design by Pierre Lallement, featuring cranks and pedals mounted on the front wheel; Lallement filed a patent for his design in 1866. By 1868 the world's first bicycle race had taken place in Paris (the winner was 19-year-old Englishman James Moore). From the late 1860s the bicycle

was highly fashionable in Europe and North America. With the modification of a larger front wheel, the boneshaker then developed into the penny-farthing – an altogether more dangerous form of transport.

Wisdom prevailed, however, and in 1885 John Kemp Starley's 'Rover' made equal-sized wheels standard. With a rear wheel driven by a chain, Starley's 'safety bicycle' provides the genetic blueprint for today's bicycles. Inventions that we now take for granted came thick and fast: the

bush-roller chain in 1880, the pneumatic tire in 1888, the freewheel and, although it wasn't adopted until nearly a century later, the clipless pedal in 1895 and panniers in 1899.

MODERN

During the 20th century, the bicycle family tree blossomed as its fortunes waxed and waned. Cargo-carrying bikes evolved for butchers and bakers, while lighter, faster bikes with more gears (the French are to thank once more for inventing derailleur gears) were developed for

recreational cycling and racing. In 1970s California, the bicycle went off-road and came back as the mountain bike (*see* p. 32), ushering in a new era of research and design that brought suspension and disc brakes.

Bikes today can fold, jump, climb mountains and carry the shopping home. They've adapted to every conceivable use, but the basic format has remained unchanged for more than a century and is unlikely to be improved upon. Why? Because in no other invention does form follow function so beautifully.

Above
Kirkpatrick Macmillan and the bike he designed in 1839.

Right
A 1950s racer.

THE BICYCLE: AN OVERVIEW

An elegant invention it may be, but how does the bicycle work? While the bicycle's engineering – its chains, cogs and wheels – is on display, the science is much more mysterious. Why does a bicycle stay upright, and how can varying just a couple of angles transform a bike's handling?

Seat angle – the steeper (closer to vertical) the seat angle, the more of your weight is pushed forward, giving a more aggressive posture.

Top tube – the longer the top tube, proportionally, the more space in the cockpit and the longer the wheelbase.

Head angle – the steeper (closer to vertical) the head angle, the quicker the handling.

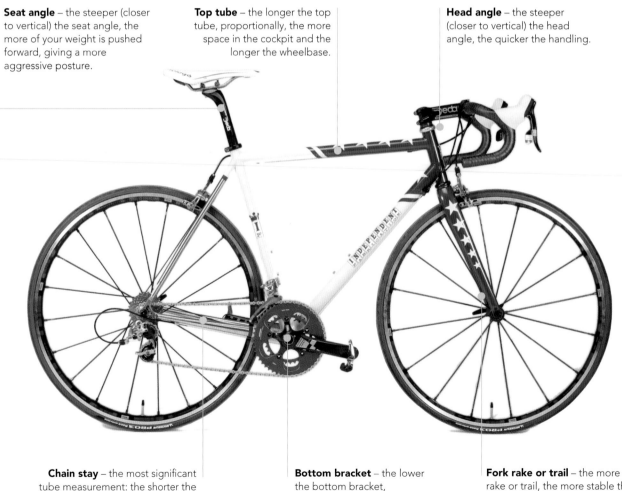

Chain stay – the most significant tube measurement: the shorter the stays, the racier the handling.

Bottom bracket – the lower the bottom bracket, the more stable the ride.

Fork rake or trail – the more rake or trail, the more stable the handling. A town bike will have more rake than a racing bike.

LAYOUT

The traditional shape of a bicycle frame is that of a diamond formed from two triangles. The front triangle comprises the seat tube, the top tube and the down tube. The head tube, into which the top of the fork (the steerer tube) is inserted, connects the top and down tubes. The rear triangle is created by the seat stays, the chain stays and the seat tube. In addition to bearing the rider's weight, the frame's purpose is to hold the various parts of the bicycle – its wheels, saddle, handlebars and chainset – in a consistent position relative to each other. Some bikes, such as full-suspension mountain bikes, have moved beyond the diamond-shaped frame; however, the basic layout is the same: two wheels with a crankset driving the rear, and handlebars controlling the front.

Below
Gears make pedaling easier.

THE SCIENCE

The mechanics of a bicycle are straightforward: a revolution of a crank turns a chainring that pulls a chain around a cog attached to the hub of the rear wheel. Varying the gear ratios makes it harder (large ring at the front and small cog at the back for a high gear) or easier (small ring at the front and large cog at the back for a low gear) to pedal. Potential energy (stored in the rider's legs) becomes kinetic energy through the application of force. What happens next is complex to understand without a degree in physics. Scientific laws, such as those that govern an object's center of gravity, mass, motion, and balance, help cyclists stay upright when all that is in contact with the ground is a pair of thumb-size patches of rubber. Taken together, they explain why the higher a bicycle's speed, the easier it is to balance.

Above
Keeping a bike upright relies on forces created by spinning.

GEOMETRY

No other factor has as great an effect on how a bike will ride as its geometry. At its heart, bicycle geometry is about the relationship between the head angle and the seat angle. Differences of just a couple of degrees can change a bike from being relaxed and stable to being racy with twitchy handling.

Geometry also covers the length of some of the tubes and the proportions. In general terms, the slacker the angles and longer the proportions, the more laidback the ride will be. Steep angles, short chain stays and tucked-in positions are reserved for racing bikes.

Below
A track bike has steep angles.

THE FRAME

If you take just one piece of advice with you into a bike shop, it should be to buy the best frame possible. The frame, a diamond-shaped arrangement of tubes, is the heart and soul of every bicycle. Components can be changed, but your new bike's frame has to fit your body and suit your style perfectly. A tall order, but as we will find out, there is such variation in the frames available that there's one out there to suit everybody.

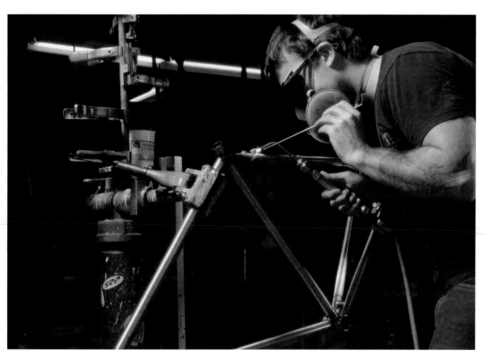

Left
Welding a
bicycle frame.

HOW ARE BICYCLE FRAMES MADE?

It has taken decades for the bicycle's design to be refined, but one country – Taiwan – has perfected their mass production. Most of the world's bicycle frames are welded in a handful of factories in Taiwan, and the island's largest frame manufacturers, Giant and Merida, make frames for smaller bike companies and other leading brands as well as their own. The advantages of this are obvious: the factories can invest in state-of-the-art processes while the bike companies concentrate on developing their designs without the expense of running a factory. The frames built in Taiwanese factories are typically made from aluminum (*see* Materials, p. 22) and range from town and mountain bikes to ultra-light racing machines. Made on vast production lines, they're finished to a high standard, with accurate alignment and functional welding.

Taiwanese aluminum frames, competent although they undeniably are, could be said to lack a certain something. Call it what you want – personality, individuality, a soul even – but for a frame with a little magic in it, you may have to look to an independent frame builder. In Europe and the USA there is a thriving network of bike builders who design and make all sorts of bike frames. These range from mid-sized companies to a man in a shed, and most will work with steel and aluminum, the easiest materials to handle. But, a few boutique companies have the skills and equipment to make titanium and carbon-fiber frames. Smaller frame builders can often include a wider spread of sizes in their ranges, or they may specialize in one or two areas. However, bikes with frames built in Europe (such as Orange, Nicolai and Thorn) or North America (for example, Litespeed, Rocky Mountain and Cannondale) are often slightly more expensive, due in large part to higher labor costs.

Left
Tubing can be made
from a range of
materials including
steel, aluminum
or titanium.

Right
Carbon-fiber
frames are both
light and strong.

Right
A handbuilt
bike blends
art, craft and
design.

CUSTOM MADE

A step beyond the
handbuilt frame is a fully
customized frame. This is a
frame that has been tailored
to your exact dimensions
and requirements after
consultations with the frame
builder. Custom frames,
whether they're for touring,
racing or mountain biking,
represent the pinnacle of
the frame-builder's art.

As we've mentioned,
nothing affects a frame's
handling so much as its
geometry (see p. 19), and
a custom frame can be
designed for a specific
feel and fit: a steeper seat
angle to make the handling
a touch livelier; a slightly
longer top tube to allow
for long arms and torso.
Of course, there's a
premium to be paid for
all this personal attention
and the cachet of having
a name like Pegoretti on
your down tube. Custom
frames can easily run into
substantial four-figure sums,
many times the price of a
good factory-made frame.

THE FRAME: MATERIALS

The days when bicycle frames could be made only from steel are long gone. Space-age materials such as carbon fiber and titanium have filtered down from motor racing to reach mid-range models from numerous bike manufacturers. But what sort of difference do these new materials make?

Right
A steel racing bike, the XCR by Independent Fabrication.

REMEMBER

While each material has general qualities, the greatest factor affecting how a frame 'feels' is what the builder has decided to do with it. Typically, those decisions are compromises. For a titanium frame to be stiff and strong, for example, extra weight will have to be added in the form of larger diameter tubing.

Ultimately it's a personal choice depending on factors such as price and personal taste.

STEEL

Often (and erroneously) associated with budget bikes, steel retains many fans, despite the fact it has been around since the penny-farthing. The most basic form of steel is a plain high-tensile steel, heavy in both weight and performance. But there is another world of steel frames, and it's a wonderful place. Steel tubing, made by companies including Reynolds and Columbus, comes in a range of different grades, and the best steel, such as Reynolds's 853, exceeds titanium tubing in strength. When steel tubes are double or triple 'butted', it means that the tubing is two or three times as thick at the ends as it is in the middle. This allows strength to be concentrated where it matters (at the welds) and weight to be lost where it doesn't (in the middle). If a frame made from good-quality steel can be said to have a certain characteristic, it is that it gives a springy, comfortable ride that is less jarring than that of aluminum. But bicycle connoisseurs appreciate steel for another, more aesthetic reason: its slim, straight tubes look great when welded into a diamond shape.

Another advantage of steel is its durability. It has a far higher yield point (the moment when it bends or breaks under stress) than aluminum, and it will bend under force rather than fail suddenly. Unlike those made from other materials, a steel frame can also be easily repaired or modified, making it a good choice for a touring bike.

ALUMINUM

The first mass-produced aluminum frames date from the mid-1980s, when the alloy was used by Trek and Cannondale. Since then it has become the material of choice for the majority of mainstream, mid-range bicycles. It's light, easy to work with and widely available. But, aluminum can't match steel for strength. So, aluminum tubing has a larger diameter and is often formed into curves and bulges to add strength. Thanks to the larger-diameter tubing, some frames have earned a reputation for a slightly harsh or jarring ride quality, although larger-volume tires or a more forgiving saddle can help.

TITANIUM

In titanium frames, the titanium is alloyed with small amounts of aluminum and vanadium, usually in the blend 3Al–2.5V (3 percent aluminum to 2.5 percent vanadium), less commonly 6Al–4V. At the top end of the market, titanium (or 'Ti') has a fashionable appeal and produces some beautiful bicycles that will last a lifetime. Harder to handle than aluminum or steel, titanium is the preserve of specialist welders whose expertise does not come cheap.

CARBON FIBER

Carbon fiber had been used on space shuttles and F1 cars before it arrived in the bike industry. Introduced in 1986 by Kestrel, carbon fiber is the most versatile material for high-end bicycle frames. Builders can control precisely the frame's characteristics by altering how the strands of carbon lie. The very best carbon frames are light, stiff, comfortable and strong. It is the default material for competition-level frames, if only because it is so versatile.

Top
An aluminum bike from Specialized.

Far right
A carbon-fiber racing bike, the XS made by Independent Fabrication.

Right top
Carbon fiber is woven.

Right bottom
Aluminum is welded.

CONTACT POINTS: SADDLE

The places where our bodies come into contact with the bicycle are crucial to our comfort. The three contact points are the handlebars and grips, the pedals and the saddle. If they are not correctly adjusted, an otherwise perfect ride can become a painful ordeal, with sore hands, blistered feet or an aching posterior. The saddle is the most important contact point, and this is where we will begin.

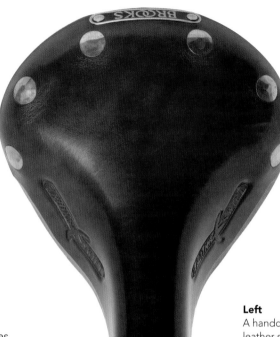

Left
A handcrafted leather saddle by Brooks.

SADDLE

Since the days of coil-sprung leather saddles, from the likes of British firm Brooks, saddle technology has changed greatly. Although a classic Brooks leather saddle, once broken in, can be sublimely comfortable, most people will opt for a more modern design. Modern saddles typically have a lightweight plastic base that is covered with a layer of padding and a synthetic (or real) leather cover. Underneath the saddle, parallel rails allow the saddle to be moved backward and forward on the seatpost, so the distance between the saddle and the handlebars can be adjusted by about 2 inches (5cm).

Saddles come in all shapes and sizes, but there are some simple rules to follow. The first rule, and the one that is hardest for new riders to understand, is that more padding doesn't necessarily make for a more comfortable saddle, particularly on longer rides. A padded saddle allows its rider to bounce around more on it, and the movement creates chafing as well as making smooth pedaling more difficult. Leg and back muscles will also be constantly trying to steady the rider's position – look out for a rocking pedaling motion in those with too-soft saddles – and can therefore tire much more quickly.

TIPS FOR CHOOSING A SADDLE

- Avoid saddles with seams and logos along the top, as these can cause friction or irritation.

- Look for a saddle that is flat along the top, not too padded and that fits correctly.

- Consider a saddle with a cutaway.

- Try as many saddles as possible to find the right fit for you.

SIZING

New riders may be surprised that a harder saddle can be more comfortable. That depends on the second rule: find a saddle that fits. Everybody has a different shape. Saddle choice is as personal as shoe choice, and each manufacturer's saddles will differ slightly. Try as many as you can in order to find the saddle that fits your shape best. This can take years, so it might be worth acquiring the help of an understanding bike shop early on. Some leading manufacturers, in addition to Brooks, are Selle Italia, fi'zi:k and Specialized. Some, such as Specialized, produce the same design in different widths; a great idea since sit bones are not standard. Women tend to have a wider pelvis, so a saddle with a wide rear and a stubbier nose may fit better than a long, narrow one.

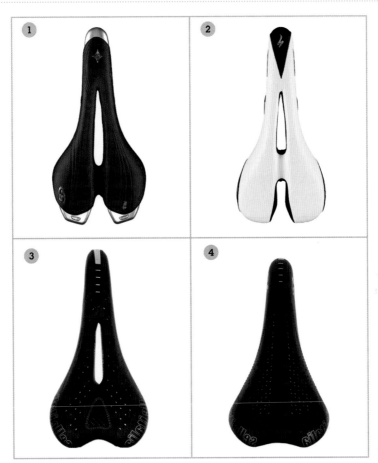

Left
1. Slim, light-weight women's saddle.
2. Flat-seated saddle with smooth contours.
3. Silicone gel-filled saddle for off and on road.
4. Gel-padded with differentiated areas.

CUTAWAYS

Another innovation has been saddles with cutaway slots along the center. These are intended to relieve pressure on the major blood vessels and nerves that run along the perineal region. Constriction of these vessels can cause temporary numbness and more serious problems (*see* p. 157). If this is an issue, a good starting point is the Specialized Body Geometry range of saddles, designed in conjunction with Dr. Roger Minkow, an ergonomics specialist.

Right
A cutaway reduces pressure on delicate parts.

Far right
Women's saddles tend to be wider.

CONTACT POINTS: HANDLEBARS & PEDALS

Not all our weight rests on the saddle; some is carried by our hands and feet. Finding the right balance and fitting the right size bars will help banish aches and pains and is an important step toward comfortable cycling.

DROP BARS

All road-racing bikes, many touring bikes and some specialist bikes (cyclo-cross and track bikes) employ drop handlebars. These curvy bars not only allow riders to get into a low, aerodynamic tuck but also offer a multitude of hand positions for a bit of variety on long rides. They're typically available in widths of 38cm to 44cm and should roughly match the rider's shoulders in width.

FLAT AND RISER BARS

Flat bars are featured on mountain bikes, hybrids, town bikes and some touring bikes. They tend to be wider than drop handlebars (around 58cm for flat bars, and from 66cm to 71cm for riser bars) to give greater control over steering. Riser bars have a slight bend in them to raise the riding position, improving visibility for the rider. Most mountain bikes are fitted with risers, although cross-country racers still prefer flat bars.

HANDLEBARS

Handlebars come in a range of styles, from curvy drop bars for racing and touring bikes to sweptback bars for town bikes and riser or flat bars for mountain bikes. The wider the bar, the more stable the ride (an effect of having weight distributed farther from the front wheel's axle). However, bars that are significantly wider than a rider's shoulders can cause discomfort and fatigue. Note that the diameter of bars also varies, so make sure you choose a set that is compatible with your bike's stem.

Above
Drop bars offer a range of hand positions.

ADJUSTMENT

Bars can be adjusted up and down, and forward and backward, by changing the stem. Stems come in a range of lengths and elevations (from zero to ten degrees or more). They can be raised by adding spacers – rings stacked below the stem. The higher the handlebars are set, the more weight is placed on the saddle (due to an upright riding position), and the lower the handlebars, the more weight is supported by the hands. Lower bars give a sportier stance but can lead to neck, shoulder and wrist pain (*see p. 154*). A shorter stem moves bars closer to the saddle and a longer stem increases the space in the cockpit.

Left
Mountain bike handlebars.

Right
A clipless pedal with a platform.

Below
Clipless pedals require special footwear.

PEDALS

At its most basic, the pedal is a double-sided platform. To secure their feet to the pedals for greater efficiency, racers used to use toe clips, an adjustable leather or nylon strap that would be tightened around their feet and the pedal. However, the advent of the clipless pedal has made the toe clip a rare sight. Simple flat pedals are still standard on town bikes and children's bikes. The 'clipless' pedal – a pedal with spring-loaded jaws into which a cleat on the sole of the shoe clicks – was invented in 1895 by Charles Hanson, who came up with the idea of twisting your foot to release it from the pedal. But his invention

didn't catch on until 1984 when LOOK applied their ski-binding technology to pedals. While the concept has changed little, there are now several competing pedal designs and brands (including Shimano, LOOK, Time and Speedplay). Shimano's widespread system, SPD (Shimano Pedaling Dynamics), gives clipless pedals their nickname: 'spuds'.

Clipless pedals can be adjusted in two ways. Most designs offer a range of 'float'. This allows your foot some degree of free movement when clipped into the pedal, and is typically tightened or loosened to increase or decrease the amount of freedom allowed and to make unclipping easier or harder, by turning an Allen (hex) key bolt.

On the sole of the shoe, the cleat also has a range of positions in which it can be set before it is fixed in place, the most effective position being under the ball of the foot.

TYPES OF PEDAL

FLAT PEDAL

Pros: Can be used with any shoes; is easy to hop on and off; standard equipment on many bikes

Cons: Feet can be bounced off on rough ground; inefficient as you can't pull up

FLAT WITH TOE CLIPS

Pros: Cheap way of fastening feet to flat pedals; don't require special footwear

Cons: Awkward to get feet into; harder to get feet out of in an emergency; unattractive design

CLIPLESS PEDAL

Pros: Aids efficient pedaling; available at wide variety of price points; a clever, refined design

Cons: Requires compatible footwear; can be costly; intimidating to first-time users

THE RACING BIKE

Modern technology allows cyclists to reach speeds of 50mph (80km/h) and climb mountains on a machine that costs more the less there is of it. Here we look at how this engineering marvel works.

Left
The state-of-the-art carbon-fiber racing bike is designed to be lightweight, speedy and efficient.

TIPS FOR CHOOSING A BIKE

- Shortlist four or five models.

- Try them out. Feel how they corner and handle at speed.

- Get fitted by a professional.

- Don't scrimp on the frame – it's the most important part.

FRAME

A road-racing frame has two aims: to enable you to deliver power in a streamlined position while weighing very little. The winner of the first Tour de France in 1903 rode a 44lb bike; today there is a minimum weight limit of 15lbs on racers' bikes. The diamond shape brings strength, but manufacturers will also reinforce certain areas, such as the bottom bracket, to ensure that no power is lost through flex.

HANDLEBARS

Drop handlebars have two advantages: they allow racers to crouch low for better aerodynamics (watch a sprinter or time trialist bend their body into the smallest possible shape) while offering multiple hand positions during a long ride. When cruising along, many racers drape their hands on the hoods of the brake levers. Today gear and brake levers form a single unit with small paddles used to flick between gears.

WHEELS

The standard wheel size is 700c – this refers to the 700-mm diameter (although the actual tire diameter is closer to 622mm). Most racing tires are about 23mm in width – wider tires have a greater rolling resistance but will absorb more shock. Typical dimensions for a tire will be 700 x 23mm. Wheels are usually made from aluminum but lightweight carbon is becoming more common on high-end racing bike wheels.

THE SADDLE

Racing saddles may look uncomfortably minimalist, but they are intended to be comfortable on long rides. Spongy, over-padded saddles allow the bottom to bounce around and can cause saddle sores. Instead, racing saddles are designed to be low in weight, with little or no padding, but perfectly fitted.

THE BRAKES

Racing bikes use side-pull caliper brakes (see p. 318) with brake blocks aligned against the rim of the wheel.

THE DRIVETRAIN

Modern racing bikes have 18 or 20 gears: a rear cassette of nine or ten cogs multiplied by two front chainrings, generally with a large ring of 53 teeth. Again, stiffness and low weight are essential, as is shifting precision.

PRACTICALITY

The road-racing bike is not the most practical choice of bicycle. It won't have fittings for racks or fenders, and lights and reflectors – a legal requirement for use after dark in many countries – are typically removed in the quest for speed.

Top
The run-in to a sprint finish can be fearsomely fast, and racers won't touch their brakes. A sprinter like Mark Cavendish will generate huge forces winding up the speed toward the finish line.

Above
The gearing on a racing bike has close ratios so the racing cyclist can find the perfect gear at any moment. The front rings will typically have 53 teeth on the larger ring and 39 on the smaller one.

THE TOURING BIKE

Touring bicycles are designed specifically for riding long distances in comfort. They're designed to carry heavy panniers in a variety of environments and are a practical option whether you're riding to work or around the world.

Left
A touring bike with racks by Independent Fabrication.

FRAME

Touring bikes are built for comfort not speed. Their frames are often made from steel rather than aluminum, not least because steel has a greater resistance to fatigue and can be more easily repaired. Steel frames can have a bit more 'give', making for a less bone-shaking ride over rough roads. The frame's geometry will be more relaxed (i.e. angles will be less steep, less aggressive) than that of a racing bike: the bike will have a longer wheelbase (mostly accounted for by longer chain stays for greater stability and heel clearance) and an upright riding position. Handling should be predictable and stable even when heavily loaded. For cycling extraordinary distances, such as expeditions across continents, around the world and the like, a custom frame may make sense.

CONTROLS

Traditional touring bikes, like road-racing bikes, have drop handlebars (although often set higher) and similar controls. Drop handlebars offer a variety of hand positions and are aerodynamic. However, for expedition-level bikes covering rough terrain, the extra width and control offered by flat bars may be welcome.

BRAKES

Stopping a fully loaded touring bike on a loose surface is nerve-wracking; riders need to trust their brakes. Most use cantilever brakes rather than caliper brakes for the extra clearance, while some prefer disc brakes, which offer greater stopping power and are effective in the wet or even when a wheel is out of shape (see p. 321). But more can go wrong with a disc brake, it adds weight and can also be tricky to repair in remote areas.

GEARS

The gearing on a touring bike is typically much lower than it is for a racing bike: wide ratio gears, triple chainrings at the front (22/32/44 teeth) and cogs at the back up to 34 teeth, enable the bike to claw its way up the steepest hills, if only at walking pace. A low-maintenance alternative to the derailleur system (see p. 328) is a Rohloff Speedhub with up to 14 gears inside, where they are safe from dirt and damage, or a Shimano Alfine hub. These internal-geared hubs are reliable but need running in and can concentrate a lot of weight in one place.

WHEELS

Robust wheels for touring bikes are generally available in 700c and 26-inch configurations. They will have steel spokes (typically with 36 spokes, more than a racing bike might have) and a wide rim for touring tires. Hub choice is important: a sealed cartridge hub from a quality manufacturer such as Phil Wood will require less on-the-road maintenance than a loose-bearing hub. Touring hubs are also designed to take the extra weight of a loaded bike.

Above
Touring cyclists with waterproofed panniers.

Left
Panniers can be fixed to bike forks.

LUGGAGE

Rack mounts brazed on to touring frames are an essential feature. Typically, there will be mounts for a rear rack and possibly a rack mounted on the forks, over the front wheel. Steel racks are the most practical. Durable waterproof panniers by companies such as Ortlieb are a worthwhile investment, as wet clothing is no joke when you're touring and don't have access to a drier.

THE HARDTAIL MOUNTAIN BIKE

Bicycles have been ridden off-road since the earliest days of cycling, but it took a group of cyclists, including Joe Breeze and Charlie Kelly, in late-1970s California to come up with a bike designed for the purpose and give it a name: the 'mountain bike'. Today its descendants are the pinnacle of cycling technology.

Left
A hardtail mountain bike by Specialized.

FRAME

A 'hardtail' mountain bike is one without rear suspension. What they lose in comfort over a full-suspension mountain bike (*see p. 34*) they gain in simplicity and responsiveness. For smooth trails and cross-country racing, a hardtail will be sufficient for most people. Hardtails can also be great fun; their snappy handling and acceleration are often preferred by experienced bikers. Hardtail frames can be made from steel, aluminum and titanium, with carbon fiber preferred for racers. Geometry varies considerably: sizing (gauged by the seat-tube length) ranges from 15 or 16 inches up to 20 or 22 inches. Seat stays will typically be short (about 16¾ inches) and the top tube will often slope down to the seat tube to increase standover height and clearance. Make sure that your frame is sized correctly, and if in doubt, err on the small side.

FORKS

The vast majority of mountain bikes have forks with suspension. The amount of movement or 'travel' available varies from 80–100mm for lightweight racing machines up to 150–160mm for more downhill-oriented hardtails. 120–140mm is standard. Suspension is provided by either an air cartridge or a coil spring, the heavier but plusher option. For how to keep suspension forks working well turn to p. 334.

WHEELS

The standard size wheel for mountain bikes is 26 inches in diameter. For taller riders, 29-inch wheels are becoming more widespread. Mountain-bike wheels are built for strength, and the wider the rim, the more robust it will be. Tires are knobby for grip on soft or loose surfaces and come in widths from 1.8 to 1.9 inches for racing and up to 2.5 inches or more for downhill and freeriding.

HANDLEBARS

Mountain bike handlebars for cross-country racers are usually flat. But most handlebars today are the slightly upward-sweeping 'risers', which give a more upright position. Bars are usually much wider than on other types of bicycle to give greater control. They can be made from aluminum or carbon fiber, and many are now over-sized (OS), with a larger diameter in the middle of the bar for extra strength and stiffness.

GEARS

Mountain bikes tend to have triple chainrings at the front and nine or ten cogs at the rear, giving a choice of 27 gears or more (although several of the ratios are duplicated). The extra-low gearing (the largest front chainring usually has 44 teeth, compared with 53 on a road bike) helps riders pedal up steep, technical climbs.

PEDALS

Mountain bikes, like road bikes, can be fitted with clipless pedals (see p. 27), but those on a mountain bike are double-sided, making entry easier.

Top and above
Hardtails can be used for a range of riding, from cross-country racing to jumping.

THE FULL-SUSPENSION MOUNTAIN BIKE

A full-suspension (or dual-suspension) mountain bike is one that has sprung forks at the front and a shock absorber at the rear, damping jolts from the rear wheel. The suspension adds weight but aids downhill and uphill performance over rocks, roots and rough terrain.

Left
A full-suspension mountain bike by Nicolai.

FRAME

Most commonly crafted from aluminum (and occasionally from carbon fiber or titanium), the full-suspension mountain bike frame uses every technological trick at its disposal. Parts are molded, cold-forged or machined before being assembled. There are numerous competing suspension designs (some developed as a way around existing patents), ranging from the single-pivot (a swingarm that pivots around one point only, usually near the bottom bracket) to four-bar linkages, with bearings at four (or more) points (*see* pp. 334–335). Each has its own advantages, while the evolution of the shock absorber, often shortened simply to 'shock', has negated many of their disadvantages.

REAR SUSPENSION

The key quality is the suspension's ability to ignore forces generated by the rider (pedaling, for example) and braking while reacting to the terrain. Technologies such as Fox's ProPedal and Rock Shox's Motion Control largely achieve this goal. Many shocks have a lockout, enabling the suspension to be switched off at the flick of a lever. Shocks are either coil sprung or air sprung.

BRAKES

Most mountain bikes have disc brakes, or the mounts to fit them. They work like those on a motorbike: a pair of pads are forced together by pistons to grip a metal disc attached to the hub. The best disc brakes are hydraulic: squeezing the brake lever pushes brake fluid around the system, causing the pistons to move (some disc brakes are cable operated). The larger the disc the greater the stopping power.

GEARS

Full-suspension bikes can have the same range of gears as hardtail mountain bikes. Downhill-oriented bikes, however, usually have fewer gears, with just a small front chainring (20–30 teeth) protected by a bashguard. In total, they may have just nine or ten gears.

FORKS

Single-crown suspension forks with travel of up to 160mm are normal for full-suspension bikes. More forks and front hubs are now using a bolt-through system rather than quick release skewers, as the 15mm–20mm-diameter axle used adds stiffness and strength.

GEOMETRY

With the absence of a traditional diamond shape and the addition of several inches of movement, the full-suspension frame's geometry becomes more complex. As the suspension moves through its travel – while heading downhill fast, for instance – the bike's geometry changes. Full-suspension cross-country bikes will be as fast and racy as hardtails, while downhill bikes are notably more relaxed in their angles.

Top and above
Full-suspension bikes are capable of tackling extreme terrain or more gentle rides.

TOWN BIKES, FOLDING BIKES & HYBRIDS

The renaissance of cycling in cities around the world has brought with it a boom in town and folding bikes. These bicycles are designed to be used daily for steady progress over paved roads; practicality and ease of use are paramount.

TOWN BIKES & HYBRIDS

Look around European cities such as Copenhagen and Amsterdam, where around 40 percent of the population commutes to work by bicycle, and one style of bike dominates: the Dutch-style town bike, which boasts an upright riding position, steel frame, sweptback handlebars and fenders. These stately galleons of the roads offer an upright cycling position (sometimes called sit-up-and-beg) that pushes the rider's weight farther back, gives greater vision and visibility and encourages sedate progress through the city.

Weight isn't a consideration for town bikes. Instead, manufacturers such as Pashley in the UK and Velorbis in Denmark have produced practical, comfortable machines fitted with lights, fenders, a rack and a kickstand for getting from A to B in style.

Above
Velorbis town bikes are very practical.

Below
Hybrid bikes combine features of mountain and town bikes.

Below
Old-fashioned town bikes have an upright seating position.

FOLDING BIKES

There's a lot to like about the folding bike. In less than a minute your two-wheeled transport can become airline luggage. They're the perfect commuting solution for those who find they are unable to take full-size bicycles on to trains. Two brands dominate the market: Brompton, founded by Andrew Ritchie, and Dahon, founded by Dr. David Hon. Brompton manufactures about 28,000 bikes a year in London and is the iconic folding bike. Dahon folding bikes are made in Taiwan and have 20-inch wheels compared to Brompton's 16-inch-diameter wheels. You get what you pay for, and the more expensive the folding bike, the less it will weigh.

The process of folding or unfolding should take no more than 30 seconds and can be as quick as 10 in practiced hands, such as those of competitors at the Brompton World Championships, who race an 8-mile course on the grounds of Blenheim Palace wearing a suit and tie.

Above
A folding-bike race between Brompton owners gets started.

Most town bikes have hub gears (from three to seven typically; gears are not a priority for city cycling on generally flat roads) with a twist-grip shifter. Rather than a full-size 700c wheel, some town bikes use the smaller 650b size or even a 26-inch wheel. Loads can be carried with a rack and panniers or a basket. Traditionally, the Dutch use panniers while the Danes prefer baskets.

Hybrid bikes are less handsome but just as practical, blending the best attributes of mountain bikes and road bikes. Accordingly, the riding position is relaxed and upright so the rider can see and be seen. Handlebars tend to be flat, while wheels are either 700c or 26-inch and will be robust. Not all models have fenders, but choose one that does, since they are essential for regular commuting. Frames, usually made from steel or aluminum, are often available in a skirt-friendly, step-through configuration. Just don't expect a town bike or hybrid to be speedy.

HOW TO FOLD A BROMPTON

Above
1. Swing the rear wheel under the frame.
2. Unclamp and fold back the front wheel.
3. Unclamp and lower the handlebars and saddle.
4. Fold in the pedals; the saddle can be used as a handle.

CHILDREN'S BIKES

From around the age of two, children can be familiarized with two-wheel transport in the form of scooters and balance bikes. By the time they are three or four they can move on to children's bikes. Choosing the right bike is very important. Here's what to look for.

BALANCE BIKES

Balance bikes, often made of wood, are light, safe and simple. The principle is also simple: the child scoots along until the speed is high enough for the bike to coast along with feet raised. They're standard issue in Scandinavian countries and are growing in popularity in the UK and USA. Without pedals or brakes (some models have a rear brake), balance bikes teach children how to steer and balance without worrying about the more complicated aspects of cycling, and there are no oily cogs or chains to catch loose clothing.

Above and right
Balance bikes in action. Without pedals it's easy for children to roll along.

LIKEaBIKE, a simple German design, is made of beech plywood, so it's light (and easy for adults to carry), strong, and there are no places where small fingers can be trapped. Features include a washable padded seat, non-marking tires, an adjustable saddle with 4 inches of movement to accommodate the growing young cyclist, and zero-maintenance wheels.

Thanks to a low center of gravity, most balance bikes are very stable; by the time the child is around four, they may be able to freewheel down hills and even small steps on their balance bike. Compared with starter kids' bikes, which are often heavy and poorly proportioned for a very young child, these are an excellent option guaranteed to spark a love of cycling in most children.

CHILDREN'S BIKES

Once the child has learned to balance on two wheels, it's time to add pedals and brakes. In Scandinavia, where children are introduced to bicycles at an earlier age than in the UK and the USA, this can be when they're about four years old. Children's bikes must have certain features: they need brakes that fit small hands and are easy to pull, a few gears if any at all, and, above all, they need to be light. The best children's bikes will be made from aluminum, with sizing adjustable using the seatpost and stem. A well-designed bike from a specialist company such as Islabikes will have shorter cranks, easy-to-use gears, and a low standover height.

BMX

BMX stands for Bicycle Motocross and is a 1970s invention. There is a variety of formats, from solo performance of freestyle (the rider performs tricks and jumps in an indoor arena, an outdoor BMX park or in the street) to racing against others around a short course of jumps.

BMXs appeal to adults and children alike and come in a variety of shapes and sizes, depending on usage. Most bikes will have an 18-inch or 20-inch wheel, the larger being preferred for racing. Freestyle bikes will be stronger, with wheels that can withstand being dropped from a height.

Above and below
BMX bikes have a low saddle and small wheels for tricks.

BALANCE-BIKE FRAME

To stabilize or not? Many parents report that their children learn to cycle much more easily without using stabilizers (*see* p. 86). After introducing their children to cycling with a balance bike, they remove the pedals of a full-size child's bike. When the pedals are re-installed, the child picks up the action quickly, having already mastered balance and control.

BMX FRAME

The best BMX bikes are made from chromoly steel, such as 4130, rather than aluminum. Steel withstands the regular impacts of a BMX's hard life better than aluminum and can be repaired and repainted easily. Weight isn't as much of a consideration since durability since BMXs tend to go with rather than against the pull of gravity.

BMX GEARS

The bikes will have a single gear (for example, a ratio such as 33 x 12) and sometimes just a single brake. The small, low profile frame – usually made from steel for strength – is designed to be highly maneuverable so that riders can perform breathtaking mid-air tricks, including a range of somersaults and twists.

THE BIKE

CARGO BIKES & TANDEMS

As bicycles have evolved, we expect them to be able to do more things – such as carry extra people or cargo – and they accomplish this with ease. Tandems, bicycles made for two, have long been used by touring cyclists, and the cargo bike sector is growing rapidly, too.

Above
Use a cargo bike to carry small
children – or whatever you like.

Left
A Bullitt cargo bike from Larry
vs Harry in Copenhagen.

Below
The tandem – a bicycle
made for two.

CARGO BIKES

It should come as no surprise that the heartland of cargo bike use lies across the bike-loving nations of northwest Europe – Denmark, Sweden and the Netherlands – where they are known as 'bakfiets' (or boxbikes). In those countries they're a familiar sight on the roads, where grandmothers use them to pick up grandchildren from school and stop by the shops on the way home. It helps that the roads in these countries are generally flat, but nevertheless the movement is gaining momentum, and cargo bikes are now also spotted in the UK and USA with increasing frequency.

There are several competing designs with two- and three-wheel options. Most place the cargo area in front of the rider, and the long-wheelbase, two-wheeled version is no harder to pedal than a regular bicycle. Modern designs have an aluminum frame into which carriers, such as boxes or childseats, can be fixed.

Loads of up to 270lbs (100kg) can be carried, and hub or derailleur gears can ease the strain. Disc brakes provide extra stopping power for a fully loaded cargo bike.

The Bullitt series, from Larry vs Harry – known in their home city of Copenhagen as Lars Malmborg and Hans Fogh – is fast, stable and stylish. The TNT is the top-of-the-range model, with an aluminum frame, puncture-proof tires and disc brakes. It can haul children, gear or just the weekend's shopping.

TANDEMS

A bicycle made for two can be the perfect solution for the couple that like to cycle together. Tandems are also available in multiple configurations (including seats for three or more riders). Traditionally, the rider at the front is called the captain and steers the tandem, while the rider at the back is known as the stoker. However, most tandem riders, stokers in particular, now prefer 'front' and 'rear' rider.

Both riders provide the power for the tandem, usually via a rear crossover drive; the front crankset drives a timing chain that runs along the left side of the bike, while the stoker's chainset is conventionally aligned on the right side, driving the rear wheel. On the flat and down hills, tandems are very quick, with a favorable power-to-weight ratio. Climbing uphill is harder as it requires more coordination.

Tandem-wheel sizes are typically 700c or 26-inch. They can be built as high-speed, road-going machines or are capable of crossing the Alps off-road. Off-the-shelf tandems are available, but those wishing to spend a lot of time riding may want a custom-built tandem to accommodate each rider's dimensions.

THE BIKE

SPECIALIST BIKES

Ever since people started pedaling, we've been refining bicycles for specific purposes. Recreationally, this includes bikes for racing off-road, around velodromes and against the clock. Here's what makes each of these bikes different.

CYCLO-CROSS

Cyclo-cross is growing in popularity in Europe and America although less so in Australia and New Zealand. The sport grew out of a need for road-racing cyclists to maintain fitness during the off-season; riding around forest tracks and muddy fields in the winter on road-style bikes has been practiced for more than a century. The cyclo-cross season runs from September to February and is dominated by the northern European nations, particularly Belgium, where cyclo-cross racers are celebrities. There are three main European competitions – the World Cup and the two Belgian series, the GVA Trofee and the Superprestige – although the toughest race is the Three Peaks Challenge in northern England. In the USA, the Cyclo-cross National Championship and the eight-race Gran Prix series are growing very strongly.

A typical cyclo-cross bike (known simply as a 'cross bike') is based on a road bike but has several key differences. It tends to have a lower bottom bracket (BB), extra mud clearance and slacker angles for stability. Its tires, mounted on 700c wheels, are knobby so they can find grip on grass and dirt roads. Its gearing will be lower, although it retains double rather than triple chainrings. Brakes may be cantilevers or even discs, which don't get clogged with mud. The appeal of a cross bike extends beyond racing, as it is highly versatile, being relatively robust and fitted with bottle cages and mounts for fenders and racks, making it a good option for touring.

Left
Time-trial bikes are streamlined for straight-line speed.

Right
A time-trial bike, impractical for everyday use.

Right
Track riders need very specific types of bike.

Right
A cyclo-cross bike, suitable for everyday use.

TRACK

Track cycling has similarly specific requirements. Again, handling around an oval, banked velodrome is not so much of a concern as outright speed. Track bikes are very light, very aerodynamic and often fitted with just one huge gear, ridden fixed (so the legs must keep turning as the wheel rotates) rather than with a freewheel.

Chris Hoy, for example, often turns a 52 x 14 setup. The bikes are stripped down to the bare minimum, to the extent that they don't have brakes. Geometry is steep, with short chain stays. The street-led 'fixie' fashion in recent years has seen track-bike frames renovated for use as either commuter or courier bikes.

TIME TRIAL

Time trialing is a British speciality, born out of the UK's mid-20th century road-racing scene, when massed start races were banned. Instead, riders competed by riding solo (often dressed in black and in the early hours of the morning), against the clock, over set distances, commonly 10 or 25 miles at a club level. These rides are called 'tests'. The Grand Tours also feature time trialing, both as team and individual time trials (also known as 'the races of truth'). Since time trials are raced alone and often on straight, flat roads, time-trial bikes are significantly different from road-racing bikes. Aerodynamics is prized over handling, so the handlebars may have an extension (an aerobar) that allows the rider to get into a stretched-out, streamlined shape, and the wheels may be bladed or discs. Geometry, particularly the seat angle, tends to be steeper, with a shorter top tube (to compensate for the aerobar), and therefore the riding position is noticeably forward. The gearing may also be higher than on a road-racing bike (time trial specialist Fabian Cancellara turns a massive 54-tooth front chainring).

Left
Time trialers use aero handlebars to reduce wind resistance.

THE BIKE

SIZING

Despite being the most important element in choosing a bike, bicycle sizing is a confusing and highly subjective area. For a start, mountain bikes and road bikes are measured in different units (inches and centimeters respectively), while many other bikes come sized as small, medium or large. Here's how to make sense of it all.

Above
Measuring yourself will help you find the perfect fit.

MOUNTAIN BIKE SIZING

Mountain bike sizing is similarly complicated. Some hardtails still use the seat-tube length for sizing but employ inches instead of centimeters: 17 inches, 18 inches, 19 inches and so on. Many manufacturers, of both hardtails and full-suspension bikes, have moved to a general description of small, medium, large and so on. A medium in one brand may equate to a 17-inch frame in one model but not another – there is no standardization, so the golden rule is try before you buy.

There's no comparison between road and mountain bike sizing, not least because mountain bike frames are smaller relative to road frames and require greater clearances. Factors other than seat-tube height may also be more important when sizing a mountain bike, such as the required reach affecting top-tube length, and the intended usage of the bike.

HOW BIKES ARE MEASURED

The standard gauge of a bike's size is the length of its seat tube. However, even this has two different interpretations: the seat tube is measured from the center of the bottom bracket to either the center of the top tube (center-center, C-C) or the top of the top tube (center-top, C-T). If it is a road bike, the measurement will be given in centimeters, usually in increments of two centimeters: 54cm, 56cm, 58cm and so on. However, just because you fit one brand's 56-cm bike doesn't mean you'll fit another brand's 56-cm bike. And the advent of compact frames (road bikes with sloping top tubes) has meant that small, medium and large sizing has become increasingly prevalent.

Left and below
Your arm span, leg length, height and arm length determine your bike's fit.

TIP
You might like to also measure your height: many manufacturers size their line according to height, which offers a good starting point for finding a bike that fits. Use the book or level again to place on top of your head and square against the wall.

THE CYCLIST

As important as knowing what size bike you have is knowing what size you are. A professional fitting service will take all sorts of measurements and even factor in your flexibility and preferred riding posture. But, for a basic fitting, the most important measurement is the inseam. To measure your inseam, stand with your bare feet slightly apart. Take a spirit level or book (hardback preferably) and push it, spine first, up between your legs as if straddling a saddle. Measure from the top of the book or level to the floor.

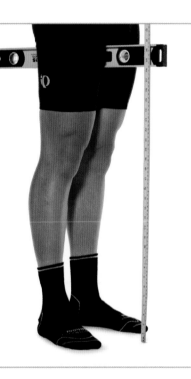

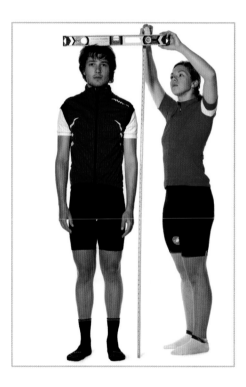

COMMON ERRORS

The wrong size bike can be the root of many problems, some quite serious. A frame that is too small may mean the saddle is too low, causing knee problems. A frame that is too big may mean the saddle is too high, causing the rider to rock from side to side as they pedal. Frames that are too long can cause sore shoulders, whereas a frame that is too short can cause hand problems. And simply fitting a longer stem and taller seatpost to a small frame increases the bend in the back, which is fine up to a point, but beyond that point it becomes a pain.

THE BIKE

SIZING & FIT

Sizing and fitting a bicycle has become a somewhat arcane science. There are competing formulas, such as Tour de France winner Greg LeMond's equation for road-bike sizes: inseam (cm) x 0.67. But, whether you're fitting yourself at home or doing it professionally (see p. 48), a hands-on approach is best.

Below left
Measuring reach.

Below right
Measuring saddle height.

THE BASICS

The key variables in ensuring your bike is fitted correctly are the distance from saddle to handlebars (reach) and the distance from saddle to the bottom bracket (saddle height), which, in conjunction with the height of the bottom bracket, will affect the standover. Get these right and you can fine-tune the rest.

STANDOVER

Start with the standover height. Stand over the frame with the saddle's nose against your back; for a road bike you want to ensure your groin clears the top tube by 2–3 inches, or a bunched fist. A road bike should have a further 2–3 inches of seatpost sticking out of the frame. Mountain bikers should give themselves about three times the clearance of a road bike.

REACH

While the proportionally shorter top tubes of town bikes allow an upright posture, racing bikes (road and mountain) demand a more streamlined posture. When positioned on the saddle, the top tube should be long enough to accommodate the length of the torso and allow the rider to reach the bars without leaning too far forward and placing too much weight on the nose of the saddle, which can lead to problems (see p. 157). Tall riders may want to go for a brand with proportionally longer top tubes for this reason. To adjust the reach, you can change the stem for longer or shorter, higher or lower varieties. The saddle can also be shifted backward and forward on its rails.

POSITION

For most recreational road cyclists, a 45-degree incline to the back is ideal when your hands are on the brake hoods. Racers may want to be slightly lower. On the bike, you should be able to look about 50 yards forward without straining your neck. A useful test is to be able to take your hands off the bars while in your riding position; you shouldn't feel like you will fall forward.

Mountain bikers and casual cyclists will have different requirements. For casual cyclists, comfort is king, and an upright position with a straight back is standard in cities such as Amsterdam.

Mountain bikers need to factor in the extra mobility required: they'll be moving around the bike much more than a road rider. When trying a mountain bike in a shop, remember to try out several positions on the bike, including standing in the attack position (see p. 118) and moving your weight behind the saddle.

SADDLE HEIGHT

Once those boxes are ticked, you can fine-tune the saddle height. At home, a simple rule is to allow your knee to be slightly bent when your heel is on the pedal at the bottom of a stroke. You should not have a perfectly straight leg at the bottom of the stroke, as this will cause the hips to rock from side to side when pedaling. Conversely, new riders often set their saddles too low, usually because they like to place both feet on the ground. If a saddle is too low, it will cause pain at the front of the knee; if it is too high, it will cause pain at the back (see p. 159).

Mountain bikers may prefer to have a slightly lower saddle, not only for the extra clearance required when moving their weight off and back, but also because a lower saddle position helps with generating more punch. A saddle at the maximum height for the rider is best for endurance. Many people have legs of slightly different lengths,

which can cause problems when setting the saddle height (look for a rocking motion when pedaling). The solution is to move the cleat of the shoe on the longer leg back, while a shim can also be added to the cleat of the shorter leg's shoe to raise it little by little.

For riders who are knock-kneed, a wedge inserted inside each shoe will tilt the legs outwards, straightening the pedaling motion. Some brands of shoe, such as Specialized, come with built-in wedges, or corrective insoles can be added to an existing pair of shoes.

Above and left
The length of the top tube is as important as that of the seat tube.

COMMON ERRORS

Avoid sitting too far forward in relation to the bottom bracket. If you need to move the saddle to its forwardmost position to reach the bars, perhaps you need a smaller bike. In such a forward position, your power delivery will be compromised (you'll underuse your glutes), and your knees will be strained by being in front of the foot at the 9 o'clock position. Watch out for frames with steep seat angles, as this will also tilt you farther forward.

PROFESSIONAL FITTING

As a rider's commitment to cycling grows, so too may their desire to be professionally fitted for a bicycle. This is like having a custom-tailored suit made. And the end result is a bicycle that is more comfortable and efficient – at least that is the aim. So, what happens at a professional bike fitting, and can you replicate the process at home?

PROFESSIONAL FITTING

The custom bicycle service begins at the bike shop with a conversation with someone like bicycle-fit specialist Roger Graver at Mosquito Cycles in London. If you think that your doctor knows a lot of personal information about you, Roger Graver is dietician, doctor, osteopath, psychiatrist and career consultant all rolled into one. 'I find out everything about them that might affect their riding,' he says. 'The first thing we do is have a coffee. Then I interview them. What do they do at work? How does it affect their posture? What is their diet like? Do they have injuries that might affect their position on a bike?'

Left
Dr. Andy Pruitt of the Boulder Center for Sports Medicine carrying out a professional fitting.

Then, Graver whips out his tape measure: height, inseam, shoulders, arm length, it all goes into his notebook. He takes a close look at the cyclist's feet: do they pronate or supernate? How are their arches? Then it's on to test hamstring flexibility and hip flexion before gauging pelvic orientation and back alignment.

What's more, the entire process is photographed and videoed from beginning to end. 'Sometimes they may have saved up for years for a new bike, and it's up to me to make sure it fits properly,' says Graver, who learned his trade on a course at the School of Cycle Fit in Saratoga, New York. When you consider that a cyclist will flex their knees up to 100 times per minute, it doesn't seem such an unusual idea to have a tailor-made bicycle.

Then it's on to the jig. This is a cycle on which everything can be minutely adjusted, from the cleats up, in order to arrive at the optimum position. The whole process can be expensive, and it's worth noting that

some experts see it as no more than a clever way of separating avid cyclists from their cash. However, the intention is worthy: a bike that fits perfectly will improve the cycling experience, in subtle or even dramatic ways.

Since all riders are individuals with different goals and riding styles, it is difficult to give specific instructions. Take crank length, one of the most important measurements after basic sizing has been accomplished. Cranks vary from 150mm to 180mm in length. Which to choose depends on the cyclist's height and length of leg. A man of 6 feet may be best suited to 175mm cranks. However, pedaling style is also a factor: longer cranks are harder to turn but deliver more power per stroke. Riders grinding out slower revolutions, such as Jan Ullrich, will favor a longer crank. Short cranks are better for spinning at a high cadence, as exemplified by Lance Armstrong (see p. 108). Having your bike professionally fitted will help with these sorts of questions.

Above
Adjusting the saddle.

Left
Checking posture on a time trial bike.

THE BIKE

BUYING A BIKE

The internet has made buying a bike both easier and more complicated. Once you've worked out what type of bike you want and even the size, the hard work begins: getting a good deal. While the internet may offer a discounted price on the bike you want, in the long term it may make more sense to buy from a local bike shop.

SHOP OR ONLINE

There's no denying that the internet will usually be cheaper than a bricks-and-mortar shop. This is fine when you're buying a component that is simple to install and requires no adjustment, such as a set of tires. Additionally, an online retailer will typically have access to a wider range than your local bike shop. But sometimes the human touch can be worth the extra cost. In your local

Left
Bike shops allow you to try out different bikes.

ADVANTAGES OF BUYING ONLINE

- Often cheaper than a shop.
- Massive choice of most brands and sizes.
- Speedy delivery across the nation.
- Typically trouble-free if you know exactly what you want and are a competent mechanic.

ADVANTAGES OF BUYING LOCALLY

- Try before you buy.
- Minor changes to the spec possible before purchase.
- Free servicing possible for new bikes.
- Fully assembled new bikes.
- Readjustment possible by a mechanic that knows the bike.
- Supports local businesses that may reward you for loyalty.

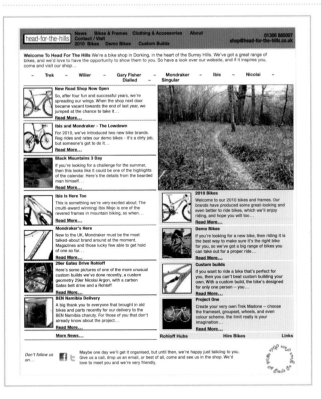

Above
Buying online offers access to a wider range of models and prices.

TIP

It can be wise to wait a year or two after a brand new model is launched. Although all bikes are thoroughly tested, many hours of real-world usage often reveal unforeseen issues – weak points in the frame in particular – that are often resolved in later models.

WHEN TO BUY

Bicycle manufacturers, for better or worse, are locked into an annual cycle of upgrading their lines. Each year, new versions of existing models are introduced and brand new bikes launched. Often the changes are only cosmetic, such as a different paintjob. From time to time, a new suspension system is introduced or a little weight is lost. But, generally, there is very little difference from one year to the next. The coming year's models make their debut from September onward, meaning that retailers become desperate to shift the current year's stock before it becomes two years out of date. Look for discounts of 20–30 percent on the current model when its new incarnation arrives. These discounted bikes are snapped up quickly, so odd sizes or unpopular colors may be the only options left by Christmas.

bike shop (LBS) you will be able to touch and try out the bikes you're interested in. You'll be able to check that they fit, and if you don't like a particular component, such as the saddle, it is usually possible to swap it for your preference. What is guaranteed to annoy your local shop, however, is borrowing a demo bike then buying it online elsewhere.

The person selling you the bike should have a detailed knowledge of the make and the model and should be able to offer useful advice. Of course, there are bad bike shops with clueless staff. Visit the shops close to you and make a judgment. In such a competitive market, the bad shops often don't stick around for long. If the staff in a specialist shop are clearly well informed but too aloof to answer basic questions, again, take your business elsewhere. But if you're lucky, there'll be an LBS nearby with friendly, positive attitude and an expertise you can't buy online. They may not have the widest choice of bikes, but they'll stock what they believe represents value. They'll be able to offer after-care and servicing in the months and years to come. And regular customers at an LBS will typically receive a 10 percent discount.

Below
Using a local supplier often results in better after-care and repair services.

THE BIKE

SECURITY: LOCKS, TAGS & TRACKING

With bike culture spreading through towns and cities, bike theft is a growing problem. At some point we will all have to leave our bikes locked outside, so here's some advice on how to do it as securely as possible. And, if the worst should happen and your bike is stolen, we look at how best to get it back.

RISK

Clearly, the best way of avoiding the theft of a bike is to avoid leaving it outside at all. The first option is always to work out if there is a secure place to stow it – indoors or in a lockable bike cage at a station, for example. If not, where is the lowest-risk spot to lock it? Thieves hate practicing their trade in the open, although this won't always deter them, and CCTV cameras are no guarantee of security. Locking a bicycle securely among other bikes may mean yours is less prominent, and thieves may go for easier targets.

Some places, such as colleges and outside pubs and bars, are intrinsically high-risk areas and require caution. Choose a well-lit area with a lot of foot traffic, but avoid places where there are signs warning owners not to leave bicycles; you may be charged a fee if your bicycle is forcibly removed, and it may be damaged in the process.

Above
When locking a bike, remove the front wheel and make sure it is locked to the frame, through the rear wheel and an immovable object.

SAFE SPOTS TO LOCK A BICYCLE

- In a busy area where it is highly visible.
- To something immovable.
- With other bikes.

TIP

Most locks come with a spare key. Keep it safe. If you lose your first key, it will save a lot of hassle.

Left
1. A simple cable lock.
2. A U-lock.
3. A heavy-duty chain with padlock.
4. A combination lock.

LOCKS

Lock manufacturers, such as Kryptonite, and bike thieves are locked in an arms race. There are two main styles of lock: U locks (also known as D locks) and heavy-duty chain or cable locks. Both are designed to resist cutting (with bolt cutters) and being levered apart (with a car jack). However, with tools, time and determination, all locks will fail eventually. So, at some point, a compromise has to be made, as we cannot all carry around multiple locks that weigh more than the bike.

If a bike has to be left outside, here's the safest way to do it. Try to use two locks of different types. This sidelines the thief who is equipped with tools for just one type of lock. Always lock a bike through the main frame triangle to an immovable object, ensuring the lock cannot be lifted over the object. Lampposts and railings are good; parking meters are bad. Best are purpose-built bike racks. Avoid locking the bike to anything that itself can be cut or broken.

Any removable parts, such as wheels and seatposts secured with a quick release, also need to be secured. You may want to take the saddle and post with you, together with your lights, bags and bike computers.

Bike locks, chains and U locks, are made from hardened steel, but the locking mechanism remains a weak point, so make a thief's task harder by fastening the lock so the keyhole is facing the ground or a wall. But don't let the lock lie against anything solid against which it could be smashed.

Many bike locks are graded according to the security they provide. Kryptonite, for example, uses a 12-point scale and offers a sliding scale of cash compensation if the lock is conquered.

Below
Kryptonite offers a range of secure locking systems.

HOW TO LOCK A BICYCLE

- If possible use two locks of different types.
- Remove the front wheel and place alongside the frame.
- Place the lock through the main wheel, around the frame triangle and a solid object.
- Thieves must not be able to lift the bike over the object.
- Make sure the shaft or keyhole is as inaccessible as possible.

THE BIKE

SECURITY: LOCKS, TAGS & TRACKING

TAGGING

There are several methods of registering and tagging a bicycle. Many police services offer a free tagging service, using a small microchip that is hidden in the frame, which can be scanned if the bike turns up after theft. There are also several bike registration schemes, although these are not free. At the very least, make a photographic record of the bike's frame number and mark your bike so that you are able to reclaim it convincingly.

If your bicycle is stolen, it may be recovered. After informing the police, contact local bike shops in case it turns up for repairs or is offered for sale, and scour online listings sites such as eBay, Craigslist and Gumtree.

NOTE

At the time of writing, we are a couple of years away from a cheap GPS tracking device for bicycles, but the technology exists and will eventually be available for bicycles.

Above
Police officers can register and protect your bike for free by placing a microchip in the frame.

HOME SECURITY

We take care when leaving our bikes in towns and cities, but we should also consider home security carefully. Thieves are aware that many bikes have a high retail value, and in some cases will follow cyclists home to find out where a high-end machine is kept. So, some basic precautions are called for. If you think you are being followed home, either in your car or on a bike, make sure you don't lead potential thieves to your door.

At home, always keep your bikes locked and out of view. Sheds are vulnerable; a garage is better. Many cyclists use motorcycle-style ground anchors to secure high-value machines in a garage. These anchors bolt into a concrete floor. Also check the garage's security. Is there an alarm with motion sensor? Motion-activated lighting? Or, most importantly, a secure door? High-security roller-shutter garage doors are becoming more popular. Don't leave a bicycle in or on a car overnight; it will be in view of passers-by, will be easy to extract and may not be covered by home insurance.

Above
Keep your bike in a locked garage or shed.

Left
A ground anchor used in a garage will increase security.

CHAPTER 2
THE GEAR

CLOTHING: COMMUTING

Rain or shine, having the right clothing for your commute will make it a safer and more enjoyable experience. If you're starting to cycle to work for the first time, working out what to wear and how to get it to and from the office can be a major headache. The good news is that you'll probably have the right clothing already; it's just a matter of planning ahead and getting the basics right.

KEEP IT SIMPLE

The perfect commuting outfit is something you can wear confidently on and off the bike. You don't have to cover yourself in Lycra and a crinkly jacket just to pedal a few miles in the morning. But the basic rules remain the same: you should wear something that will wick away sweat (draw sweat from the skin), allow lots of freedom of movement, be breathable and not get caught in chains or wheels. You don't need to overcomplicate things. As Mikael Colville-Andersen, chronicler of urban cycling at www.copenhagencyclechic .com, says: 'Open your closet, it's full of cycling clothes. Anything you can walk in, you can cycle in.' Even in Copenhagen (see p. 244), a famously pro-cycling city, with plenty of rain and genuinely cold months, 80 percent of the city's many commuting cyclists continue riding during the winter.

If you live in some of the drier areas of the world, in parts of the USA or Australia for example, you may not need to worry about inclement weather.

Right
Visibility and waterproofing are important considerations for commuters.

Left
Commuting cyclists in Copenhagen tend to wear everyday clothes rather than expensive cycling gear.

LAYERS

The under layer is as important as the outer layer. Cotton soaks up moisture and holds it, leaving you damp and chilled. It should be the last resort of any cyclist. Instead, next to the skin, wear lightweight wool, polyester mixes or even silk. These transport sweat away from the skin. Depending on the weather, a good outer layer will be anything light in weight, windproof and breathable. A bright color will help motorists spot you. On the legs, avoid voluminous skirts (or baggy bottoms) that may get caught in the chain (even with a chainguard). Slim-cut trousers, for both men and women, work well; denim jeans – which are hot, abrasive and inflexible – do not.

Whether you wear special cycling gear for a journey to work may depend on the length of the commute and whether your workplace has changing rooms and a shower. If not, just wear everyday clothes and take it easy. Those lucky enough to have a bike-friendly workplace are able to take several office outfits to work by car at the start of the week, ride in for the rest of the week, and pick them up at the end of the week. With a large car, it's possible to drive the bike and clothing in on Monday morning, ride home in the evening and leave the car at work, ready for a rainy evening later in the week.

Henry David Thoreau once said: 'Beware of all enterprises that require new clothes.' But there's one item of clothing that all cyclists could benefit from, and that's a merino-wool base layer. Woven into a tight-fitting top, merino shares some of its unique properties: it wicks moisture away from the body, is warm when wet, breathable and, unlike polyester, it's highly odor resistant. And people with sensitive skin often find they get on better with merino's natural fibers than with artificial fabrics. Merino base layers are available in varying grades of thickness.

Above
1. Waterproof jacket and trousers.
2. A wicking top.
3. Waterproof outerwear.
4. A vest.

Right
Courier bags are designed for cyclists so that they can carry heavy items such as laptop computers.

LUGGAGE

Luggage carrying is an important consideration when toting laptops around. Many courier-style bags, such as those by Crumpler, hold laptops securely; in addition to the shoulder strap, some have an extra strap that runs around the torso to hold the bag in place. Laptop-friendly backpacks spread the burden over both shoulders, but for bulkier luggage, a set of waterproof panniers (see p. 292) will take the weight off your back altogether.

THE GEAR

CLOTHING: ROAD RACING

Love it or hate it, Lycra (or spandex) is to cyclists what denim is to cowboys – only less flattering, unless you have the legs of Chris Hoy. From Sunday morning social rides to the Grand Tours, the default outfit for roadies is a pair of Lycra shorts, a tight, bright top and a pair of iridescent shades. But what makes it such a practical option? And do you have to have a tan and less than 5 percent body fat to pull off the look?

Left
Skintight shorts and tops wick sweat away from the skin.

HISTORY

It wasn't always this way. Back in the early days of the Tour, the cyclists would wear thick woolen shorts, heavy shirts and motorcycle goggles. It was a reflection of cycling's working-class origins. Sponsors' logos were banned, and the overall ethos was very utilitarian. Even by the 1950s, in Britain, racing cyclists were forced to pursue their sport clandestinely and would wear plain black clothing to escape notice during their early morning time trials. This is probably why black is the basic color for Lycra shorts, instead of red, white or blue.

Lycra was invented by Dupont in the 1950s, although it didn't make its way into cycle clothing until the 1980s.

FUNCTION

With the advent of man-made fabrics, the cyclist's world was revolutionized. Cycling clothing has to balance several different requirements: it has to be light, comfortable, allow freedom of movement, be streamlined and wick away sweat from the skin.

Lycra, now frequently used as the generic name for any stretchy material, is admirably suited to this task. Lycra shorts, which fit closely to the skin, provide support to muscles and won't get snagged on anything. Inside, most cycling shorts will have a padded crotch, giving a little extra comfort during a long, hard day in the saddle.

Once this would have been made from chamois leather (softened with an anti-bacterial cream), but today most are a honeycombed foam pad. They can be stitched or welded to the shorts, the latter to be

EXTREMITIES

Only Lance Armstrong can carry off the long-black-sock look; for the rest of us, short white socks are the default option (avoid cotton). On the hands, fingerless cycling gloves should have a ventilated topside, a soft leather underside to protect the palm from blisters and a patch of terry cloth over the thumb for mopping the brow. On the head, a short-peaked cycling cap can be worn under a visorless helmet for extra style.

preferred where possible. The very best shorts, from firms such as Assos, are very comfortable when you're in the bent-over riding position. Bibshorts have shoulder straps, removing the need for a potentially uncomfortable elastic waistband, and are cut low down below the navel (to make up for the absence of a fly).

WEATHER

In winter you can wear bibshorts under a pair of thick thermal tights or a pair of tights with a padded insert. The best of these will be shaped from a windproof fabric.

On the top, a cycling jersey will typically be made from polyester. Most will be cut longer at the back, where there will be a couple of pockets for stashing snacks, tools and a vest.

The vest is a useful addition to the wardrobe: a zip-up, sleeveless garment with windproof panels at the front that keeps the chill off your chest on long descents, although pros are still known to stuff a newspaper down their jerseys at the top of a climb.

Below
Layering clothing allows you to dress for different conditions:

1. Long-sleeved top with vest.
2. Long-sleeved windproof top.
3. Summer outfit.
4. Waterproof jacket.
5. Three-quarter length tights and vest.
6. Spring outfit with base layer.

THE GEAR

CLOTHING: OFF-ROAD

Mountain bikers make many demands on their clothing: it has to be durable, protect the rider from the elements and unscheduled dismounts and carry extra cargo. There is also the small matter of appearance. Mountain bikers like to make a statement – 'I ride on dirt not pavement' – and will dress accordingly in looser outfits than their road-going cousins.

HELMETS

Starting at the top, helmets for mountain biking differ from road riding helmets in several key areas. The protective coverage is increased, particularly at the back of the head, as mountain bikers are more likely to land on that part of their head. The helmets are also tougher, although they can be just as well ventilated as a road helmet.

Mountain biking helmets will also feature a visor, useful for keeping sun, rain and dirt out of the eyes. Roadies rarely wear a visor. There are also free riding helmets, produced by the main manufacturers such as

Giro, Bell and Specialized, that are designed to withstand greater impacts, plus motorcycle-style full-face helmets that protect the whole of the face. These are used by downhillers.

A Buff is a versatile tube of fabric that can be worn under the helmet bandana-style or around the neck, in cool weather or to mop up sweat.

Right
Many mountain bikers prefer baggy shorts.

Below
Hydration packs are designed for mountain bikers.

Below

1. Waterproof jacket.

2. Vest.

3. Short-sleeved top.

Below
Protective knee pads provide a
sense of security but can be bulky.

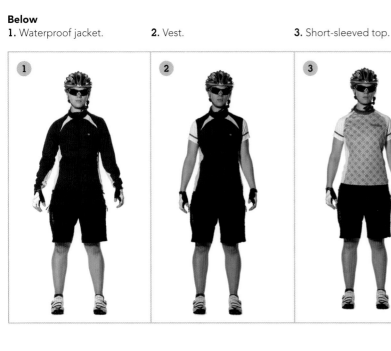

LAYERS

For the jersey, mountain
bikers have the same
requirements as road riders:
it has to wick moisture away
from the body as effectively
as possible, and it has to
dry quickly. The cut is often
loose, allowing greater
range of movement, and
long-sleeved jerseys are
worn more widely. Pockets
at the back can be used
to store snacks and tools,
but because mountain
bikers often carry more
gear (shock pumps, spares
for breakages, maps) many
will wear a small backpack
that also doubles as a
hydration system. Most
mountain biking jerseys are
made from polyester mixes,
although body-hugging
base layers of merino wool
are growing rapidly in
popularity, thanks to their

odor-resistant properties
and warmth even when
they are wet.

The range of jackets
suitable for mountain
biking is huge. Styles range
from lightweight shells
that can be stowed in the
backpack to heavier padded
or waterproof jackets
fashioned from GoreTex or
eVent, depending on the
conditions. Layering lets you
add or remove clothing as
the temperature changes.

Below the waist, mountain
bikers typically wear baggy
shorts. Under the 'baggies'
the best option is to wear
good-quality Lycra bibshorts
(see p. 61). In cold weather,
mountain bikers wear
thermal tights or three-
quarter length shorts.

HANDS
AND FEET

On the hands and feet,
the watchword is 'rugged':
gloves are invariably full-
finger and can feature
protective panels on the
top of the hand. They may
have rubbery patches on
the palm and fingertips to
help grip the handlebars in
wet weather.

Shoes range from light-
weight racing shoes, not
dissimilar to road-racing
shoes, to all-season
waterproof boots, such as
those made by Shimano.

AN OPTIMUM MOUNTAIN
BIKING OUTFIT

- Merino-wool base layer for warmth and comfort.
- Good-quality Lycra bibshorts.
- Tough, baggy shorts in a rip-stop fabric.
- Long-sleeved jersey.
- Lightweight, breathable jacket.
- Hydration pack or small backpack.

WOMEN-SPECIFIC GEAR

As more women start cycling, so demand is growing for clothing designed for the female body. That doesn't mean the same clothing in feminine shades, but structurally different pieces. Not only do women tend to have smaller hands and feet than men, but also the proportions of the female body are different. Thankfully, these days, there is a far wider range of women-specific gear to try compared even with ten years ago.

CLOTHING

In general, in addition to the more obvious differences, women have proportionally shorter torsos and longer waists and thighs than men, making women-specific clothing vital for comfort. The most important item to get right, as always, is the shorts. Like men, women will benefit from good-quality, padded Lycra shorts, which are constructed from panels designed to fit while in the riding position (so remember to test them this way). The same rules apply: the shorts should be supportive, wick away sweat and have a padded insert that fits. However, the details may be quite different. Women often prefer a more supportive fabric, and the cut for women's shorts differs to accommodate female proportions. Many different types of shorts cut with longer and shorter legs

are available, but avoid the hipster style, as a higher waist will keep the lower back covered (and warm) when cycling. An extra flap of fabric can even transform shorts into a 'skort'.

As with men's shorts, the internal pad, once made from chamois leather, is made of foam these days. The pads vary in thickness and width, so try a few in the shop. As always, you get what you pay for. Some of the best brands for women are Sugoi and Assos. Cheaper pads are sewn into the shorts, while higher up the range the pad will be welded on to the Lycra, avoiding abrasive seams.

Cycling shorts are not designed to be worn with underwear, as this would impede the wicking effect and create friction. Always check the care instructions

Left
Some cycling clothing is cut specifically for the female shape.

before you wash them: only use cold water, no spin and no spin driers.

Tops for women have the same basic features and requirements as those for men: a tight fit with pockets at the back, made of a breathable, wicking fabric that doesn't irritate the skin. A comfortable, ideally

seamless, sports bra is essential for cycling, and mountain bikers will want extra support and stability.

The range of crop-top sports bras available from manufacturers such as Sugoi and Shock Absorber combines firm support with fabrics that wick away any moisture.

ACCESSORIES

The best women's cycling gloves will not only be smaller than men's versions, but also have different proportions in the palm width and finger lengths. Some styles also have a gel insert on the heel of the palm to relieve pressure on

the ulnar nerve, which can cause numb or tingling fingers if pinched. Like men's gloves, women's cycling gloves should have a mesh topside for breathability, a terry cloth-covered thumb for wiping away perspiration and a soft, grippy palm.

Women's shoes and helmets should also be sized appropriately. The US bike company Specialized has a particularly well-thought-out range of gear for women, including shoes, helmets, gloves and other clothing.

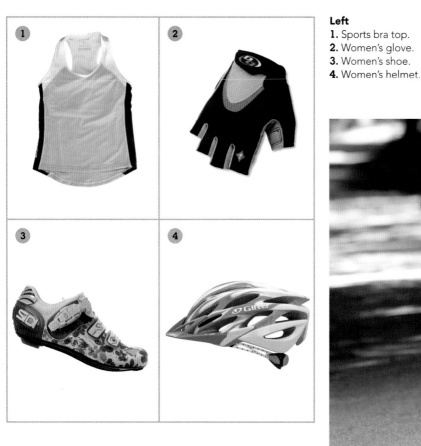

Left
1. Sports bra top.
2. Women's glove.
3. Women's shoe.
4. Women's helmet.

Right
Specialized's Body Geometry line offers a great choice of women-specific gear.

SHOES

Off the bike, you hear them before you see them: the tip-tap of cycling shoes on hard floors. They're a source of fear and confusion for novice cyclists but, once mastered, will improve comfort and performance considerably. So how do cycling shoes work, and what should you look for?

Any shoe, boot or sandal can be used for cycling. If you're just cycling to work or the store, there's no real need for a pair of cycling shoes. But, if you want to go farther, having your feet attached to the pedals will be more efficient, enabling you to apply power for more of the pedal stroke while pulling up with the other foot. Thanks to a stiff sole and supportive uppers, they also reduce fatigue in the foot by reducing unnecessary flex. Cycling shoes today are used with 'clipless' pedals (such as SPDs, *see* p. 27), which have a mechanism into which cleats slot. They've largely replaced toe clips, the old-fashioned straps attaching the foot to the pedal.

Above
A cycling shoe's cleats click into and out of clipless pedals.

TECHNIQUE

The principle is simple: a cleat on the shoe's sole locks into a catch on the pedal. Twist the heel of the foot to release the cleat. It's a rite of passage for most cyclists to topple over at an intersection just after remembering their feet are attached to the pedals.

Below left
Cleats on a mountain biking shoe; note the studs at the toe for extra grip.

Below right
Cleats on a road-cycling shoe: note the larger platform.

FIT

The fit should be snug. Although feet do swell on a long, hot ride, any sort of movement will cause a hotspot or blister. Those with wider feet may be tempted to go up a size, but instead try extra-wide shoes from Shimano or Sidi.

Left
1. Casual cycling shoe.
2. Mid-range road-riding shoe.
3. Top-end road-riding shoe.
4. Mountain bike shoe.

TYPES

Whether it be mountain biking, road racing or riding around town, cycling shoes have evolved to meet the specific demands of each type of riding. At the performance end of the market, shoes will have a stiff but lightweight carbon-fiber sole; the shoe does not need to flex (which will lose energy) but must be supportive. The upper is usually leather and may be secured with laces, Velcro or ratchets.

Commuters should pick shoes that are comfortable for walking; there are several that are as flexible as regular shoes but simply have recessed cleats. Cleat covers will protect polished wood or stone floors from the metal cleats.

Mountain bikers will find robust shoes and boots available; pick a pair designed for mountain biking rather than road-riding and they'll have a longer lifespan.

COMPATIBILITY

The most complicated part of choosing a pair of cycling shoes is compatibility. With several major clipless pedal designs on the market (including Shimano, LOOK, Time and Speedplay) you'll need to make sure your shoes are compatible with the pedals you want to use: each design has its own style of cleat. Cleats are fixed to the sole of the shoe via bolts and small threaded holes on the underside of the shoe. The position of the cleat holes varies from brand to brand, although there is a small degree of adjustability. The received wisdom on where to place the cleat is to fix it just behind the ball of the foot (*see* p. 27 to learn more).

THE GEAR

HELMETS

There's little doubt that wearing a helmet will protect your head in the event of a crash or accident. This protection can prevent superficial bumps and bruises and even serious brain injury. Many people feel that wearing a helmet is a wise precaution; modern helmets are light, well ventilated and comfortable. However, many observers agree that compelling people to wear helmets is counter-productive; in most places cyclists are free to make their own minds up.

Below
Cycle helmets have a hard outer shell and dense foam to protect the head. Ventilating slots allow in cooling air.

Most cycle helmets are made from expanded polystirene foam with an outer layer of thin, hard plastic. The foam absorbs the force of any impact, often cracking. Cycle helmets are not designed to take repeated blows, so even if there is little visible damage after an impact, the helmet should still be replaced. Most manufacturers offer a crash-replacement discount.

In a few places, such as Australia, cycle helmets are mandatory for all ages. In approximately 20 US states they are required for all young cyclists (mid-teens and younger).

There is evidence that forcing people to wear helmets can discourage cycling; and for cyclists there is safety in numbers. However, most cyclists choose to wear a helmet

HELMET FITTING RULES

- Having measured your head, try on a few helmets; there are subtle differences in the shape of both heads and helmets.

- A helmet that fits correctly will sit comfortably when level on your head. It should extend down to a couple of finger-widths above your brow but not impair your vision.

- Fine-tune the fit by tightening the straps under the chin (leave just enough wiggle-room for a finger so that you can open your mouth) and the V sits just under your ears. The strap behind the ear controls how far forward the helmet will tilt; the strap in front of the ear governs how far back it will tilt. There shouldn't be more than 1 inch of movement in either direction.

- If there is one, tighten the ratchet or clasp at the rear. Your helmet should not move from side to side.

TIP

A helmet that doesn't fit properly is useless. Cheaper helmets are available in just one size, although they will have adjustable straps. Measure your head size by wrapping a tape measure around the widest part of your head; this is the circumference. More expensive helmets are usually available in two or more sizes and will have an adjustable clasp at the rear as well as chin straps.

TIP

There's little point spending more than you need on a racing helmet if you're only wearing it to ride around town.

as they offer extra safety for minimal cost and inconvenience. When selecting a helmet, look for a model that conforms to national standards: the Consumer Product Safety Commission (CPSC) in the USA, the British Standards (BS) mark in the UK, and Australian or New Zealand Standards (AS/NZS). Standards set by the US organization Snell are especially rigorous.

Many of the major helmet manufacturers, including Giro, Bell, Specialized and Met, offer helmets for every sort of cycling, from commuting trips to downhill mountain biking. The first step is deciding what your helmet will be used for and how much you want to spend on it.

Above
Adjust the helmet for a safe and secure fit. A helmet should not move around on the head:

1. Level the helmet.
2. Fasten the chin strap.
3. Tighten the chin strap.
4. Tighten the rear clasp if there is one.

(Also *see* Helmet fitting rules opposite).

TYPES OF HELMET

For city cycling a mid-range helmet will suffice. It will have to be robust enough to take knocks and scrapes as you carry it around. A basic mountain biking helmet would be fine but not one so expensive that you would regret its loss to a thief. A bright color will make you more visible in traffic.

ROAD RACING

Ventilation and weight are the key criteria. Most top-of-the-line road-cycling helmets are so light – under 250 grams – as to be almost unnoticeable when worn.

MOUNTAIN BIKING

These offer more coverage, extending farther down the back of the head and around the sides. Downhill bikers often wear full-face helmets for extra protection.

BMX

Nicknamed 'skidlids', helmets for BMX have a tougher outer shell that means they can be used again after a knock.

THE GEAR

CHILDREN'S CYCLING GEAR

We looked at how best to introduce children to cycling on p. 38, but even before they have a bike of their own, there's an array of gear that can get them out and about on two (or more) wheels. And, in addition to the child-carrying options, there are ways of ensuring they remain safe and comfortable.

Above right
Children can be seated on the front or rear of the bike; or both.

Below right
A strap will secure the child in a seat.

Most experts agree that children should not be using a child seat on a bicycle before the age of one year and perhaps not until the second. This is because, as a proportion of their bodyweight, very young children's heads are too heavy for their weak neck muscles to support, especially when coupled with a helmet and bouncing along a rough surface. But once the child has grown sufficiently to hold its head up, parents can look at either adding a child seat to a bicycle or a tag-a-long trailer. This enables parents to get some fresh air and exercise while the child experiences their first taste of two-wheeled travel.

COMFORT

Perched on a seat, a child is exposed to the same sun and wind as an adult cyclist, so don't forget to apply sunscreen and clothe the child in warm, windproof clothing or a sunhat. It is important to remember that as the child is not exercising, they can grow cold quickly.

Pedaling on a tag-a-long, the child will be working up an appetite, so bring food and drink on every ride. For larger children, Camelbak produce a child's version of their hydration packs (the Skeeter).

CHILD SEATS

There are two main options: front- or rear-mounted seats. Rear-mounted seats are affixed to a rack with the child facing forward. These seats tend to be secure and stable but have the disadvantage of placing the child out of the adult's field of vision. The best seats have a five- or six-point harness, and so long as this is correctly adjusted there's little chance of the child slipping out. Many of the better seats have footrests and side supports to prevent lolling heads. Choosing the correct size of seat is determined by the child's size and weight rather than age.

The front-mounted seat, such as the WeeRide, sits on the crossbar, between your arms. These seats keep the child in view and free up the rear rack for luggage carrying. The child gets a better view and won't feel quite so ignored. Try a couple of styles to see how the weight distribution feels. Look for removable padding (for washing), adjustable footrests so the seat can be used as the child grows, and that it meets the national safety standard (confirmed by the CPSC stamp in the USA, the BS mark in the UK, and the AS/NZS mark in Australia and New Zealand).

TAG-A-LONGS

For older children (four to five), an alternative to a seat mounted directly on to the bicycle is a tag-a-long trailer. These are typically fixed to the seatpost or rear rack and pivot with a simple bearing attachment. The rack-mounted models have a superior range of movement. Look for both horizontal and vertical movement. Tag-a-longs typically provide the child with handlebars and pedals. Unlike a tandem, the pedaling action is independent of the main drivetrain but it allows the child to practice pedaling or just freewheel. The child will also learn road sense from watching the adult.

Remember to fit fenders to the towing bicycle. To prevent little feet flying off pedals, you can try fitting Power Grips (simple pedal straps). An increasingly popular child-carrying alternative is the two-wheeled trailer (or chariot), which is towed behind a bicycle, usually hitched to the rear axle. For young children they have several advantages: a low ride height for stability, a cover for shade and a robust construction. The best convert into strollers, making them perfect for errands and full days out. Look for an aluminum frame and good quality hubs with smooth bearings.

Right
Cycle trailers (or chariots) are a good option for longer rides.

THE GEAR

MOUNTAIN BIKING ACCESSORIES

With the prospect of challenging terrain, complex equipment and long days in the saddle to consider, it's no wonder that mountain bikers tend to carry more gear than their road-riding cousins. What you carry with you will depend on your style of riding, how far you're going and what you're riding. Find out what's essential and what's not.

Left
A mountain biker wearing a hydration pack and a helmet with a visor.

Below
Hydration packs have a special compartment for water and a nozzle that allows riders on-the-go drinking.

SAFETY

Dehydration is a hazard for mountain bikers, especially since they may find themselves far from civilization. Most bikers use a backpack fitted with a hydration system, an idea popularized by Camelbak. The system comprises a plastic bladder or reservoir that can carry 1–3 liters of fluid. This fits into a pouch inside the pack and a tube (with bite valve) curls over the shoulder to enable the biker to sip water as they ride without taking their hands off the bars. To keep them free from bacteria they should be cleaned and sterilized regularly (sterilization kits for baby bottles are useful). Avoid putting sweetened drinks (or sports drinks) inside, as they'll encourage bacteria or leave a sticky residue. They are made from rip-stop nylon and are very durable.

MAINTENANCE

In addition to the basic tools carried by all cyclists (see p. 302), mountain bikers on full-suspension bikes often carry a shock pump to adjust their suspension on the go (shock pumps are much smaller, and more precise than a tire pump). Zip ties are useful for securing out-of-action components, such as a damaged derailleur. A multi-tool, such as a Leatherman with pliers and

Left
Mountain bikers often wear protective gear:
1. Long-fingered padded gloves.
2. Waterproof gloves.
3. Knee pads.
4. Elbow pads.

Below
Baggy clothes are best for mountain biking as they don't hamper movement.

TIPS FOR EXTENDED BACKCOUNTRY ADVENTURES

Whether you're in the Scottish Highlands or the wilds of North America, there are certain items or gadgets that may make an important difference in a survival situation:

- GPS unit (pre-programmed with useful waymarks).

- Fully charged mobile phone (like the GPS, not to be relied on).

- LED headlamp (small, helpful for signaling rescuers).

- Compass (and the knowledge to use it).

- Foil survival blanket (compact and potentially lifesaving).

PROTECTION

a knife, can prove useful on longer rides. The pliers can be used to bend chainrings back into shape and the knife for trimming zip-ties. And, in the expectation of punctures occurring, mountain bikers often pack a spare inner tube.

When riding over rocks, roots and logs, many mountain bikers choose to wear protective pads on their knees and elbows in case of a crash. The most popular varieties, from companies such as Dainese, have a hard outer shell and a padded lining. However, they're a hot, bulky option and impede pedaling. Some riders carry pads in their backpacks and only wear them for difficult

descents. They can help boost skills by allowing riders to take risks without too many consequences, but they're no substitute for skill.

More important, perhaps, is protecting eyes from dust, dirt, bugs and twigs with a pair of wraparound shades. There's nothing worse than negotiating a steep slope with one eye closed. Serious downhill mountain bikers

wear ski-style goggles, such as those produced by Oakley. It's worth noting that, as mountain biking involves moving in and out of shaded and bright areas on a typical ride, it's wise to select a tint that can be used in both conditions. A yellowish tint to the lenses will brighten darker areas and increase definition.

ACCESSORIES: LIGHTS

Some basic accessories make life safer for all cyclists. Top of the list is a set of lights. Wherever you live, bicycle lights are essential for riding after dark – as much for making you visible to others as illuminating the way forward. Bike lights range from the basic to retina-burning bright: we'll shine a light on the options and the relative costs.

Different locales may have their own requirements for cyclists' visibility, but most bikes sold by a shop will comply with specific regulations. At the most minimal level, this means new bikes will be fitted with front and rear reflectors. However, to cycle after dark will require a separate set of lights. In most places, and as a matter of self-preservation, cyclists must use front (white) and rear (red) lights at night. These have to be mounted where they are clearly visible to other traffic.

Left
Lights and high visibility clothing are vital at night.

Lights come in varying degrees of brightness, which is measured in lumens, while the light's power is measured in watts.

Standard LED (Light Emitting Diode) lights are inexpensive, adequate for city riding and enjoy a long battery life. These compact lights click into a bracket mounted on the handlebars and on the seatpost so they can be easily removed at the end of a journey. They'll usually have a variety of modes, including flashing, which has been shown to

Above
Knog lights clip on to handlebars and seatposts and can be easily removed.

HEADLAMPS

These can be extremely useful for cyclists. Not only does the beam, when the light is mounted on a helmet, follow the rider's gaze, unlike handlebar-mounted lights, but it provides hands-free lighting when making repairs. Headlights from Petzl and Black Diamond are highly recommended for cyclists, and such companies frequently team their front lights with helmet-mounted flashing red LEDs for the rear, for extra visibility.

Left
1. Front light.
2. Rear LED light.
3. Madison rechargeable front light.

be more visible to drivers in constant traffic. The preferred tactic is to use one flashing and one steady light at the rear. It's a good idea to ensure that your front and rear lights can also be seen from the side, and in some places this may be a legal requirement.

Basic LED lights are highly affordable and are usually powered by standard AA and AAA batteries, although more expensive, rechargeable LED lights are available.

In Europe, lights powered by a dynamo, run from either the hub or in bottle-dynamo form by rotating along the tire, are more widespread. Batteries are not required, but their power output is low and the bottle-dynamo's performance is particularly patchy. Lighting for more extreme night-time cycling requires a brighter, more reliable solution.

Below
Mountain bikers often use high-powered helmet-mounted lights.

MOUNTAIN BIKE LIGHTS

Lights for night-time off-road riding, from companies such as Niterider and Lumicycle, are extraordinarily powerful; indeed, so powerful that in some cases they may be illegal on the road (check your local laws if you suspect your mountain bike lights exceed restrictions). As well as the latest generation of powerful LED bulbs, super-bright options include halogen and halide bulbs. These lights can range from 700 to 1,000 lumens, ten times the power of a standard bike light, and cost as much as an entire new bike.

Their advantage lies in great depth, enabling riders to judge distances and see the route ahead even on the darkest nights. However, their power consumption is considerable, and a fully recharged set of batteries may last for only three hours at a time. For powerful LED lights, halogen and halide (HID), battery power is provided by lithium-ion (li-ion) or acid (NiMH) batteries. Bulky battery packs may be housed in the waterbottle cage on the bike's frame.

ACCESSORIES: GADGETS

This category covers the more advanced accessories: non-essential but an asset to many cyclists. These gadgets will tell you where you've been, where you're going and how fast you're getting there. With the means to share data – from training rides, commutes and sightseeing rides – online with friends and club-mates, these gadgets are becoming increasingly popular with all sorts of cyclists.

COMPUTERS

Once a high-tech luxury, cycle computers are now highly affordable. Even basic models are wireless, beaming information from a sensor mounted on the fork to the handlebar-mounted unit. Entry-level computers inform cyclists of their speed (maximum and average), distance traveled and time. Mid-range models add an altimeter for elevation gained and lost. They need to be carefully set up and calibrated (using the size of wheel).

HEART-RATE MONITORS

The heart-rate monitor (HRM) measures the work your heart is doing on a ride and is especially useful for training cyclists who want to stay above or below a certain level of exertion for training purposes. Most feature a sensor, held in place on the chest by an elastic strap, that feeds data to a wristwatch. Polar are market leaders, but many smartphones now carry HRM apps.

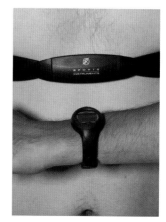

Above left
Cycle computers provide speed, time and distance data at the touch of a button.

Above right
Smartphones can become versatile cycle computers.

Left
Heart-rate monitors (HRM) are useful for training cyclists.

WHAT IS GPS?

GPS stands for Global Positioning System (GPS). The technology was developed in the 1990s. The first of the 24 GPS satellites was rocketed into orbit on Valentine's Day 1989, and the satellites, plus several spares, orbit 12,400 miles above the earth. The more satellites a signal can be received from, the more accurately a position can be calculated. In 2000, GPS was opened up to civilian use, and it is now widely used by hikers, climbers and cyclists.

Below
The Edge 705 cycle computer from Garmin uses GPS for navigation.

POWER METERS

Still the preserve of professionals, power meters measure a rider's power output (in watts). They're useful for gauging performance during solo exertions such as time trials, but have limited use for recreational cyclists.

GPS

The greatest advance in gadget technology has been GPS. In recent years, it has revolutionized how we navigate, plan trips, maximize our time and effort and even conduct rescues. With the development of smartphone apps and social media, GPS has also enabled us to share detailed data, making cycling much more of a communal activity.

Many smartphones have a GPS function today and, coupled with a free software application, this is enough to plot a route (using waypoints), and collect the data after a ride to share with friends.

All-in-one gadgets, such as the Garmin Edge series, can measure speed, distance, elevation and power, while keeping an electronic eye on your heart rate. While most GPS units designed for the outdoors are robust, don't neglect to ensure that the unit is securely mounted on your handlebars (using a purpose-built mount). There's nothing quite so heartbreaking as watching an expensive little gadget bouncing downhill.

HOW TO READ GPS COORDINATES

The Greenwich Meridian divides the world into east and west along lines of longitude, much like the segments of an orange, while the equator splits it into degree-sized segments in northern and southern hemispheres (90°N latitude is the North Pole). Each degree can be broken down into 60 minutes then 60 seconds; at the Equator a minute represents about a mile in distance. The first number of a traditional GPS coordinate will give the degree of latitude followed by minutes and seconds, then the degree of longitude followed by minutes and seconds. For example, the GPS coordinate of London's Canary Wharf tower, 51° 30' 19"N by 0° 1' 10" E, tells you that it is just over 51 and half degrees north of the equator (the '30' represents half a degree) and a fraction of a degree east of the Greenwich Meridian.

CHAPTER 3

TECHNIQUES & SAFETY

LEARNING TO RIDE

Learning to cycle, or returning to cycling after several years or even decades, need not be an intimidating process. A solid grounding in basic techniques will smooth the transition, for young and not-so-young, from wobbly beginner to safe and confident cyclist.

Right
As cities get more congested, using bicycles to commute to the office is becoming a popular option.

FIVE REASONS TO RIDE

1. It's fun.

2. It's practical.

3. It's healthy.

4. It's green.

5. It's sociable.

As cycling moves from sport to transport, many more people could become born-again cyclists. London, for example, has set a target of a 400 percent increase in journeys by bike by 2025 (from levels in 2000). In New York, the city's Department of Transportation aims to triple the number of commutes by bicycle over the decade to 2017; by 2010 more than half a million New Yorkers were riding bicycles. In Australia, the City of Sydney Council spent A$70m over four years on cycling facilities and from 2009 A$115m was spent on improving Victoria's cycling network. Also in 2009, New Zealand's government committed NZ$50m to creating a national network of cycleways. As David Byrne, the Talking Heads singer and long-time bicycle advocate, notes, bicycles are no longer only for the 'athletic and risk-prone'.

It stands to reason that there is an army of new cyclists preparing to do battle on the roads of towns and cities around the world, except it is precisely this image of cycling as confrontational – a war waged between those on two wheels and those on four – and the perceived risks of riding on the road that will put many of them off for good.

Right
For the young or old,
cycling is great exercise.

ENVIRONMENT

Of course, there's more to
cycling than getting from A
to B quicker than a car in
rush-hour traffic. A cyclist
riding to work in the
morning is one less driver
adding to congestion. The
environmental benefits of
cycling are obvious, but so
is the benefit to the ebb and
flow of a city. Studies show
that cities with a high
proportion of cyclists
typically rank higher on
a quality-of-life index.
Bicycles enrich the urban
environment in a multitude
of ways, not just by being
emission-free. As cult
cycling blogger Mikael
Colville-Andersen says: 'If
you're standing shoulder to
shoulder at a red light with
100 cyclists, so close you
can smell perfume, that
must give some sense
of community.'

FITNESS

As a form of exercise,
cycling is of immense
benefit, not just to the
young and sprightly but
also the elderly. Unlike,
say, jogging, cycling is
not a load-bearing activity,
making it an excellent
low-impact form of exercise
for those with joint or
bone problems (*see also*
p. 154–158), such as the
elderly or overweight.
It's also a good form of
cardio-vascular exercise,
increasing endurance and
burning calories. The
amount of calories burned
will depend on the weight
of the cyclist and the level
and duration of the
exertion, but it will
be several hundred an
hour (although fewer,
usually, than jogging).

FUN

The real, enduring appeal
of cycling, though, is
the same as it was when
most of us sat astride our
first bicycles as children:
it's fun. More than that,
it gives us freedom and
independence.

No matter the technological
innovations of computer
games or ever-busier urban
areas, the sheer fun to be
had when cycling will always
be something worth sharing
with the next generation.

Below left
Cycling is good for the
environment by reducing
car pollution.

Below right
Independence is a key
part of the fun of cycling.

LEARNING TO RIDE AS AN ADULT

The adage that you never forget how to ride a bike isn't always completely accurate. Returning cyclists can expect to be a bit rusty. As an adult getting started on two wheels, it's important to begin with the basic principles, such as controlling the brakes and dismounting, and from there everything else will start to fall into place.

OLD DOGS, NEW TRICKS

The learning curve is always steeper for adult beginners. Not only can adults be slower to pick up new skills, but being taller, heavier and less agile, they are at greater risk of injury in a fall (*see p. 101 for how to minimize injuries*). This is especially important to remember when older people are taking up cycling again. Many organizations – for example Bike New York and various other city-based groups across the USA, Bikeability in the UK, and the City of Sydney local government authority in Australia – offer classes (sometimes free) and one-to-one instruction to adults.

Above
Instruction can give confidence to new adult cyclists.

PATIENCE

Impose no time limit; people learn at different rates. Break it down into one-hour sessions at most, and many adults will be cycling within four hours.

SETUP

Bike choice is important. It is better to use a bicycle that's slightly too small than one that's too large and ungainly, as it will be easier to maneuver and control. Similarly, the saddle height should be slightly lower than a seasoned cyclist would prefer, enabling the beginner to place both feet on the ground comfortably. It's also important to make the usual safety checks (see pp. 92–93), particularly making sure that the brake levers are within easy reach of the handlebars.

FIRST STEPS

Don't underestimate the fear factor for adult first-timers. What is second nature to an experienced cyclist can be a frightening experience for a new cyclist. Work out what the main anxieties are: falling off; losing control?

One strategy to combat these fears is to practice braking and dismounting before turning a pedal. Try removing the pedals from the cranks (see p. 324); many cyclists prefer to coast down a gentle slope to find their sense of balance. Braking should be gentle and steady. The front brake delivers the greatest stopping power (in a ratio of about 70:30, front to rear). But jamming on the front brake abruptly will result in a trip over the handlebars. Posture is key. The head, which has a huge effect upon balance and stability, should be up, and the rider should be looking ahead. Don't move the head around. Select an easy gear, one with moderate resistance. Start with the leading foot's pedal at the two o'clock position, i.e. up and slightly forward. Push down with the leading foot and quickly place the second foot on its pedal. Don't look down! It's natural to wobble. Beginners rarely fall over forward or backward. That's the preserve of mountain bikers attempting steep hills. Instead, the first-time cyclist is most likely to topple over sideways. Speed will improve balance, but if increasing speed isn't possible, another tip to try when you begin to fall is to steer in the direction you're falling.

CORNERING

Once the rider has found their sense of balance and is comfortable pedaling in a straight line, it's time to make a turn. Cornering a bicycle is as much about shifting bodyweight by leaning in the direction you wish to turn as it is about turning the handlebars. Again, this can best be practiced in a safe, open area free from vehicles.

Above left
Learning to pedal is best done on a gentle grassy slope.

Above right
Keep your fingers covering the brake levers so you can stop quickly if you want.

TECHNIQUES & SAFETY

CYCLING WITH CHILDREN

It's a rite of passage for most children: the first bike-riding lesson shortly followed by the first crash. A few bumps and bruises can be expected when introducing children to cycling, but the end result should be a youngster reveling in two-wheeled freedom.

THE RULES

There are no rules. There are a variety of approaches, and what works for one child may not work for another. Getting hung up on a particular tactic won't necessarily be successful. The key is to read the child's responses, adapt and respond. And something that the children of avid cyclists may suffer from is a surfeit of pressure. Be patient. Not every three-year-old is ready to ride.

Left
A balance bike for two- to three-year-olds.

Below
Tag-a-long attachments give children a sense of independence.

TIMING

As any parent knows, children develop at wildly differing rates. From the age of two, most children are eager to scoot along on ride-on toys, but usually it's not until they're three that they have the coordination to make turns. From around four to five, strength and coordination increase – remember that to ride a bike several things need to done at once (balancing, pedaling, steering and braking). The majority of children will be ready to learn to ride by six.

In Scandinavian countries, many children use a balance bike (*see* p. 38) from the age of three. This is a basic bicycle, often wooden, with a low seat and no pedals. It allows slow, gradual progression from scooting along flat ground to freewheeling at a higher speed, teaching balance and steering.

In addition to a balance bike, using a tag-a-long can familiarize children with pedaling.

FIRST BIKE

When the time comes, it's important that a first bicycle should be the correct size. The task will be much harder on a bike that is too large. A low weight is also crucial; many low-quality children's bikes are overbuilt and too heavy for little legs to pedal, but a children's bike from a specialist such as Islabikes will be light with the correct dimensions, such as child-sized brake levers. A first bike will typically have 12- or 14-inch wheels; 16-inch wheels are acceptable for larger children (four to five years).

FIRST RIDE

After some months of practice on a balance bike, remove the pedals on the child's bike. Running alongside the child with a steadying hand between their shoulder blades (not holding on to the bike itself) will help them get a feel for their center of gravity on the new bike. Encourage them to relax and remember that wobbling is OK. It's a good idea to practice braking and dismounting before the pedaling starts and speeds get higher.

Left
Children love the freedom of a bicycle.

Location is important: a wide, grassy area (for soft landings) with a slight downhill slope is perfect. Start part of the way up the slope, going farther uphill as the child's ability grows. Replace the pedals. Again, as with the adult's lesson, start with the lead foot's pedal in the two o'clock position with their head up and hands on the brakes. You may need to remind them to keep pedaling after each turn. Encourage them to look ahead and not look down or turn their head to the side to look at you.

Keep running alongside the child, offering praise and encouragement. At first it may be easier for the child to coast downhill with their feet on the pedals, but repeated practice will result in pedaling sooner or later. Once this stage has been attained, you might like to make the lesson into a game by adding small cones they can ride around to reinforce balance and steering control.

Left
A steadying hand on the back helps young riders find their balance.

CYCLING WITH CHILDREN

TRAINING WHEELS

Training wheels pose a dilemma for parents. While they may make things much easier for the child in terms of not falling off (although the wheels can catch obstacles and topple the bike), in the long term they may be less helpful. Experts are split: Isla Rowntree, founder of Islabikes, believes that the use of a balance bike from a young age renders training wheels unnecessary. The London Cycling Campaign also argues that learning to balance on a bike without pedals makes it easier for children to progress to a bike that has pedals but not training wheels.

Momentum is certainly swinging away from training wheels. However, if you decide to use them (there are no rules, remember, and many parents have great success with the technique), attach them to the rear hub and raise them gradually so the child can lean over farther and farther. The greatest problem with training wheels is when they're removed and the child forgets that they're no longer there.

Above left
Schools and local organizations may offer lessons.

Above
Training wheels can boost confidence.

ROAD SENSE

Parental supervision for young cyclists is essential. But once the child is proficient on the bicycle, usually at around the age of six, they will want to range further from parental control. Even while remaining on driveways or sidewalks, this is the time to introduce road sense; the habit of safe cycling will last a lifetime. Safe cycling falls into two categories: what you do and what other people do, and this is covered from p. 96 to p. 101.

FALLING

Falling is an art and children may get a lot of practice, but at a certain point instinct takes over. Rather than stretching out a hand to stop the fall – an easy way to fracture a wrist – children should try to break the fall gently while protecting the head and face. Keeping the body loose and rolling with the fall is important. They should step off the bike if possible. Extra safety equipment, such as gloves and kneepads, is optional. Most children are not put off cycling by a graze or two.

Below
Accidents happen, but falling off a bike safely is a good skill to learn.

Above
A helmet is a basic precaution and children should be encouraged to wear one.

PERSONAL SAFETY

Many people learned to ride without a helmet, but a helmet is a precaution with no downside. If wearing a helmet becomes a habit, like fastening your seatbelt in a car, then it won't deter children from getting out on their bikes. Always buy a helmet with the national safety standard marking on it, so you know it conforms to national safety standards.

Encouraging your child to wear a helmet while sitting in a child seat on your bike is a useful way of introducing your child to helmet-wearing – and besides, in safety terms, children are a lot higher off the ground in this situation than they would be when riding their own bicycle.

Put your helmet on first; children love to imitate, and if you don't put yours on, they will also be very quick to ask why they have to wear a helmet and you don't. Take care fitting the helmet: it should be level on the head, covering the forehead. Movement should be minimal, but avoid pinching skin. Make it 'their' helmet; do let them choose the color and personalize it with stickers. Don't let them choose your helmet!

RIDING AS A FAMILY

Riding as a family group is one of the joys of cycling. Short journeys and longer expeditions with children, partners and pets are possible, and with just a little bit of thought and planning to make sure things run smoothly, cycling outings could quickly become a favorite family activity.

Above
A family bike ride on a traffic-free bike path.

Right
Child seats are the best solution for toddlers.

PLANNING

Shared activities are great opportunities for families to spend more time together. But beware the friction that occurs when one member is clearly a lot more passionate about the activity than the others. Exciting others about bicycles often means going at their pace and listening to what they want to do.

A bike ride for those who don't often ride bikes very far (this includes children) needs to be planned with their limitations in mind. Plan food and entertainment or play stops and avoid cramming too much in. A short distance with a special destination is best. Family cycling is not the same as simply cycling on your own or with other cyclist friends.

TOURING

Riding for several days at a time with children is possible, so long as the route is carefully planned. Don't expect to do more than 20 to 25 miles per day. This sort of distance can take up to four or five hours with food and toilet breaks. The most enjoyable routes are those on quiet roads and bike-only paths. Sustrans (see p. 105) has created a number of safe, scenic cycle routes around Britain. Other countries also have bike routes, although not organized on a national scale. Rail trails also make good routes for family rides, being free from cars and often quite flat.

To start with, select a route with fewer hills. It can be a good idea to base yourselves in one spot and do loops without having to carry luggage. Involve children in planning the route; show them the map, answer their questions and point out attractions on the way where you can all stop for a break. When riding, listen and react; children will be interested in all sorts of things they see on the ride, and it's not fair to whizz past them. After all, the joy of cycling is doing all the things you can't do in a car, and this includes stopping and exploring on a whim.

Right
Child seats are good for shorter family trips.

GEAR

Children under three can happily occupy a child seat on a bicycle (see p. 70) for an hour at a time and will often fall asleep. But for longer trips, a trailer is much more versatile, not least because of the paraphernalia that needs to be carried. In a trailer, a child is also protected from the elements, and it is a safe and stable form of transport. Dress children in layers that can be removed or added to, depending on the weather. Without exertion, children will feel the cold more than pedaling adults. A blanket in the trailer, for example, will give warmth and cushion the ride.

Trailers can also be used for children from three to five or six years, although older children will be more active and impatient. At this age a tag-a-long hitched to an adult's bike will involve them more in the activity. Gear can be carried in panniers.

Clothes for kids on tag-a-longs should be carefully chosen not to chafe or catch in wheels. A windproof outer layer is essential, as are waterproof shells if it's wet – nothing chills as quickly as a damp top. Pack a change of clothes just in case, plus hats and sunscreen, whether it's sunny or not.

OLDER CHILDREN

From the age of six, children will be too large for a trailer, and it'll be time to think about letting them loose on their own bike. The advice from the UK's national cyclists' organization, CTC, is to ride with the child between two adults. Or, a solo adult should ride just behind and to the outside of the child, protecting him or her from traffic and being ready to act quickly at intersections. Skills taught at this age will remain with children for the rest of their lives.

Above
Quiet, safe paths or roads make the best bicycle routes for families.

RIDING AS A FAMILY

FOOD AND DRINK

Every cyclist gets grumpy without sufficient food or drink. Whether children are in a trailer, on a tag-a-long or riding their bikes, it is crucial to keep them hydrated. Provide them with their own water bottles, but remind them to drink. Kids burn a lot of energy cycling, so keep up a supply of snacks, and don't wait until they're hungry. Sugary foods such as candy will send their blood sugar stratospheric before it then plummets. Fruit, nuts, seeds and crackers are better options for a more steady release of energy, while wholesome sandwiches are fine for larger meals. You can pack cold pasta salads in plastic boxes before setting off. Don't give food to children in trailers as they may choke on it as they go along.

Above left and right
Refuel with energy-rich foods.

Right
Stopping for water and a snack is important for children.

Left
Off-roading
with a trailer.

Below
Some dogs can
be trained to run
alongside a bicycle.

DIVERSIONS

Children can become
bored in a trailer, but giving
them books and toys (even
games) can stave off the
worst symptoms. Bring an
MP3 player with speakers
to play talking books or
music. Experienced tourers
use headphone intercoms,
although walkie-talkies
are a low-cost alternative.
Children can record the trip
in their diary or journal at
the end of the day.

DOGS

Dogs are inherently risky
companions for bike riders.
They can be unpredictable
and will not be aware of the
implications of a collision.
But it can be possible to
take canine companions
on rides with you. Certain
breeds are more capable of
being trained to run freely
alongside bikes than others:
collies, hunting dogs, such
as spaniels, and smaller
dogs such as Border terriers.
However, there are leashes
available that can be fixed
to bicycle seatposts with
an attachment that always
keeps the dog at a distance.
With familiarity, these can
be effective in exercising
the dog by bicycle on wide,
quiet trails.

PRE-RIDE CHECKS

Even if you use your bicycle regularly, it's sensible to check it frequently before you ride because bolts can work loose and cables lose their tension. There are some basic checks you can do to ensure your bike is roadworthy, and they can be completed with the minimum of mechanical aptitude.

CONTACT POINTS

Use an Allen (hex) key to tighten the bolts holding the handlebars in the stem. Ideally, these delicate bolts should be tightened using a torque wrench (*see p. 303*), particularly if the bike has carbon handlebars, although doing up these bolts to finger tightness is fine. The same applies to the Allen (hex) key bolt through the stem's top cap; this need only be tightened sufficiently to remove any play. Pull the front brake and rock the bike backward and forward on its front wheel; any knocking sounds or movement may indicate a loose headset. Slacken the bolts holding the stem to the steerer tube and use the Allen (hex) key to tighten the top-cap bolt. Don't forget to then re-tighten the stem's bolts.

Is the saddle at the correct height (*see p. 47*)? Adjust it using the bolt or quick release around the seatpost, then tighten it.

Pedals can come undone; check that they are tightly bolted into the crank, taking care to remember that the rider's left pedal is reverse threaded and is therefore tightened counterclockwise; the drive-side pedal on the right is tightened clockwise, as normal.

Top
Checking the handlebar bolts.

Above
Tighten the top-cap bolt with an Allen (hex) key.

Above
Lubing the chain.

Right
Checking a
quick release.

Below
Adjusting the brake
cable's tension.

DRIVETRAIN

Is the chain dirty or rusty?
A poorly maintained chain
won't last as long as a clean,
lubed chain and is more
likely to skip gears or jam.
Lightly lube the chain and
check that it runs freely.

For bikes with gears (see p.
328), check that the top
pivot bolt on the derailleur
(the shifting mechanism),
where it is attached to the
frame, is tight.

Above
Checking disc-brake
pad wear.

BRAKES

Pull both brakes. If the
levers can be pulled all the
way back to the handlebar
you will need to make
adjustments (for disc brakes
see pp. 322–323). Check
that the pads are not worn
out. To do this, remove the
pads (see p. 321), and if
they have been worn down
to the point where you can
no longer see the grooves
in them, you'll need to
replace them before the
metal shoe grinds into the
wheel's rims. What is more
likely, however, is that you
simply need to tighten the
brake cable. Most cable-
operated brakes have a
barrel adjuster where the
cable meets the brake –
give it a turn until the brake
pads have moved closer
to the rims. Check that the
pads line up with the rims.
On older bikes, you may
need to tension the cable
by undoing it, pulling more
of it through the brake and
tightening it up again.

WHEELS

Make sure your tires are
inflated; most tires have a
suggested pressure range
printed on the sidewall.
Heavier riders should inflate
the tire to the upper end
of this range. Simply giving
the tires a squeeze with your
fingers is enough to find out
whether they need some
more air. Also, check the
tread of the tire for shards
of glass or thorns that may
not yet have penetrated
the casing. These can be
removed with pliers. Give
the wheels a spin to check
that they are true (straight).

A wobbly wheel is weak but
can be repaired (see pp.
332–333). Most wheels are
secured in the dropouts
(the notches in the frame)
by quick-release skewers.
Check that each one is
tightened, ensuring the
lever is folded backward
in a position where it can't
be flipped out easily when
hit by branches.

WHAT TO CARRY

Even if your bicycle is in perfect working order before a ride, a number of things could happen to it – from a puncture to a broken chain – that will require on-site repairs. A basic toolkit should help you get the bike moving again.

TOOLS

The key areas to consider are the wheels and the drivetrain; if either fail, it could be a long walk home. Punctures are unpredictable (although ensuring the tires are properly prepared and inflated will help), so always carry a puncture repair kit with patches, a vulcanizing glue for rubber, and tire

levers (minimum of two) with which to remove the tire (*see* p. 304). A tire boot can be used to repair gashed tires.

Multi-tools made by companies such as Topeak may also have in-built tire levers. A shortcut that is recommended by many

cyclists is to carry a spare inner tube, which can simply be installed in place of the punctured tube in a couple of minutes. Match the valve type (Presta is long and narrow, Schraeder is short and fat) with the existing tube. It's still a wise idea to carry the repair kit too; bad luck often comes in threes.

A spoke key (or wrench) is small and can be used to repair a bent wheel.

Always carry a pump, whether it's a pocket-sized mini-pump or a larger pump that can be attached to the bike's frame. Most modern pumps work with either Presta or Schraeder valves.

Left
1. Saddle bag.
2. Spare inner tube.
3. Tire levers.
4. Allen (hex) keys.

Rather than a jangling assortment of Allen (hex) keys, take a cycling-specific multi-tool. This will have a selection of Allen keys in the most useful sizes (typically from 2mm to 8mm) and may also have flat-head and Phillips screwdrivers as well as a chain-breaking tool. This tool is used to split bicycle chains so that damaged links can be removed (see p. 326–327). A master-link (check that it is compatible with your brand of chain) is useful for replacing a damaged link.

Below
Snack on fresh fruit and cereal bars.

Below
Mountain bikers need to be self-sufficient.

COMFORT

On rides of more than an hour in duration, it's wise to take a snack and some water. Typically a muesli bar or a piece of fruit, such as a banana, is enough for rides of two to three hours. Take note of the weather — you can lose up to 2 liters (3.5 pints) of fluids an hour cycling hard on a hot day. Sunblock may be useful too.

HOW TO CARRY

Packed together, your tools should fit into a small pouch that can be attached under the saddle. Many cyclists can fit the kit into their jersey pockets or attach the pump to their bike's frame. Small backpacks are more commonly used by mountain bikers, since they tend to carry more tools.

MOUNTAIN BIKING

Mountain bikers tend to ride in more out-of-the-way places and therefore need to be more self-sufficient than their road-going counterparts. While the basic toolkit is enough for a two-hour spin, many mountain bikers will pack a little more to cope with the different trail conditions. Suggested extra equipment includes spare spokes, zip ties and a shock pump in addition to a tire pump. A multi-tool with pliers, such as a Leatherman, may also come in handy, for example when bending chainrings back into place.

Left
A mini-pump can be carried in a jersey pocket, a backpack or attached to the frame.

ROADCRAFT: SAFE CYCLING

The basics of safe cycling on public roads should be instilled in every young cyclist. Sadly, it can make the difference between life and death. Position yourself on the road properly, exercise awareness and adhere to a few simple practices.

As soon as you are on the bike you should start to think like a cyclist. This means being able to recognize your vulnerability. Taking a chance you might take as a driver, such as crossing an intersection on yellow, can have far more serious consequences. As a cyclist you will have to look out for a whole new series of hazards: car occupants opening doors, treacherous "street furniture" and even wayward pedestrians unaccustomed to the silent approach of a cyclist. Another way of looking at it is to think of everybody else on the road as an idiot, capable of unpredictable, stupid actions, and to ride accordingly. This approach is the essence of 'defensive' cycling.

POSITIONING

Cyclists must travel in the same direction as motorized traffic, and whether that's on the left or the right side of the road, the best place to be is about a meter from the gutter. Riding in the gutter, right next the curb, is undesirable because it is where the detritus of the road (grit, glass, cans) accumulates and because it gives you nowhere else to go in an emergency. By riding at least a meter into the roadway, you occupy your rightful space in the road and compel car drivers to think clearly about overtaking rather than simply whizzing past. It also gives you time and space to take evasive action if something moves into your lane. It also makes you, and the signals you make, more visible.

Give the car in front a couple of meters of space; this allows you to brake or get out of the way if it makes a sudden and unpredictable move.

Right
Use bike lanes where available.

HAZARDS

Being aware of your surroundings is the first step in safe cycling. Here's what to watch and listen for.

- When riding in car-lined streets, be alert to the possibility that the door of a parked car could swing open at any time.

- Look ahead for brake lights. This will tell you what the traffic is about to do and help you anticipate events.

- Crossing side roads is potentially hazardous. Make eye contact with drivers waiting to join a main road.

- Don't be blind to dogs or children, as both can dash in front of cyclists with painful consequences.

VISIBILITY

See and be seen. It is every cyclist's responsibility to ensure they are as visible as possible to car drivers. Modern cars have wide door pillars, impairing the driver's field of vision, so aim not to blend into the background. This means wearing bright clothing and using lights front and rear at night. (A flashing light is more obvious in steady traffic, while a steady light is usually a legal requirement; ideally use both.) Reflective material is most effective on moving parts, such as the legs and arms.

AWARENESS

It's important to use your senses when cycling, as you may be encountering several potential hazards at the same time. This is just one of the reasons why it is foolhardy to wear headphones or use a mobile phone when you are cycling.

Top
You can ride two abreast on shared-use lanes, but give way to pedestrians or other cyclists.

Right above
Look out for car doors opening.

Right
Dual-use traffic lights are becoming more common.

ROADCRAFT: SAFE CYCLING

Left
Riding two abreast is allowed in most places.

OVERTAKING

Before overtaking other cyclists, look behind you. Passing stationary traffic, particularly trucks, which have a limited field of vision, on the left is exceptionally dangerous. Vehicles may turn across your path before they have spotted you.

Ride predictably; avoid weaving in and out of parked cars.

Below
Getting into the habit of giving clear signals helps road users around you and makes journeys safer.

GROUPS

In most places, cyclists are permitted to ride two abreast. Legally, in many places, drivers are required to treat bicycles as equivalent to other vehicles and accord them the same space when overtaking. Clearly, however, on narrow, congested roads, riding in single file is the less obstructive option. In certain situations, it may be safer for large groups of cyclists to break into smaller groups so vehicles waiting to pass are able to overtake bunch by bunch.

TURNS

Cyclists use arm signals, which may differ slightly from country to country, to indicate that they're about to make a turn. Turning from a main road into a side road on the same side is straightforward; take a look around for other traffic, indicate using your outstretched arm, slow down and make the turn.

However, turning across the flow of traffic from a major road into a minor road is one of the most exposed maneuvers a cyclist needs

Above
Whether you're turning left or right, signal your intentions clearly with an arm.

INTERSECTIONS

At intersections, positioning is extremely important. City-center intersections are high-risk areas for cyclists, which is why advance bike boxes have been introduced widely. An error many new cyclists make is to wait just in front of large vehicles, such as trucks, at the offside front corner, where they are invisible to the driver. The driver starts off without realizing a cyclist is in front. The solution is to occupy a more forward and central position at the intersection. Don't be afraid to assert yourself. Make sure you have been seen by and are still visible to the driver of the vehicle behind you.

to perform. About 100 feet before the turn, look over your shoulder to see what traffic is approaching. If the road is clear, indicate your intention with your arm, move into the center of the lane and, if the opposite lane is clear, cross the road. If the opposite lane is busy, you will have to wait for a break in the traffic. It's an exposed position, and ideally, on a busy road, you will be able to find a traffic island.

In some cases, it's worth going a little out of your way to find a safe crossing spot. On exceptionally busy roads with fast traffic, it is often safest to pull off the road and walk your bike across using a pedestrian crossing.

Above right
Take care overtaking buses and trucks; never pass them on the left.

Right
Waiting at the lights in front of other vehicles is a good way to make sure you can be seen.

TECHNIQUES & SAFETY

ROADCRAFT: SAFE CYCLING

LAWS

Nothing infuriates drivers more than seeing cyclists flouting basic rules of the road. The most obvious example is jumping red lights. It's notable that in pro-bike cities, such as Copenhagen and Amsterdam, where cycling has permeated the culture deeply, red-light jumpers are noticeable by their absence. Some will argue that cyclists jump red lights as a means of self-preservation, getting away from the intersection without having a large truck breathing down their neck. But the moral high ground is occupied by cyclists who do stop at red lights, believing that it's illogical to demand respect from drivers without behaving as a law-abiding road user.

Another contentious issue is cycling on sidewalks. Generally, only young children should be riding among pedestrians, unless on a mixed-use path (see p. 103). Adults must walk their bikes.

In the USA, each state has its own rules of the road. In the UK, cyclists and drivers have to follow the Highway Code (available from government websites). It's

a good idea to familiarize yourself with local traffic laws, governing, for example, turning on a red light if going with the flow of traffic.

One area of law worth checking is the use of helmets. Helmet use is not compulsory in most European countries, but certain US states require children to wear helmets, and helmets are compulsory in Australia and parts of Canada. Depending on where you live, cyclists may also be penalized for cycling while under the influence of alcohol, for speeding or for riding without lights.

Above
Helmets are not compulsory in the most cycling-friendly countries, such as Denmark.

Above
There are plenty of helmets to choose from if you decide to wear one.

Below
The best technique is to stay loose and roll with the fall (top). Breaking a fall with an out- stretched arm can break your wrist or other bones (bottom).

Above
A helmet can protect you from a serious head injury in a slow-speed crash.

ACCIDENTS

If you are involved in an accident or come across one, check for injuries, feel for broken bones and find out if there are any shooting pains. With suspected spinal and head injuries, keep the victim as still as possible while waiting for medical assistance. Always call for an ambulance if you are in any doubt.

If there are no obvious serious injuries, and you are able to, get the injured party off the road. Cyclists who have been in an accident are often dazed and disoriented and may stumble into further danger.

Once off the road, give yourself or whoever has had the accident a thorough check. When the adrenalin wears off, the full brunt of the pain will be felt. Concussions can cause confusion, nausea or more symptoms for minutes or hours after the event.

In certain situations, such as after being hit by a car or when damage has been caused, you may be obliged to inform the police of the accident. Don't leave the scene even if you are unharmed; this is illegal in many places.

Following such an incident, take the contact details of witnesses and exchange details with the other party. Try to remain calm and do not discuss the incident; the police will determine blame.

If you are unable to continue, get someone to pick you up and remain with you to check for signs of concussion or shock.

TECHNIQUES & SAFETY

CITY CYCLING

Right
Bike-specific lights.

Below
A car-free path
shared with pedestrians.

The urban environment in many cities across the USA is changing in favor of cyclists. Features such as bicycle traffic lights, advance bike boxes at intersections, bike parking and bike lanes are being added as urban planners accommodate the increasing number of cyclists.

BIKE PATHS AND LANES

Congestion, the cost of motoring and an increased awareness of its health and environmental benefits means more people are cycling in inner cities. In response, cities across the world are being reconfigured to make bicycle travel safer and quicker. Many world cities are emulating Copenhagen (*see p p. 244–245*), probably the world's most bike-friendly capital. One of the key areas of improvement is in bike lanes. These come in several flavors.

Bike lanes run alongside roads. They can be marked out by paint and signage, or segregated entirely by curb stones or posts. The painted variety carries a degree of risk due to complacency: just because the lane has its own paint scheme doesn't mean that cars won't park in it, cross it without looking or move into it. Cyclists

Right
More cities, such as Brisbane, shown here, have high-quality bike routes today.

in bike lanes should still ride defensively. Separate bike lanes alongside but protected from roadways are safer, but they may add confusion by carrying cyclists in both directions. Keep an eye on signage. In some cases, the bike lane will be broken by an intersection where cyclists have to give way to other vehicles entering or leaving side roads.

Rare in the USA, cycle paths are bike-only routes through the city, passing through parks, residential areas and beside canals or rivers. Some cities have wide paths able to funnel cyclists into them in great numbers at peak times. In certain cities, you may be able to devise an almost entirely car-free route by linking cycle paths. Most metropolitan transport authorities (see p. 105) publish cycle maps.

Shared paths, where cyclists and pedestrians mingle, are more common in the US. A modicum of etiquette makes the experience enjoyable for both.

CITY BIKES

The perfect city bike is reliable, comfortable and theft-proof. Speed isn't a priority. A reconditioned old bike is perfect. Essential accessories for urban riding include front and rear lights, a bell (a legal requirement in many places), a repair kit (spare tube, tire levers, pump, multi-tool) and, most importantly, a bike lock.

RULES FOR CITY CYCLING

- Moderate your speed. Pedestrians, especially the elderly, can feel spooked by fast cyclists. Children may behave unpredictably and dash in front of you.

- Try not to surprise people. A friendly 'hello' or the ring of a bell warns pedestrians of your approach. Anger is a common reaction to shock.

- Smile: a 'thank you' costs nothing.

- Give way to pedestrians on shared paths.

- Give space to pedestrians and other cyclists as you pass. In the same way cyclists feel threatened by vehicles that pass too closely, so pedestrians can feel uncomfortable surrounded by speeding cyclists.

Left
A two-way cycleway is a safe option for cyclists.

CITY CYCLING

CITY HAZARDS

City cyclists encounter a variety of potential hazards daily. These can include anything from wild boar in Berlin to wild bears in Vancouver. However, the most common hazards are "street furniture."

Metal drain covers can be slippery when wet. Watch out that your wheel doesn't get caught in one of the gaps; inexplicably in some cities (hello Sydney!) these run parallel to the curb. Manhole covers and painted areas can also be slippery in the rain.

After a dry spell, rain can cause roads to be extra slippery as residual oils are washed away. When cycling in wet weather, add a bit more braking distance. Water on brake rims can

delay braking; the first few turns of the wheel just clear water off the rim before the pads bite.

Public transport is also a risk. Trolley tracks are particularly treacherous and should be crossed at right angles (or as close to perpendicular as possible). Proficient cyclists may lift their front wheel over. Buses will be pulling into and out of stops frequently and won't necessarily signal. Taxis may make U-turns even in places where they are not permitted.

Above
Potholes, drains and train tracks are common hazards for urban riders.

Right
Safe riding means staying visible.

Right
Using an advance
bike box puts you in a
good position.

Right
Using an advance
bike box puts you in a
good position.

INTERMODAL COMMUTING

The goal of many urban cycling advocates is the adoption of coherent transport policies that allow people to reach their destination using a combination of public transport and bicycles. This remains the most effective way of moving from outlying or suburban areas into and across major cities. In densely populated countries such as Britain, where it's often an impossible task to take a bicycle on a train at rush hour, this vision seems unattainable. But progress is being made: from Chicago to Vancouver, public buses across North America have bicycle racks. And while Londoners can't take their bicycles on the Tube, they can carry them on to the Thames river boats.

Secure locking areas are becoming widespread, and streets are being redesigned to reflect the growing use of bicycles.

A number of organizations promote cycling in cities and are good sources of further information, advice and classes in safe cycling and maintenance. In the USA, the League of American Bicyclists is an all-encompassing advocacy group that pays particular attention to legislation affecting cyclists. At a city-level, Bike New York is a very thorough resource for all urban cyclists, offering classes, information and events such as the world's largest annual mass-participation bike ride, the Five Boro Bike Tour. The San Francisco Bicycle Coalition is a west-coast counterpart (*see* p. 340 for details for specific countries).

The aim of the London Cycling Campaign is to make Britain's capital a world-class cycling city. It offers a huge amount of advice, hosts regular rides and distributes maps. Transport for London, the government agency responsible for London's transport network, has a handy journey planner, sponsors annual cycling events and offers free advice and mapping. Sustainable transport crusaders Sustrans plot routes around Britain to rouse the inner explorer.

In Australia, Bicycle Victoria and Bicycle New South Wales are prominent, not-for-profit advocacy groups dedicated to making cycling safer and more popular.

Below left and below right
Most cities provide bike racks, but taking your bike on a train is another option.

BIKE-HANDLING SKILLS

Tricks such as trackstands and bunnyhops are not just for showing off; they can have useful applications. Practicing them will also improve your general bike-handling skills as you grow to understand how your bike works.

Below
A bunnyhop.

NO HANDS

USE FOR:

Riding one-handed when you need to signal direction changes. Riding without holding the handlebars at all helps racers pull on a vest at the top of a descent but is of little use to the average cyclist. It is fun and easy to learn, though.

HOW TO:

Start with both hands on the grips. Then try riding with one hand and just a finger lightly guiding the bars on the other side. On a smooth, safe road, let go with one hand. Speed makes you more stable, and keeping your head still and your movements smooth will also prevent wobbles. Practice and try switching hands. To ride with no hands, it helps if you're sitting up straight with your weight centerd. A moderate speed and slightly downhill slope will also make it easier. Splaying your knees increases stability and you can steer by sticking a knee farther out or leaning slightly into a shallow corner.

TRACKSTAND

USE FOR:

Balancing on a stationary bike without unclipping a foot from a pedal when waiting at lights, for a quick getaway. Mountain bikers can also use this for a tricky corner or obstacle.

HOW TO:

With your leading foot forward, come to a halt, ideally on a very slight uphill slope. Turn your front wheel so it is pointing away from your front foot. Keep your brakes on and pressure on the pedals – if you start to fall on the leading pedal side, let some pressure off the pedals and rock backward. If you start to fall on the side your wheel is pointing, you can put more pressure on the pedals and rock forward. Shift your bodyweight to help stay balanced.

WHEELIE

USE FOR:

Lifting your front wheel over an obstacle either on- or off-road.

HOW TO:

It's not essential, but it helps to have your saddle lowered. As you're riding along at a moderate speed, with your leading foot at 11 o'clock, lean forward, then pull up on the handlebars, give a turn of the pedals and shift your weight back in one fluid movement. If you have suspension forks, leaning forward gives you a bit of upward assistance when the spring releases. Your weight needs to be pivoting over the rear wheel. Lean forward to put the front wheel down again. If you keep your finger over the back brake lever, you can feather the brake to help control the wheelie – a quick touch on the brakes will bring the front wheel down if you feel you're in danger of going off the back. It takes practice to find the perfect balance point. A 'wheelie' is when you pedal on one wheel; a 'manual' is lifting the front wheel and freewheeling.

BUNNYHOP

USE FOR:

Hopping over obstacles on- or off-road, without stopping or hitting them.

HOW TO:

The bunnyhop is a sequence of well-timed movements. At a low speed, and with your saddle lowered, practice lifting the front wheel. The next movement is to help the rear wheel rise too, which can be achieved by pointing your toes down on the pedals and pushing back with the feet. Try this with the bike stationary and the rear brake on: the rear wheel will rise up. Finally, put these movements together: lift up the front wheel, push down and back with the pedals, and then push down at the front so the bars follow an arc. Let your arms and legs flex on landing. It takes a while to get the timing right. Practice hopping over sticks before progressing to bigger obstacles.

Far left
A trackstand.

Left
A wheelie.

TECHNIQUES & SAFETY

ADVANCED ROAD RIDING: HOW TO PEDAL

It sounds too obvious, doesn't it? But thinking about how you pedal, from finding a rhythm to selecting the most efficient gear, will make a big difference to your riding.

CLIPLESS PEDALS

Several components of the bike will affect your pedaling technique. Using clipless pedals allows the rider to pull up with one foot while the other is on the down stroke. If you only push down, you are only generating power for around a quarter of the revolution. One technique to increase the duration of the revolution when power is delivered is called 'ankling'. This involves keeping your ankle level (or even slightly lower) at the top of the revolution and pushing through the top of the pedal stroke from about the 11 o'clock position.

CRANKS

Crank length is also an important factor in cadence and power delivery. Cranks range from 150mm to 180mm in length; the longer your femur, the longer the crank should be. There are many crank length calculators online, which use your inseam to suggest an optimum crank length. A longer crank gives greater leverage, more torque and theoretically, more power. However, bear in mind that long cranks (175mm and more) are harder to turn. They also require a lower seating position and greater flexibility. If your pedaling style is to spin a high cadence, you will prefer shorter cranks.

Far left
Generate power by pulling up with the pedal.

Left
Try out different seating positions.

Left
1. Cassette.
2. Crankset.
3. Derailleur. The derailleur moves the chain from one cog of the cassette to another.

Below left
A shorter crank can help generate a quicker cadence.

CADENCE

Many new riders tend to underestimate the role of cadence and pedal at around 50 to 60 revolutions per minute (rpm), but pro racers won't go below 90 revolutions and some stay above 100 revolutions. This is because mashing a big gear at a low cadence takes cyclists into anaerobic exercise (*see* p. 130). A fast cadence in a lower gear consumes less oxygen and puts less stress on the leg muscles and knees. However, it is a skill that needs to be learned. Some bike computers can measure cadence, so find a flat stretch of road and use the data to focus on increasing your rpm gradually.

GEARS

With often more than 18 gears to choose from, making the right selection is important as it affects cadence and speed, especially when climbing. Most road bikes have two front chainrings with 53 and 39 teeth and rear cassettes with a range of 12 to 25 teeth. Replacing a cog with one of 27 teeth will help riders struggling up steep hills. Another option is to use a compact crankset (50/34 at the front) or a triple (such as 52/39/30). This can allow riders to maintain a higher cadence. On an undulating ride, use the gears to maintain a constant level of effort; there's nothing more tiring and inefficient than varying cadence and effort. On shorter climbs, you can get away with a bigger gear thanks to momentum's helping hand, but never let the gear stall you.

Experiment with different combinations. Many cyclists feel that a bigger gear rolls more efficiently on the flat, but a smaller gear gives rapid acceleration. Being aware of what gears work best for you will help with the most important part of gear selection: being ready for attacks and getting into the right gear quickly. Changing under load in a hurry can cause the chain to slip, so slacken off the pedal stroke for just the instant you change gear.

Right
1. A compact crankset.
2. A triple crankset.

Both compact and triple cranksets can give riders a wider selection of easier gears to choose.

TECHNIQUES & SAFETY

ADVANCED ROAD RIDING: HOW TO CLIMB

The hills are where races are won and lost. Climbing an Alpine road for mile after mile requires not only suffering but also skills: reading the climb, deciding on gearing and tactics and finding a rhythm.

RIDING POSITION

Don't worry about being aerodynamic. Instead, the priority must be a relaxed and efficient style. With your hands up on the brake hoods or the bar tops, creating a riding position that opens the airways and lungs, maintain a light, relaxed grip. This informs the rest of the upper body;

the more relaxed it is, the easier your breathing and more focused your effort. It's fine to push forward a little on the bars. Try sitting toward the back of the saddle, to lengthen and straighten the back. Shifting your position every now and then will also give muscles a break.

To sit or to stand? Well, standing on the pedals delivers more power but is more tiring and cannot be sustained for entire climbs by mortals. It also raises the heart rate and burns more energy. If you do need to stand for an extra exertion, don't let your arms bear too much weight, keep the

power flowing through the core and legs; the arms should be providing a little stability. Try to find a rhythm led by the turns of the pedals and keep the upper body still.

Below
Find your rhythm climbing out of the saddle.

Left
Lightweight climbing
specialists such as Andy
Schleck can accelerate
up a mountain road.

CADENCE

Riders will have different
styles; Lance Armstrong
preferred to spin a low gear,
while his long-time rival
Jan Ullrich opted to grind
out the climbs at a slower
cadence in a higher gear.
On shorter climbs, you
are more likely to select a
higher gear and get out of
the saddle, although you
will soon find your legs
swimming in lactic acid
as a result.

BREATHING

Being able to regulate your
effort and your breathing
is very important. Fill your
diaphragm; it may help
to take a couple of deep
breaths with full exhalations
before the road turns
uphill. This is also a useful
relaxation technique. If
you find yourself puffing,
slacken off the speed, relax
your arms, straighten the
back and shift into an easier
gear for a while. Focus on
your breathing, giving slow,
complete exhalations, and
spinning the pedals.

STRATEGY

Good climbers are clever
cyclists. They understand
about pacing their effort,
saving energy where
possible, using techniques
such as riding within the
pack or on someone's wheel
(directly behind them) to
reduce wind resistance (see
p. 201). They will be able
to read other riders and
the road ahead. On long
climbs in a race situation,
stay at a pace that keeps
you at the front of the main
pack where you can monitor
the situation. Successful
climbers often use a feature
of the road – a tight corner,
a suddenly steepening
gradient – to launch an
attack, accelerating hard
until they're free of the
group then finding a hard
but sustainable pace. It's
essential to read the climb
and its place in the route.
Most pros will prefer one
or two long climbs to
numerous short, steep,
energy-sapping hills. On the
shorter hills, when riding
in a group, start the climb
at the front, and you can
let yourself filter backward
through the pack and still
be in the group at the top.
This means you won't drop
out the back and have to
work on your own up to
the top, watching the rest
disappear into the distance.
Look at the profile of the
course; big climbs toward
the end of a race are where
attacks will occur.

ADVANCED ROAD RIDING: HOW TO DESCEND

Left
Descending at speed, racers need to keep their fingers over the brake levers.

In the same way that climbers are celebrated, so riders such as Jens Voigt and Fabian Cancellara have carved a reputation for fearless descending. It's a skill that allows riders to make up seconds or even minutes on rivals in a race and involves more than just switching off any instinct for self-preservation.

THE BIKE

Geometry makes a difference on descents. The longer the wheelbase and the more relaxed the geometry (*see* p. 19), the more stable the bike will be at speeds of up to 50mph which is the speed that professionals can hit on some descents.

Below left
Find the fastest line through a corner.

Below right
Jens Voigt is an expert at descending.

THE BODY

Descending involves more of the upper body and core than climbing, since you'll be crouching in an aerodynamic tuck. The position involves putting your hands in the drops, tucking the elbows into the sides of the body, lowering the chin to the bar and raising your backside. A relaxed body is essential; the bike will respond negatively if you are locked stiff with fear. In a straight line, cyclists will keep their cranks level when freewheeling. In corners, keep the inside pedal up.

CORNERING

Watch out for corners with a camber that slopes away from the direction you want to go. Enter the corner wide and cut the apex; this will help you carry the most speed and minimize the need for braking.

BRAKING

Brake before a corner. Braking during a corner will do terrible things to your center of gravity (shifting weight forward) and unsettle the bike. If possible, brake in a straight line. Use both front and rear brakes. On long descents, rims can become very hot through friction, so hot in fact that blowouts are not unheard of.

SPEED WOBBLES

Sometimes a bicycle descending at speed develops a speed wobble, an uncontrollable side-to-side shake. To correct it, try clamping your thighs to the top tube and slowing down very gently by feathering the brakes. Letting a little air out of your tires or even installing better quality wheels can prevent it from occurring again.

TECHNIQUES & SAFETY

ADVANCED ROAD RIDING: HOW TO CORNER

To the casual observer, it might appear that climbing prowess or a powerful sprint finish defines a successful cyclist. However, insiders know that the skill of cornering efficiently is vital in conserving energy and keeping up with others.

Does cornering make the difference between winning and losing? Yes. Just ask Mark Cavendish and Mark Renshaw, who wound up their one-two win on the Champs Elysées for team Columbia-HTC in the 2009 Tour de France with a perfect final corner. Or Levi Leipheimer who dropped out of that year's Tour with a broken wrist after crashing on a corner on stage 12. The very best riders, such as Cavendish, don't even appear to slow down.

Right
Keep your inside pedal up.

Left
Follow the racing line.

Below
Look toward the exit of
the corner.

THE CORNER

Keep your head up and look through the corner to the exit point. Don't brake during the corner; this will upset your balance, cause the bike to become more upright and destroy any momentum you've maintained.

THE APPROACH

Positioning is crucial. If it's a familiar corner, visualize your entry and exit points. How tight does it get? Look at the road surface: loose gravel, wet paint or shiny surfaces where oil has spilled or asphalt has melted can have the bike sliding sideways in a second. Commit to the racing line which allows you to retain as much speed as possible. On fast, sweeping corners, it won't necessarily be the shortest line you should choose but will involve entering the corner wide, cutting across the apex and leaving wide. (On slow switchbacks uphill, you can afford to take a tighter line, although it's worth noting that the inside line is usually steeper.)

If you can see the exit, pick the exit gear in advance so that you're ready to put

power down. On a fast corner, the angle at which the bike will lean means you won't be able to turn the pedals and change gear during the corner. On a racing bike, your hands should be in the drops for streamlined control.

Once you enter the corner, keep your weight balanced. The inside pedal should be at the top of its revolution for maximum clearance and the outside pedal should be down to keep most of the weight on your outer foot. You can stick the inside knee out a little for extra stability.

When braking, use both levers gently to avoid either locking up or losing traction. The best riders will corner so smoothly that they appear to brake only for the tightest corners.

THE EXIT

In a race, as you come out of the corner, prepare to accelerate hard. Corners have the effect of stringing riders out with an accordion effect causing riders at the back of a bunch to need to accelerate harder than those at the front. If you've selected the right gear in advance, you can get out of the saddle and start pushing the pedals. Don't look at the wheel in front, look ahead: if there's another corner on the way, stay seated and get ready to shift your balance again.

ADVANCED OFF-ROAD RIDING: CLIMBING & CORNERING

For many mountain bikers, climbing is just a means to an end, and the payoff is a thrilling descent. But there are subtle pleasures to be found in climbing a technical trail without putting a foot down. For competitive riders, climbs are where you can hurt other racers.

Below
Power up short climbs
out of the saddle.

TERRAIN

Reading the surface of a slope is the key to maintaining traction. A loose surface, from dirt and gravel to fist-sized rocks, means concentrating on preventing the rear wheel slipping. Distribute your weight between the front and rear wheels so that the rear tire bites into the ground and the front wheel doesn't rise. You can do this by sitting on the nose of the saddle, bending your elbows and crouching low over the top tube. Standing up to climb can unweight the rear wheel: change into an easy gear and pedal smoothly in circles so less torque is coming through the rear wheel, reducing the likelihood of it slipping on loose, slippery or uneven surfaces. Look for the line with the most solid terrain. This may not necessarily be the shortest, but you are less likely to lose traction.

TIMING

The art of climbing a technical trail cleanly lies in the timing. When you encounter rocks, roots and other small obstacles, try to time your pedal strokes so that as you arrive at the obstacle you are in position for a downstroke with your leading foot. Simultaneously unweight the front wheel by moving slightly back in the cockpit (even just sitting upright will achieve this) and push down on the pedal. The front wheel will rise up and on to the obstacle. Now, get ready to throw your weight forward, giving another full turn of the pedal to get the rear wheel to follow.

Right and below
Shift your weight to find traction for both wheels.

STEEP CLIMBS

A relaxed upper body is helpful. Channel all your power into your legs. And if you do stall? On a steep slope it may be very difficult to get started again. But before pushing to the top, try angling the bike across the slope, clipping in with your leading foot and turning your easiest gear. By traversing the slope, you are taking some of the sting out the gradient.

Switchbacks are where the trail itself zig-zags up or down a hill. Riding these tight corners uphill at a slow speed can be a challenge. As you approach the switchback, aim for the outer edge and steer the front wheel around the widest part of the corner, keeping your weight over the outer side of your bike. As you emerge from the switchback, cross back over the trail and go uphill.

BERMS

You don't need to understand centrifugal force to ride a bermed (banked) corner, but it helps. Descending, the bike's speed and mass will push it into the banked corner, so long as you hold off on the brakes and keep your body in the 'attack' position: knees and elbows bent, cranks level, elbows out, body hovering over the saddle. The higher and steeper the berm's banks, the faster you can go. Keep your eyes focused on the exit to the corner; your head will be slightly angled. By putting more weight on the outer pedal and moving it down to the six o'clock position if necessary, you'll be forcing the tires to bite more deeply, maintaining traction.

TECHNIQUES & SAFETY

ADVANCED OFF-ROAD RIDING: DESCENDING

Gravity-assisted descents are where mountain bikers explore the boundaries of their comfort zones. Having some solid skills to fall back on is essential when the adrenaline is flowing.

POSITION

The default stance for a mountain biker is the 'attack' position: knees and elbows bent, cranks level, elbows out, body hovering over the saddle. On steep descents, you should move your center of gravity back – but don't go too far. Many bikers have been told to get way off the back of the bike, risking abrasion from the rear tire. In most cases this is not necessary. Instead, it's more important to keep your weight low. And keeping your elbows bent rather than locked straight gives you the option of moving farther back if required.

DROPS

Ranging in height from 1 foot to many times that, drops are where the ground falls away from you. For those that can't be rolled, you will need to get airborne and land the drop. For small drops of 1–3 feet two contrasting techniques can be used. The wheels-in-the-air technique means getting into the attack position: shifting your weight slightly back (but not right over the rear wheel), arms bent but not locked, knees bent, with your best foot forward as your front wheel goes over the lip. You can give an extra pedal stroke as you go over, but the main thing is to let

LINE CHOICE

Let a mountain bike run downhill and, like water, it will find the path of least resistance. This may not be the ideal line, but it's useful to remember to let the front wheel move around. Stay loose and grip the handlebars securely but without tension. Shift your body weight to change direction. Look where you want to go, not at the obstacles; this is called target fixation and is a surefire way of crashing into them.

Above and top
Move your weight back on descents, staying in the 'attack' position.

HOW TO DO A DROP-OFF

Left
1. Approach in the attack position, pedals level.
2. Lift the front wheel, moving your weight back.
3. Bend your arms and knees when landing.

BRAKING

your bars rise at the same time. The worst-case scenario is having too much weight over the front and landing front wheel first. Focus your attention on the landing spot. Speed is your friend for this maneuver. Aim to land both wheels at the same time.

If you want to keep your wheels on the ground, you can use a slightly different technique that allows you to negotiate surprisingly large drops. Stay in the 'attack' position, but instead of shifting most of your weight backward, crouch as low as possible in the cockpit, keeping your arms very bent. As the front wheel goes over the edge, extend (push away) your arms, letting the front wheel fill the space beneath it. With a lower center of gravity you shouldn't feel too top heavy. Without stalling, allow the bike to roll on and let the rear wheel follow, extending your legs. The

idea is to keep your body still (and low) and then let your legs and arms contract and extend as required, so that your bike undulates beneath you.

The first technique can be applied to larger drops. For extreme drops (more than 10 feet), and especially if you're being filmed for a DVD, it's often known as 'hucking'.

Don't 'drag' your brakes by keeping them on all the time. Instead, on steep descents brake hard then release and repeat. This allows the rotors to cool and avoids the brake fluid heating up too much. If your brakes overheat, you may experience brake 'fade', a serious loss of braking power. In an emergency, try slowing your bike with a foot on a tire. Or bail out.

Controlled braking takes place before a change of direction is needed or an obstacle, not in a sudden panic during the maneuver. The art of mountain biking is timing.

Below
Negotiating a drop-off is a useful skill to learn.

TECHNIQUES & SAFETY

ADVANCED OFF-ROAD RIDING: JUMPING & OBSTACLES

There's nothing quite like it: the sensation of weightlessness as you soar through the air. Jumping is one of the most exciting elements of mountain biking, and it's actually not as difficult as it might appear.

Above
Getting airborne is the most exciting part of mountain biking.

of the take-off to increase the height the front wheel reaches. Look ahead and pinpoint your landing spot. On a tabletop, coming up short is not a disaster but you should aim to hit the down-slope. By pushing the handlebars forward in mid-air your rear wheel will become level with the front. You can now adjust for the landing, aiming to put both wheels down at once (or the rear wheel just ahead). Get ready to absorb the bump with your bent arms and legs. Skilled riders land smoothly by extending their arms and legs into the landing area.

Overcoming fear – a perfectly natural emotion – will help you stay relaxed, which in turn will help you stay loose. Tense up with anxiety, and the jump is less likely to work out satisfactorily. If you get the chance to practice the same jump, start by rolling it then gradually pick up speed as your confidence builds.

JUMPS

Man-made jumps come in two forms: tabletops and doubles. The area between the up and down slopes on a tabletop is level; on a double there is a gap, forming two mounds. If you know you will be jumping, it can help to lower your saddle in advance, giving you more clearance. When approaching a tabletop, assume the 'attack' position and maintain a steady speed. Stay loose and relaxed. When you reach the up-slope, extend your arms and legs into the face

Left
Unweight the front wheel
to clear small logs.

OBSTACLES

Gracefully overcoming obstacles such as logs and rocks on the trail not only looks good but also saves energy and maintains the rhythm of your ride. A dash of skill and timing makes all the difference. The technique Jessica Douglas, an Australian National Champion, teaches is to unweight the front wheel.

As you approach the obstacle, pedal up to a comfortable speed – too slow and you'll stall – then get into the 'attack' position. This is off the saddle, knees slightly bent, both feet level on the horizontal cranks. Your elbows should be bent and sticking out, and your weight should be centered down through the balls of your feet.

When you get to the log, don't pull up on the bars. Instead, shift your weight backward in the cockpit in a firm but smooth motion. The effect is closer to pushing the handlebars away from you. As the wheel rises up and over the log, extend your arms to guide the front wheel down into the space on the far side of the log and move your weight forward, allowing the rear wheel to rise and follow you over the log. You should keep your head up and be looking 20 feet down the trail for the next corner or obstacle.

MOUNTAIN BIKING CODE OF CONDUCT

- Stay in control.
- Give way to walkers.
- Use a bell or greeting when approaching others.
- Ride shared-use trails in small groups.
- Only ride shared-use or MTB tracks; stay off closed trails.
- Carry tools, and be prepared for mechanical problems.
- Obtain permission from the landowner.
- Leave gates as you find them.
- Don't skid, cut corners or make new lines, as this degrades the trail.
- Avoid riding in mud and rain, as both bikers and walkers damage soft trails.
- Take trash home.

Right
The 'attack' position is needed for tackling obstacles and corners.

CHAPTER 4
FITNESS & NUTRITION

FITNESS & NUTRITION

RETURNING TO CYCLING

People take up cycling for many different reasons, but increased fitness is a side effect shared by all. Male or female, young or old, cycling has a hugely positive effect on the human mind and body, and promotes vitality.

Above
Starting to ride again can be fun, sociable and boost your fitness.

FITNESS BENEFITS

Riding a bicycle is a superb form of exercise for two reasons: it boosts health and wellbeing, and it does so without putting too much stress on joints. This makes it suitable for the elderly or even people with limited mobility. At the most obvious level, cycling conditions the legs and buttocks and, by burning calories (see p.127), can also aid weight loss. Most returning cyclists notice a new-found trimness, although a minimum of two hours' exercise a week is required to see an effect.

But, in addition to the more externally obvious changes, riding also has a positive effect that is less evident to the naked eye. Coronary heart disease poses an increasing threat to people in the USA, Britain and Australia and to some extent other European countries. Cycling builds cardiovascular fitness, helps strengthen the heart, lowers blood pressure and is even thought to lower cholesterol. Regular exercise is also prescribed to diabetics (see p. 151) and the obese.

Even on a cellular level, it has been shown that endurance exercise enhances mitochondrial function (mitochondria are the engine rooms of individual cells). But even if it can't guarantee a longer life, cycling can be an enjoyable component of an active life and can be easily incorporated into a busy lifestyle.

Right
Age isn't a barrier to being able to enjoy cycling.

OTHER BENEFITS

The positive effects of exercise on depression, anxiety and stress are well documented, and cycling is no exception. Strenuous exercise releases endorphins (also known as the 'happy hormones') shown to combat stress. Add to that the therapeutic benefits of getting outdoors into the sunshine (itself an important source of vitamin D) for a few hours, and the bicycle suddenly seems more like a treatment tool. It is thought that endorphins are only released after an hour or more of hard exercise, but even moderate cycling is beneficial: exercise can improve the quality of regenerative sleep, so long as you leave a gap of five hours or more between exercise and bedtime.

CHECK-UP

Older men and women returning to cycling should have a medical check-up if they have pre-existing health problems. Gentle cycling places fewer demands on the body than many other sports – there's a saying that cyclists aged over 50 are runners whose knees have given up – but there are certain issues to be aware of. For those that are elderly or overweight with a history of heart problems, any sort of strenuous exercise should be discussed with a medical professional. If you are on diabetes medication, for example, this should also be discussed as it may require adjustment.

Additionally, men in their 40s, 50s and 60s may have an increased risk of prostate problems (see p. 157) that can be exacerbated by bicycle saddles. And, both men and women of mature years will find it harder for bones and skin to heal in the event of an accident. On the bright side, cycling is a good activity for arthritis sufferers, as it causes less stress to bones than many other sports.

Basic safety precautions should prevail: try to find a local cycling group so you're not going out alone initially. Choose a bike with an upright riding position, a wide range of gears and, for those with a weak grip, consider a twist-grip gear shifter: your bike may also benefit from a check-up.

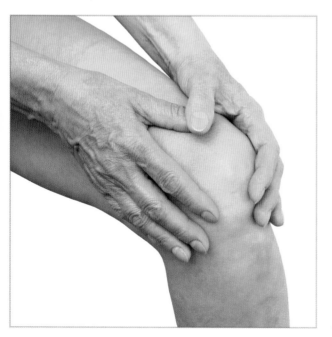

Above
Cycling is low-impact and easy on the joints.

FITNESS BASICS

General all-round fitness comes not from doing one thing obsessively but several things pretty well. Cycling is just one component of a healthy lifestyle: it's also important to understand what to eat and when to rest.

sport such as cycling and burn calories week after week. But, with regular exercise comes responsibility. Hard exercise damages muscles, which must be repaired to grow stronger, and they're best repaired with a full and balanced diet.

Food can be broken down into three categories: carbohydrates (the primary energy source), protein (the primary repair material) and fats, of which many fatty acids are essential for the synthesis of various substances and the maintenance of cell membranes and the nervous system (*see* pp. 160–165).

FOOD IN, ENERGY OUT

Think of the body as a simple engine that needs to be fed with fuel regularly. The energy derived from this fuel is measured in calories (or kilocalories, units of 1,000 calories known as Kcal). The human body, through respiration and other processes, converts calories into energy: Kcal is the unit of measurement for the body's metabolic rate, so the output of energy is measured in Kcal per minute. Energy is expended by the body doing anything from sleeping or watching television to doing a long-distance bike ride; the more active you are, the more calories you'll need to eat.

However, appetite and the body's actual requirements are rarely matched, and surplus energy is stored in the body, as glycogen (glucose) in the liver and muscles, and as fat. Counting the calories ingested is one way of controlling weight gain; another is to take up a

Above
Steamed vegetables are rich in nutrients.

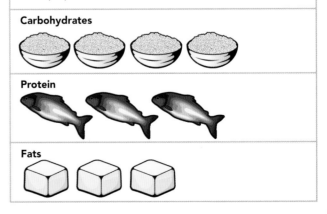

Sports nutritionists typically recommend consuming carbohydrates, protein and fats in the ratio of 4:3:3 in an average meal. However, each person's requirements differ so be prepared to tweak that formula.

Carbohydrates

Protein

Fats

Below
Racing cyclists require a consistent training schedule.

REST

As important as diet, rest and recovery are when the body takes time off to repair itself. Regular exercise places demands on your metabolism, and by ignoring what your body is saying, you risk burning out or even falling ill. The fittest cyclists are those who look after themselves, and that includes taking time off the bike and getting plenty of sleep. When you're resting – and even the most serious athletes make sure they schedule a couple of days off per week – your body is getting stronger and fitter.

RESULTS

Eat well, exercise and rest regularly, and the end result will inevitably be a higher level of fitness. But how long does this take? Everyone responds differently and it will depend on your goals (*see* pp. 134–135). You may notice a change in fitness – for example, being able to jog up a flight of steps without breathlessness – within a month. The longer you work at it, though, the greater the gains. There are plenty of veteran cyclists who have spent decades steadily working on and maintaining their fitness, and as a result will out-ride cyclists half their age. Fitness is a life-long project.

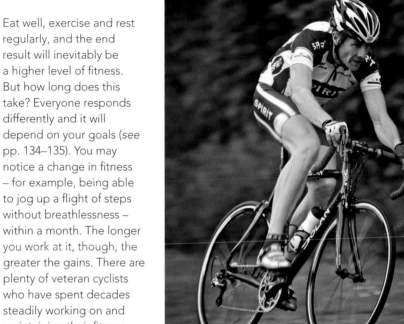

Left
Allow your body more rest after exercise so that it recovers fully.

Above
Replace burned calories with carbohydrates, the primary energy source.

THE CYCLING BODY

If cyclists were a tribe, then their bodies could be said to bear the hallmarks of initiation: taut hamstrings, thick thighs and unfortunate tan lines. So, what parts of the body are used in cycling, and how are they adapted to a life on two wheels?

The human body can transform an inanimate assortment of tubes into a machine that can travel great distances through muscle power alone. And, conversely, even after just a moderate amount of cycling, the bicycle can make great changes to the human body. The part of the body most used by cyclists may seem obvious – the legs – but the actual process of transferring power to the pedals involves a complex series of movements.

Left
Leg power comes from several muscle groups.

MUSCLES

Cyclists' most important muscles are behind them. The glutes – the derrière in French – are the motors of a cyclist's body. During each pedal stroke, they are responsible for pushing the crank through the first stage of its revolution. The gluteus maximus is one of the largest muscles in the human body and is attached to the pelvis, the base of the spine and the back of the femur.

Like all muscles, it is composed of fibers, each almost as thick as a human hair (as a point of reference, an arm's bicep muscle has about 100,000 muscle fibers). These fibers contract and expand with the movement of the body, consuming energy in the form of glycogen.

Quads
These include the rectus femoris, the vastus medialis and the adductor muscles.

Glutes
These include the gluteus maximus, medius and minimus muscles, which form the backside.

Calves
The bulky calf muscle is the gastrocnemius; deeper inside the calf lies the soleus.

Hamstrings
Hamstrings can refer to the muscle running the length of the back of the thigh or its associated tendons.

JOINTS

All the parts of our bodies that move – knees, fingers, feet and so on – use joints of varying complexity. While cycling is certainly easier on most people's joints than more impactful exercise such as running, it's wise to take care of our moving parts, especially given the repetitive workouts they get: six-hour ride at a fast pace adds up to more than 30,000 pedal strokes per leg. So a minor problem can easily be amplified by overuse. Mountain bikers also face other joint-related problems, in particular handlebar palsy, which is compression of the ulnar nerve at the wrist causing numbness or tingling. To maintain joints, ensure the bike is correctly set up for you and that your diet aids flexibility: fish rich in omega 3 oils are helpful, while ginger and acidic fruits (such as cherries and berries) are thought to have anti-inflammatory properties. Oats and whole grains also boast beneficial properties, while calcium is found in dairy products.

Glycogen is how energy is stored in muscles and, primarily, the liver. Energy for cycling also comes from glucose in the bloodstream, fat and, if all other sources run out, eventually the muscle protein itself.

The glutes power approximately the first third of a pedal revolution; then the quadriceps take over. The quads are a group of four muscles that sit at the front of the thigh. Again, they're enormously powerful and drive the remainder of the pedal revolution. Despite cyclists being renowned for their sculpted calves (the gastrocnemius and the soleus are the most prominent muscles here), these muscles do little in terms of power generation except at the very end of the pedal stroke. Instead, they are an important conduit for the forces produced by the glutes and quads, while smaller muscles control the movement of the foot.

Hamstrings are the muscles at the back of the thigh, connected to the pelvis and the knee. With the kind of work they do on a bike (and simply sitting down at a desk), tight hamstrings are a notorious problem for cyclists. A stretching routine (see pp. 142–143) can help. Lunges and squats work these muscles and are good for building strength.

TENDONS AND LIGAMENTS

Tendons are the connective tissues that attach muscle to bone, while ligaments link bones to other bones, for example at the knee joint. Both get a lot of use during cycling, which is a very repetitive activity (frequently requiring an average of 5,000 pedal revolutions per hour). Tendonitis is inflammation of a tendon through overuse, while knee pain can be caused by a poorly set up bike and, in some cases, rest is the only cure.

Right
Cyclists use both fast- and slow-twitch muscles.

THE CYCLING BODY

AEROBIC AND ANAEROBIC

During aerobic exercise, the body uses oxygen to produce energy. If the rate of exercise outstrips the supply of oxygen (for example in a sprint), muscles generate energy anaerobically – but the by-product of this chemical process is lactic acid. When lactic acid floods muscles (and to a lesser extent the bloodstream) it causes a painful, burning sensation. The point at which this occurs is called the lactate threshold and is a useful guide for determining exercise intensity. Regular training will prompt the body to build more blood vessels to deliver more oxygen to the muscles.

CARDIOVASCULAR SYSTEM

It is easier for the human body to convert glucose into energy with oxygen (aerobically) rather than without (anaerobically) – and the more oxygen the better, making the cardiovascular system of the heart and lungs the engine room of a cyclist. Oxygen is gulped down into the lungs and is absorbed into the bloodstream through the alveoli. Many of the most successful cyclists have gargantuan lung capacities: five-time Tour de France winner Miguel Indurain's was about 8 liters – 2 liters more than is average for a man. The oxygenated blood is pumped around the body to the muscles by the heart. Again, top cyclists have above-average readings: Lance Armstrong's heart is about a third larger than average, and his resting heart rate, a good indicator of cardiovascular fitness, was 32 to 34 beats per minute, half that of an average male. Measure yours to compare.

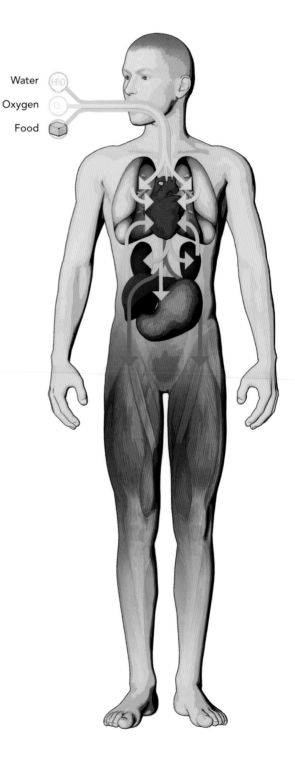

Water H₂O
Oxygen O
Food

Right
Food, water and oxygen combine to generate energy in the human body, which is distributed around the body by blood vessels.

EYES

Many road riders use protective shades to prevent watering eyes thanks to the wind and sun, or simply to avoid bugs getting in their eyes. For mountain bikers, protective glasses (or goggles) are even more important, preventing grit and dust from damaging the eyeball. A yellow or orange tinted lense will aid vision in low light, brightening up a trail.

THE CHANGING BODY

The same changes that occur in a professional cyclist's body happen to a casual cyclist, only on a less dramatic scale. Regular riding of just half an hour, three or four times a week, will tone legs and buttocks, improve cardiovascular fitness and aid weight loss.

UPPER BODY

Compared with the glutes and legs, a cyclist's upper body has relatively little to do. Sprinters and mountain bikers tend to have a bulkier build than climbing specialists, due to the sudden bursts of power and strength required in their disciplines, but chiefly the arms, shoulders and torso are used to hold the body steady while the legs do the work. However, that's no excuse to ignore the upper body, as it still plays a vital role and can be a source of aches and pains if neglected (*see* p. 154).

WEIGHT

Racing cyclists have to fight gravity in every race, so body weight is a crucial issue for them. Lugging a few extra pounds up a hill is going to hold back even the most talented rider. The skinniest male pro road racer may have a body-fat percentage of just 5 percent, and his female counterpart a body-fat percentage under 15 percent. However, cycling is not the most efficient means of losing weight; by some estimates, running is almost twice as effective at burning calories.

Neck
A shorter cockpit with a saddle that is not pushed way back can help a sore neck (and lower back).

Right
Mountain bikers use their upper body to move the bike.

Shoulder
With a wider arm position, a mountain biker's shoulders can feel stressed or stretched.

Torso
Offroaders use their upper bodies much more, not only to move the bike around obstacles but also to carry hydration packs. So it needs to be stronger: exercise to build core stability (*see* p. 136).

Arms
A mountain biker's arms withstand much more pounding than those of a road rider. A good suspension will take out some of the sting of a rough trail, but elbows and delicate joints in the fingers and hands can suffer.

FITNESS & NUTRITION

MEASURING FITNESS

How do you know whether the riding you're doing is making you fitter? Casual or competitive cyclists can measure their progress using various techniques. The results can be motivational and even form the basis of a training program.

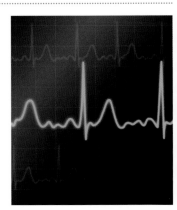

Above
Regular exercise should reduce your heart rate.

WHAT IS FITNESS?

Fitness is about more than stepping on the scale; after all, muscle weighs more than fat, so you can get fitter and heavier at the same time. For cyclists, fitness is a combination of cardiovascular health and muscular strength. Improve both and you'll be quicker.

FITNESS TESTS

Time trials (*see* p. 208) are known as 'tests' for good reason: there's no clearer gauge of a rider's fitness than their speed from A to B. Riding the same circuit at intervals during a year will highlight the peaks and valleys of a rider's fitness; this information can then be used to plot a training program that will deliver the rider to the start lines of their target events in the best possible shape.

Consistency is the key. The standard distance for a fitness test is three miles (five kilometers). Set an easily replicable course, preferably on flat terrain. Your preparation has to be the same each time you ride it. Warm up for the same amount of time (generally around half an hour) and eat at the same time (at least two hours) before the test. Then ride the course as fast as you can.

There are also fitness tests you can do in your home. The step test involves measuring your pulse rate after stepping up and down on a bench for three to five minutes. After a month or more of regular exercise, you should notice your heart rate falling.

GAUGE YOUR FITNESS

For a 3-mile course the following times indicate your general level of fitness:

MEN

- **Very fit:** Under 8 minutes
- **Above average:** 8 to 10 minutes
- **Average:** 10 to 12 minutes
- **Unfit:** More than 12 minutes

WOMEN

- **Very fit:** Under 10 minutes
- **Above average:** 10 to 12 minutes
- **Average:** 12 to 14 minutes
- **Unfit:** More than 14 minutes

WHAT IS VO$_2$ MAX?

In a laboratory setting, fitness tests can be performed very accurately. The standard test for cyclists is to establish VO$_2$ max. This test measures the maximum volume of oxygen (in milliliters) a person can consume (per minute, per kilogram of body weight) while exercising at maximum capacity. The greater the cardiovascular fitness of a cyclist, the more oxygen they'll be able to use to produce energy. The test is administered on a stationary bike with the athlete required to pedal at their top rate until they reach the point where they can no longer continue, while their oxygen consumption is measured by machines. At 82ml of oxygen per kilo per minute, Lance Armstrong had one of the highest VO$_2$ max levels recorded, in a league table dominated by endurance athletes such as cross-country skiers, cyclists and marathon runners. The VO$_2$ max of an average male is about half Armstrong's.

VO$_2$ max declines with age, but it can be boosted by doing just half an hour of exercise, three times a week, at 70 to 80 percent of your maximum capacity. The test provides a set of numbers, but they may not translate into better performances on the bike, where skills, experience and tactics also play a part.

Above
Top athletes such as Lance Armstrong are genetically gifted.

Left
Measuring VO$_2$ max is the best way of establishing a cyclist's level of fitness.

FITNESS & NUTRITION

SETTING GOALS

The most important requirement of any fitness-building program is an achievable goal. Without a goal, whether it's losing a certain amount of weight or winning a local race, motivation will ebb away. Any training program should revolve around the goals you set.

GOALS

There are as many types of goals to choose from as there are cyclists. You can have a personal goal – to lose weight or keep up with a friend or partner – or a more specific goal, such as riding a first century (100 miles) or competing in a 24-hour mountain bike race.

What is important is finding the balance between a goal that is challenging and one that is attainable with hard work. Once you've decided on a goal, commit to it, write it down and tell someone. Announcing it will set the goal in stone, providing motivation, and double the sense of satisfaction when you achieve the goal.

BIG RIDES

Mass-participation events offer great goals for new cyclists. The supportive camaraderie of such events, whether it's a short ride with 50 people in support of a local hospital, or a 5,000-strong, multi-day tour, can prove to be a huge boost to cyclists who may have found the challenge too much if attempting it alone.

Such events also offer the opportunity to train with a group and share the ups and downs. Most areas will have charity bike rides taking place throughout the year, from the UK's 54-mile London to Brighton Bike Ride for the British Heart Foundation (with Ditchling Beacon en route), to Lance Armstrong's Livestrong Challenge series in cities around the USA, to the 345-mile Great Victorian Bike Ride in southern Australia.

Once you've identified a suitable event, set a target. For example, if you can ride 50 miles comfortably, commit to completing a hilly century like the Susan G. Komen Ride for the Cure in Aspen. Ask yourself

Above
Charity rides, such as the UK's London to Brighton Bike Ride, are a popular goal for cyclists.

what you want to achieve. To finish? To set a personal best? The target has to inspire you to get out on the bike at your lowest point, on a dreary morning when an extra hour in bed is all too tempting.

MOTIVATION

During the winter months, when it's cold and there's less light, it can be all too easy to slide into a rut where you feel like eating rather than exercising. Instead, put the bike aside for a month or two and freshen up your fitness regime with new activities. If you live in a snowy area, cross-country skiing offers an unbeatable all-over workout. Indoors, swimming is a great way to work on the whole body without stressing joints. Spinning classes are also excellent at jump-starting the metabolism and introducing a degree of intensity to your routine.

TRAINING PROGRAMS

When you've committed to a goal, one that is going to test and develop your fitness and abilities, devise a training program. There is no such thing as a one-size-fits-all plan, but there are common elements to all programs. For most cycling goals, you will want to build stamina and improve speed. Each week you will need to complete long rides for endurance at a steady rate, short, hard rides (see p.145) for speed and strength and gentle recovery rides, an essential part of any fitness program. If time is tight, think laterally: you may not find an extra two hours on the weekend for a session, but adding a weighted trailer to your daily commute is resistance training, or take a hillier route back from work. Focused training is better than hours grinding out the miles: just 20 to 30 minutes of aerobic exercise a day builds fitness.

Ask how much time you have before your event. A grueling race such as an Ironman triathlon will require up to a year's preparation for an average person. A mountain bike marathon will be easier with a couple of months of training under the belt. When plotting a training plan, use a spreadsheet and work backward from the goal event. You should be building up a good base level of fitness from the outset with increasing weekly mileage. Top-end speed can be sharpened closer to the event.

Ignore Oscar Wilde's witticism that consistency is the last refuge of the unimaginative. Consistency is crucial to a training program. Work out how much time you can set aside a week (eight hours is ideal, less is probably more normal for everyday cyclists). Professional riders train to peak at certain points during their season; they'll identify the races they want to win and those they're happy to use for training. Casual cyclists can do the same. You should aim to be exercising at your maximum capacity four to five weeks before the event; from that point to the event you will need to gradually taper off your workouts by doing 20 percent less per week so you are not burned out before the big day.

Listen to your body; feed it and rest it properly. Vary the training to keep your interest levels up and set interim challenges, such as setting a personal best up a steep hill. Note the time it takes to recover from such exertions; there is no better guide to fitness levels. Ride with people better than you and with a group on occasion. Cycle computers can download data recorded from a ride straight to a home computer and this can be shared with other riders to compare progress.

Above
Racing cyclists dedicate their lives to winning.

TRAINING RIDES

- **Recovery ride** = able to hold a conversation comfortably.
- **Endurance ride** = able to speak and breathe normally.
- **70 percent pace** (below lactate threshold) = able to speak a few words, breathing heavily.
- **Maximum rate** (above lactate threshold) = unable to talk.

TRAINING: OFF THE BIKE

CORE STABILITY

Cycling is a lot of fun and delivers great cardiovascular fitness. It doesn't build strength and stability in the upper body, and yet it makes big demands of it. These exercises will reduce aches, pains and potential injuries, while building a more balanced body and all-around fitness.

The powerful leg muscles may do most of the work, but the rest of the body plays its part in pedaling by supporting the upper body and providing a stable base for the lower body's exertions. Unfortunately, the typical cycling position is unnatural. Bent over the handlebars, back muscles, such as the multifidus, which runs the length of the spine, are extended, while the abdominal muscles, such

as the transverse abdominis, which wraps around the waist from the ribs to the pelvis, aren't worked at all.

Taken together, the lower back and abdomen form the body's core; a vital link in a chain of movement from top to bottom. Core stability exercises are designed to strengthen these often-neglected muscles.

How do you know if you need to work on your core? Aside from lower-back pain, a rocking motion while

seated on the saddle, plus locked elbows and straight arms as a result of their need to compensate for this lack of stability, suggest a core problem. A weak core is associated with many lower-back injuries.

These exercises are designed to require the minimum of equipment, and to be able to be performed in the home or outdoors.

Shoulder
Shoulders benefit from an exercise routine to prevent a rounded appearance.

Lower back
A well-known trouble-spot, a cyclist's lower back is locked in one extended position for hours at a time.

Neck
To see forward, a cyclist's neck is usually tilted back for long periods, which can cause aches and pains.

Knees
As the legs piston away, the knees can suffer from overuse if the bike's set-up is slightly incorrect by being too high, low or forward.

Wrist
Select handlebars and grips with care: the wrist is a delicate joint around which nerves pass.

Left
Areas of the body that need care and exercise.

Right
The plank:
1. Place your hands together and rest your weight on your elbows.
2. Lift up on to your feet and rock forward, drawing in your core.

THE BRIDGE

The bridge is good way to locate and understand your abdominal muscles. Lie on your back, with your knees up (in an inverted V) and your feet flat on the floor. Raise your pelvis until your torso forms a straight line down from your knees to your shoulders. With your pelvis in the air, draw your abdomen inward, as if a thread from your belly button is being gently pulled toward the ground. This is more than just breathing in; try to feel the muscle working deeper in the core. Hold for at least 10 seconds then relax. Repeat.

THE PLANK

The plank is one of the best internal-muscle exercises for cyclists. Lie face down and stretch out, resting your weight on your forearms and toes. Raise your pelvis, holding your body in a straight line by using your abdominal muscles. Lean forward on your arms, pivoting on your toes.

The forearm and upper arm form an L-shape under your shoulder, and you can lock your hands together or leave them flat on the ground. Look at the ground (not ahead), extending your neck in line with the rest of your spine, and don't stick your bottom in the air or let it sag. In this position, engage the core muscles as you did in the bridge, drawing in the stomach. Breathe in and out while doing this so you're using the deep core muscles rather than simply holding your breath. Hold for at least 10 seconds then relax. Repeat.

A variation of the plank is a lateral hover: essentially, the plank on its side. Lie on your side, feet together and resting on one forearm.

Raise your pelvis off the ground, holding your body in a straight line from your head to your toes. Hold for at least 10 seconds then relax. Repeat.

TIP

Remember that stretches and exercises are not supposed to be painful.

TRAINING: OFF THE BIKE

SWISS BALL

A large Swiss ball is an excellent tool for core exercises and can be used in a multitude of ways. A deceptively simple exercise to start with is to sit on the ball, feet slightly apart and with knees forming a right angle. First, raise the heel of one foot, using your abdominal muscles to hold your body as still as possible. If you can do that, try raising the whole foot off the ground, holding still using your core. The Swiss ball also adds extra work for the core to push-ups and crunches.

CRUNCHES

Sit on the ball, rolling forward until you're perched on one edge, with your legs shoulder-width apart and slightly bent. Bend your back over the ball and place your hands beside your head. The key to the exercise is to keep the ball as still as possible. Using your core muscles, sit up a couple of inches. Hold it, then return to the flat position slowly, without letting the ball move. Repeat.

Swiss-ball crunches:
Left
1. Sit on the edge of the Swiss ball.

Right
2. Slowly roll forward on the ball.
3. Keep the ball still when it's under your back.
4. Sit up and return to the horizontal position in a slow and controlled way.

PUSH-UPS

Get into the push-up position – hands under your shoulders – but with your feet resting on the ball. Keeping your core muscles engaged, bend your arms and bring your chest to the ground, then back up, in a controlled manner rather than with a jerk. The key is to keep the ball as still as possible using your core muscles. Repeat.

Left
Push-ups:
1. Start with your feet on the ball and hands on the floor.
2. Slowly lower your body to the floor and return to the horizontal position.

YOGA AND PILATES

Both yoga and pilates are outstanding for reinforcing core stability and improving flexibility – which can be a major problem for cyclists thanks to their tight hamstrings and calves. Newcomers should sign up for yoga or Pilates classes with an instructor to learn correct technique and help avoid injury. However, one basic and useful exercise to try at home is the downward dog position, which works the rectus abdominus muscle – which forms the so-called 'six pack' in the super-toned – at the front of your stomach.

Start on your hands and knees, with your feet shoulder-width apart. Straighten your legs and raise your pelvis into the air to form an inverted V. Holding the stomach muscles in, gently extend your heels so your feet are flat on the ground – cyclists may have trouble with this move, which stretches the backs of the legs, so don't overdo it.

Above
Yoga aids flexibility and breathing. This is the downward-facing dog pose.

TRAINING: OFF THE BIKE
NECK AND SHOULDERS

The neck and shoulders can suffer just as much as the lower back when cycling. The human head weighs about 11lbs and when your body is at a 45-degree angle over the handlebars, much of the weight is supported by the arms and hands, stressing the shoulders. Combine that with the need to tilt your head back to see where you're going, and it's easy to see how stressed the neck can become.

Left
Shoulder rotations:
1. Hold light dumbbells with straight arms and back.
2. Bring your arms back, up and forward clockwise.
3. Repeat counter-clockwise.

SHOULDER ROTATIONS

Holding a pair of small dumbbells, stand with your feet shoulder-width apart, your shoulders back and your back straight. Rotate your shoulders clockwise and counter-clockwise in a controlled, steady movement.

NECK STRETCH

This simple stretch releases tension in the neck's trapezius muscle. Sitting or standing, gently tilt your head to one side. Count to ten then repeat on the other side. Keep your movements slow and smooth to avoid a strain.

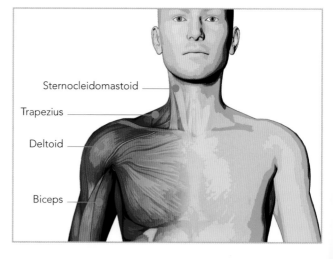

Sternocleidomastoid

Trapezius

Deltoid

Biceps

Right
The main muscles in the human neck and shoulders.

SHOULDER STRETCH

Standing with your feet shoulder-width apart, take one arm and bring it horizontally across the upper body. Place your other hand above the elbow (palm flat) and bring it in toward your body. This will stretch the deltoid muscle. Hold it and relax. Repeat with the other arm.

Left
Shoulder stretches relax the upper body.

TRICEP PRESS

A tricep press with a dumbbell also works the upper arms. Holding a dumbbell in one hand, move your arm up and back so your elbow is pointing up and your hand is behind your shoulders. With your other hand, support the upper arm. Keeping this part of the arm still, extend the rest of your arm into the air then bring the dumbbell slowly back down. Repeat then switch arms.

Left
A tricep press with dumbbell:
1. Place one arm in the air, using the other arm to support the tricep underneath the raised arm.
2. Keep the upper arm still and bring the dumbbell back down.

DIPS

Dips will work the shoulders and triceps. You can do this exercise using a park bench. Sit on the bench with your hands gripping it on either side, next to your hips. Shuffle your feet forward until you can lower yourself off the front of the bench, keeping your knees at a right angle and thighs parallel to the ground. Push yourself back up by straightening your arms.

TIP

Pain and tingles (pins and needles) can also be caused by pinched nerves in the hands and lower back. Setting up your bike correctly can combat some of these problems (*see* pp. 46–47), but preparing your body with some simple exercises and stretches will also help.

TRAINING: OFF THE BIKE STRETCHES

There's no evidence that stretching before exercise has any benefit at all. However, getting into the habit of stretching after cycling is a good idea because cycling doesn't fully extend some muscles and stresses others. This routine of basic stretches can be repeated after any prolonged bike ride.

Below
Calf stretch.

QUAD STRETCH

Stand with your feet shoulder-width apart. Flick the heel of one foot up behind you to stand on one leg. Catch your ankle or top part of your foot with one hand and hold it, keeping your body straight and tall, looking forward and stretching through the hip.

Right
Quad stretch.

CALF STRETCH

This stretches the lower leg. Stand close to a wall or flat surface, lean forward and rest your palms on it. Step forward with one leg, bending the knee. Move the other leg back and, keeping the heel flat to the floor, lean forward. Hold it, then relax and repeat with the other leg.

Below
Lower-back stretch:
1. Get down on your knees and elbows.

2. Curl into a tucked position and reach forward, flexing the spine.

HAMSTRING STRETCH

Standing up, step forward with one leg, bow forward and place your hands on the opposite knee. Lean forward but don't arch your back or reach down to your toes.

Right
Hamstring stretch.

LOWER-BACK STRETCH

Sitting on your knees, curl forward so the spine is flexed. Move into a tucked position and reach forward with your arms. This is a good post-workout stretch. An alternative is to lie on your back and bring your knees up to your chest.

EXTRA STRETCH FOR THE ARMS

Standing up straight, bring one arm up and over your shoulder so your hand lies between your shoulder blades. With the other hand, grasp your elbow and pull gently.

FITNESS & NUTRITION

TRAINING: ON THE BIKE

For cyclists, there's no substitute for simply 'getting the miles in'. Time in the saddle, turning the pedals, brings fitness. But the level of fitness gained depends on how that time is spent. A carefully planned program of on-the-bike training will bring your cycling goals within reach.

Below
Emilia Romagna, in Northern Italy, is a popular training ground, used by Marco Pantani.

Even gifted cyclists need to train. Professional racer Marco Pantani would do laps of his favorite training climb, Cippo Carpegna in Italy, again and again – in the snow, the rain and the wind. Lance Armstrong had the same single-minded approach, pounding the French and Spanish hills around his base in Girona all winter with one objective in mind: winning the Tour de France. But such riders don't get to the top of their game without making sure they get the most out of their training time, which is why a week-by-week training schedule is essential, whatever your goal. You can follow a specialist training program, tailored to the time and ability you have, or you can sketch out your own, following some basic principles.

SCHEDULE

Whether your goal is three, six or nine months away, the point of a structured training plan is to ensure you are at peak fitness at the right time. This is called 'peaking', and it is what bike racers base their season around. It takes discipline to train during the winter months, but this is when summer races are won or lost. A fitness schedule needs a solid foundation, which means gradually building fitness with steady mileage before you can begin pushing yourself. Opportunities for cycling over the winter months are likely to be fewer, so be prepared to do another

activity (swimming, spinning class, gym work, indoor climbing) to stay in shape, and use the time to work on other areas of your fitness, such as flexibility or upper-body strength.

As the year warms up, so should your training. Instead of doing four steady rides per week and an indoor activity, you can add a couple of intensive sessions of climbing or sprinting. As the weeks go by, do fewer rides at a moderate pace and add more testing rides, going further, riding harder. All the time, however, remember to schedule rest days – at least one

per week, two if it suits you – and recovery rides, again, at least one per week. Overtraining (*see* p. 149) now will set back your progress towards your overall target level of fitness. A month before your goal or target event, you should begin to taper your

Above
A spinning class is a good way to train during the winter.

efforts. The idea is that you will cut back on harder rides until you are fully rested, fit and at peak strength for the big day.

SAMPLE TRAINING PLAN

A sample training plan, over three months, for an average rider (someone who can do 20 miles without too much difficulty) wanting to complete their first century (100-mile) ride, might look like this:

Key:	(R) Recovery ride: Ride of your choice at a social pace	(E) Easy: No breathlessness
	(I) Intervals: 2- to 10-minute max efforts such as sprints or hill climbs	(M) Medium: Limited talking possible
		(H) Hard: Talking difficult

	Monday	Tuesday	Wednesday	Thursday	Friday	Saturday	Sunday
Week 1	Rest day	10m (M)	10m (M)	Recovery ride	Rest day	20m (E)	20m (M)
Week 2	Rest day	12m (M)	12m (M)	Recovery ride	Rest day	20m (E)	20m (M)
Week 3	Rest day	15m (M)	15m (M)	Recovery ride	Rest day	25m (M)	25m (M)
Week 4	Rest day	15m (E)	15m (E)	Rest day	Rest day	20m (E)	20m (E)
Week 5	Rest day	15m (I)	15m (H)	Recovery ride	Rest day	30m (M)	35m (H)
Week 6	Rest day	15m (H)	15m (I)	Recovery ride	Rest day	30m (M)	45m (H)
Week 7	Rest day	20m (I)	20m (H)	Recovery ride	Rest day	40m (M)	60m (H)
Week 8	Rest day	15m (R)	15m (R)	Rest day	Rest day	15m (R)	40m (R)
Week 9	Rest day	20m (H)	20m (I)	Recovery ride	Rest day	30m (H)	70m (M)
Week 10	Rest day	20m (I)	20m (H)	Recovery ride	Rest day	30m (H)	80m (M)
Week 11	Rest day	15m (H)	15m (I)	Recovery ride	Rest day	20m (M)	40m (H)
Week 12	Rest day	15m (I)	15m (M)	Rest day	Rest day	15m (I)	Event day

TRAINING: ON THE BIKE

KNOW YOURSELF

Right and below
Your heart rate is a guide to your fitness and can indicate overtraining.

A key element of an effective training plan is having an accurate picture of your own capability. Discovering your lactate threshold (the point where comfortable aerobic effort becomes painfully anaerobic, see p. 130) and VO_2 max would enable you to tailor your training – however, for those of us who don't have the support of a pro team, a fitness program is best built on your maximum heart rate (HR max). There are several formulas for calculating your HR max.

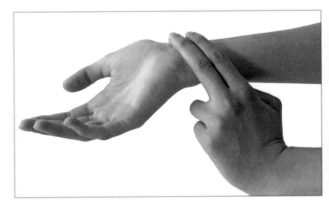

The most well known is 220 minus your age, but there are variations that can give more accurate results depending on whether you're male or female, young or old. The other option is to find out for yourself, using your own heart rate monitor (HRM) to record your maximum effort. This is best done with the guidance of a personal trainer and after taking a doctor's advice if your health, age and family background give cause for concern.

Knowing your HR max allows you to train at a certain percentage of it: a recovery ride will be at about 60 percent of your HR max; a steady training ride will be at about 70 percent of your HR max; and a breathless pace at your lactate threshold will be at about 80 to 90 percent.

This information makes it much more simple to calibrate your training effort to your schedule.

TIP

Another measurement worth taking, if you have the means, is your power output in watts. Top-end road bikes are often fitted with power meters today, and they will unambiguously inform you of your maximum output, whether you like the numbers or not!

TIP

Remember that the more you stress your body, the more rest and recuperation it will require.

VARIETY

Consistency in training need not mean endless repetition. Every training plan should take into account the mental as well as physical effort involved, and a tedious routine will not be motivating or inspiring. Instead, try to add a bit of variety to your routine, whether that means joining a 'chain gang' (group ride) or cross-training by doing another complementary sport. A clever tactic is to address one of the weaker aspects of your riding each week: if you're a poor sprinter, focus on racing for telephone poles and road signs; if you don't feel confident cornering while descending, find some downhills and practice.

Varying the pace of your cycling during a training ride is called 'doing intervals'. For a couple of minutes, two or three times a ride, push yourself up to an uncomfortable level of exertion (80 to 90 percent of your HR max) then back off and ride at a gentle pace for a couple of minutes to let the lactic acid subside. This is an essential training technique for several reasons: it develops fast-twitch muscle, it is good preparation for a race situation, such as chasing down a group or sprinting for the finish line, and builds power rather than just building endurance.

BALANCED TRAINING

A balanced training schedule will include all of the following each week:

- Base miles at a steady heart rate

- Sprints or intervals where you hit HR max

- Recovery rides and rest days

Above top
Off-season training means wrapping up warmly.

Above
The months of training pay off on race day.

FITNESS & NUTRITION

TRAINING: ON THE BIKE

GROUPS

There are plenty of benefits to signing up with a cycling club for training rides, sometimes called 'chain gangs'. The extra support and competition offered by other riders can be highly motivating – there's a form of collective responsibility when it comes to turning up on even the bleakest of days. It can also be enjoyably sociable compared with doing the same miles solo. Riding as a group, especially at a fast pace, also builds group-riding skills and familiarity with riding at speed among large groups of cyclists.

Left
Joining a group training ride can be good for motivation.

Below
Train at your own pace and to your own requirements.

OVERTRAINING

Overtraining can be a genuine problem and is not to be underestimated. Caught up in the pursuit of your goals and with an accelerating fitness schedule, it's easy to overlook the signs that you're overdoing it. But others may spot them: lethargy and fatigue, personality changes, such as a shorter temper, persistent illnesses, disrupted sleep. All these symptoms indicate that you are doing too much training. Check your numbers too: an elevated pulse, taken on waking over several mornings, and a lower maximum heart rate can add to the evidence.

The fatigue that is brought on by overtraining is pervasive and entirely different from the three or four hours of tiredness after a hard ride. The cure is rest, for as long as it takes to return to vitality, which may be weeks. If it persists, look again at your diet and ensure you're getting the right nutrients.

TIP

Remember that the training objectives of a group ride may not correspond to your training plan. There's a tendency for a group ride's speed to edge upward, when you may be better off with a more relaxed pace. Many organized groups are quite specific about their planned rides, for example doing 60 miles at an average of 17mph.

Right
Overtraining brings fatigue and even illness.

FITNESS & NUTRITION

RIDING WITH A DISORDER: ASTHMA & DIABETES

Rates of asthma and diabetes are increasing worldwide, but having a chronic health problem need not be a barrier to enjoying cycling. Sensible precautions taken before and during a ride can ensure a safe day out.

Below
Asthma or diabetes doesn't stop riders from reaching the top of the world.

ASTHMA

Asthma seems increasingly prevalent in the modern world (for example, up to 7 percent of the US population is affected and only slightly less in the UK, while over two million Australians suffer from the condition). Symptoms include acute shortness of breath, coughing, wheezing and tightness in the chest, caused by muscle spasms in the lungs. All this can be extremely frightening on a bike ride. Attacks can be triggered by a number of things, from cold, dry winter air to pollen in the summer. Apart from staying off the bike during these periods, there are several things you can do to minimize the chance of an attack mid-ride. The first is to visit your doctor to check whether your medication routine needs to change if you take up cycling. Many asthmatics use a steroid inhaler before exercise to prevent an attack and bronchodilator medicine to relieve an episode. It's important to warm up properly (*see* p. 152) before a ride, and practicing breathing exercises may help. When you can't get on the bike, swimming in warm water is the next best form of exercise. Neither Paula Radcliffe nor David Beckham let asthma stop them from reaching the top in their sports.

Below
Carry an inhaler on rides.

Far left and left
Diabetics need to monitor their blood sugar levels, and may need insulin.

DIABETES

It's the same story with diabetes: the condition is on the increase in the Western world, driven perhaps by lifestyles and diet. Diabetes is a failure of the body to regulate its blood sugar levels, either because the pancreas isn't producing enough of the hormone insulin or because the body is resistant to insulin (among other factors). Diabetes is classified into type 1 and type 2; generally type 1 diabetics suffer from the condition from a young age, while it tends to affect type 2 diabetics later in life. All sorts of generalizations are made about type 2 diabetics, who form the bulk of sufferers, but, although obesity and sedentary lifestyles are often contributory factors, the condition can affect anyone.

Many successful athletes have not let diabetes stop them from reaching the pinnacle of their sport, among them Sir Steve Redgrave, the Olympic rower who cycled in the 2010 Race Across America, and Wade Simmons, the star freeride mountain biker, both of whom are type 1 diabetics.

The most important adjustment diabetic cyclists have to make is getting into the routine of monitoring their blood sugar levels: diabetic cyclists will always carry a blood sugar testing kit, and experience helps them recognize the warning signs of a hypoglycemic (low blood sugar) attack. It takes time to understand how exercise will affect each diabetic. Diabetic cyclists will also carry dextrose tablets or candy to ward off sudden drops in blood sugar. Another wise precaution is always to carry ID that notes the condition. Many riders will carry insulin with them, while others may be tempted to put off taking insulin in order to avoid a hypoglycemic episode/attack and will have a high blood sugar instead for a while. Ask your doctor or dietician for advice about managing your blood sugar level with increased exercise. And speak to other diabetic cyclists: riding with the condition is a learning process, but it can be done.

Below
British rower Steve Redgrave won five Olympic gold medals despite suffering from diabetes.

AVOIDING INJURIES: WARMING UP

An important way of preventing injuries is to warm up properly. This gets the heart pumping, muscles become more supple and joints gain a wider range of movement, all of which benefits cyclists.

The most basic way to warm up is to gradually increase the intensity of your activity over about 30 minutes. If you're warming up before a race (*see* p. 212), the session should culminate in a few minutes of cycling approaching your maximum effort. Professional cyclists will use a turbo trainer before a time trial (*see* p. 208), but even casual cyclists will find that doing a few exercises will reduce the risk of strains or tears. There's no evidence that stretching cold muscles before exercise does any good (although a stretching routine after exercise is a good habit to acquire). Instead, warm-up exercises should focus on dynamic stretches with gentle, swinging movements.

CALF RAISES

To warm up the calves, find a step (a low box is fine) and stand with your toes on the edge. Lower the heels and then rise up on your toes, working the leg muscles in a controlled way. Repeat.

Below
Calf raises:
1. Stand with your toes on a step.
2. Slowly rise up on your toes and go back down.

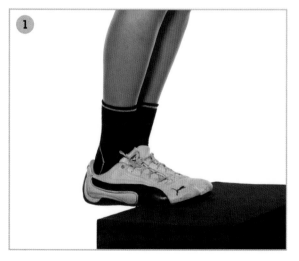

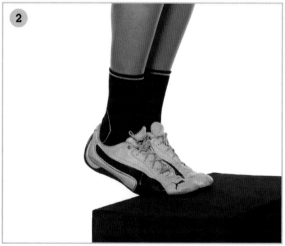

GLUTE KICKBACKS

Warm up the big gluteal muscles with a simple swinging exercise. Hold on to the back of a chair and, making sure you keep your back straight, kick your leg backward in a steady, controlled movement. Change legs. Repeat.

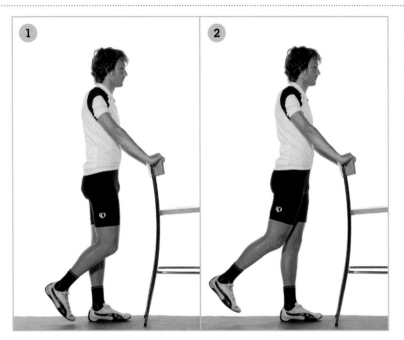

Left
Glute kickbacks:
1. Holding on to something, raise a foot.
2. Swing your leg back.

STANDING HIP FLEXION

To warm up the hip flexors, which attach to the hip and lower back, stand with your feet shoulder-width apart and your back straight. Lift one knee, gradually increasing the height. Swap legs. Repeat.

Left
Standing hip flexion:
1. Stand with feet a shoulder-width apart.
2. Raise one leg, keeping the pelvis square.

LOWER-BACK FLEXION

Riders with back problems may benefit from warming up the lower back before a ride with this simple exercise. Place your feet together and your hands on to your thighs. Bend the knees, keeping them together, and bend your back forward, pivoting at the hips. Return to upright and repeat, gradually increasing the range of motion of your lower back each time.

FITNESS & NUTRITION

AVOIDING INJURIES: ACHES & PAINS

A correctly fitted bike goes a long way toward avoiding a variety of aches, pains, tears and strains (see p. 46). But sometimes, whatever we do, something doesn't feel quite right. Working out what's going wrong is the first step toward resolving the problem.

The body sends signals in the form of aches, tingles, pains and numbness when a position is not only uncomfortable but also possibly harmful. Listening to those signals is vital to understanding what's happening. From top to bottom, the following are the most common complaints and how to remedy them.

Above
With mountain bike handlebars, angle the brake levers downward so that your wrists and hands are in line with the lower arm.

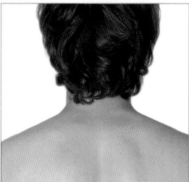

Above
The tendons and muscles around the upper cervical vertebrae can become painfully stressed.

NECK

A stiff, painful neck and tight shoulder muscles are often caused by a top tube that is too long, stressing the upper trapezius muscles, and handlebars that are set too low, requiring the head to be tilted too far back, compressing the vertebrae at the top of the spine. Contributory factors include a heavy helmet or low visor, or handlebars that are too wide, minimizing shock absorption by the arms. In addition to some simple strengthening exercises (*see* pp. 140–141), try raising the handlebars by adding spacers beneath the stem (*see* p. 26) or replacing the stem with a shorter one. When riding, change your position regularly, sitting upright to allow the neck and shoulders to relax. Off the bike, perform basic stretches after a ride. And work on your posture throughout the day, holding your shoulders back and your back straight.

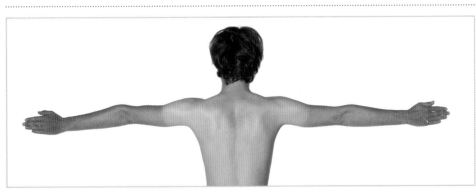

Left
Hands and arms as
well as the back, neck
and shoulders may be
subject to strain.

Below
Drop handlebars offer
a variety of positions
for the hands.

HANDS

Many riders complain of prickly pins and needle sensations in their hands and fingers, or even numbness in the outer fingers. There are several possible causes, but one of the most common is compression of the ulnar nerve (also known as 'handlebar palsy'). The ulnar nerve runs along the forearm, passing through the elbow and wrist and along the outside of the hand; the third and little fingers are those that can be affected. Compression of the nerve can occur at the elbow if the arm is stretched out, at the wrist (carpal tunnel syndrome) and, most likely of all, at the base of the palm where it meets the grip – many cycling gloves, such as those in the Specialized Body Geometry range, now have a small pad at this point. Relieve pressure points by changing the orientation of your handlebars, for example, to give a more backswept layout, and perhaps raising them to reduce the weight borne by your hands. You can experiment with ergonomics: different grips (thicker, thinner or contoured) and different brands of cycling glove.

Bikes with exceptionally stiff forks and handlebars – such as bars with an oversized diameter – may transmit more of the vibrations from the road up to the hands. Some road bikes, such as Specialized's Roubaix range, have small shock absorbers fitted in the forks; alternatively, a carbon-fiber handlebar with a bit of give may reduce the buzz. Remember not to grip the bars too tightly; a firm but relaxed grip is best.

ARMS

One cause of aching arms is handlebars that are too wide. Mountain bikers tend to prefer wide bars for extra control over rough ground, but having your arms splayed places greater stress on them and inhibits their ability to absorb shocks.

BONES

This is a rare problem but one worth being aware of: studies show that there is a correlation between serious cyclists and early-onset osteoporosis, a condition where the bones lose density and become thin and brittle. Cycling is not thought to cause the osteoporosis, but rather the low-impact, non-weight bearing nature of the exercise, at the expense of other activity, doesn't prevent it.

As a precaution, mix cycling with a load-bearing activity (such as weights) and make sure your diet is rich in calcium.

AVOIDING INJURIES: ACHES & PAINS

Above
The correct posture will minimize aches and pains.

Right
Pack your equipment into panniers rather than a backpack to avoid causing back pain.

BACK

Lower-back pain can be a persistent problem for cyclists, especially taller riders. Serious cyclists aim for as low and streamlined a position as possible, extending the lower back for longer periods of time, while jarring jolts are passed up the seatpost, so it's no wonder the back can complain. In addition to core-strengthening exercises (see pp. 136–139), bike setup can be tweaked for extra comfort: raising the handlebars and reducing the reach with a shorter stem will give the back a break. Shift position regularly to relieve tense muscles, getting out of the saddle and straightening the back. Check that your saddle is not too high – suggested by a rocking motion of the hips – because any loss of stability here will require the back muscles to work harder. And it may help to avoid placing extra weight on the spine by carrying cargo in panniers rather than a backpack.

GROIN

The groin is an area subject to much rumor and innuendo. But the fact is that both men and women can suffer awkward and annoying problems here and, as one of the key contact points with a bicycle, it's important to pay attention to any hints it's giving you.

Male cyclists have been on high alert for impotence-related issues since a series of medical studies, such as Dr. Irwin Goldstein's 1997 report and Dr. Steven Shrader's 2005 study in *The Journal of Sexual Medicine*, hit the press. Dismissed as unfounded hype by some, anecdotal evidence alone suggests that men can experience problems caused by cycling.

So, what's the issue? The male body isn't designed for sitting on narrow saddles: important blood vessels and nerves run along the perineum, right where it meets the saddle. There's no protective padding on the body here, and regular, constant pressure on these blood vessels is thought to be a possible cause of erectile dysfunction. Certainly, men do report numbness in this region during cycling, due to the constriction of nerves and blood supply. It's important to note this issue may only affect a tiny number of very serious cyclists who spend many hours a week in the saddle – and that there are other factors that may have affected the results of the studies, such as age differences.

Since the issue gained prominence, many saddles have been redesigned with cut-outs along the center; Specialized's Body Geometry line is a good example of carefully researched saddle design. The cut-out is intended to reduce pressure on the specific area affected. However, we're all different shapes, so you may need to try a few saddles before finding one that fits. Remember that comfort isn't always the best indicator of whether a saddle is restricting your blood supply or not. A good habit to develop is getting out of the saddle regularly (every 15 minutes) for a few pedal strokes. A riding position that places less weight on the front of the groin can also be helpful, as is a saddle that is flat, rather than tilted down at the front.

Another potential problem area in the groin is the prostate. This large gland, again situated exactly where the saddle meets the body, can get temperamental in later life and become inflamed, a painful condition called prostatitis. Cycling can exacerbate and even cause prostatitis, the symptoms of which include a painful and intermittent flow of urine and, in serious cases, a fever. Antibiotics and time off the bike may be needed for a full recovery.

Right
Get out of the saddle regularly to give your groin a rest.

FITNESS & NUTRITION

AVOIDING INJURIES: ACHES & PAINS

SADDLE SORENESS

New cyclists of both sexes can suffer saddle soreness as their bodies adjust to the saddle. This can be in the form of abrasions, sores or even (rarely) boils. A good quality pair of padded cycling shorts, such as those from Assos or Rapha, will make a huge difference to comfort levels. Applying special chamois cream (from Assos) or even Sudocrem (intended for babies' diaper rash) can help, too.

Above
Sitting correctly, on your sit bones, will help to avoid saddle soreness.

BEATING SADDLE SORENESS

- Wear a good quality brand of cycling shorts, such as Assos or Rapha.

- Find a saddle with a cut-out that suits you.

- Don't lean too far forward; sit on your sit bones.

- Get out of the saddle every 15 minutes.

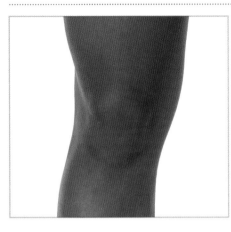

Left
Knee pain can be cured by using wedges in shoes or checking the alignment of your leg's pedaling action.

Left
Cleats can be adjusted for comfort.

KNEES

The knee joint is especially susceptible to exercise-induced pains – which is why many runners turn to cycling. But even riding a bike stresses the joint, especially when turning a big gear. The extension of the leg is the most important factor in knee pain, so to diagnose the cause and therefore the solution, the general rule is that pain at the front of the knee suggests that the saddle is too low, and is not allowing the leg to extend enough; while pain at the back of the knee indicates a saddle that is too high, resulting in over-extension.

A saddle that is too far forward can also cause knee pain by placing the knee ahead of the foot when the pedals are at the 9 o'clock position. Also check whether your cleats are straight; most cleats allow a bit of sideways movement (float), but having your knee twisted from the beginning is not a good start. Another variable is 'the Q-factor' – the width between the pedals – which will affect the alignment of the legs and knees, depending on the individual. And the length of the crank will also affect the relative position of the knee during a pedal stroke. A professional bike fit will work through all of these issues.

FEET

Composed of numerous small bones and tendons, the foot and ankle combine to form a delicate piece of anatomy. The shoe is the most common cause of foot pain: stiff soles prevent too much flex, but the uppers should also offer support. Shoes that are too small can pinch nerves and cause numbness. And a hotspot can develop underneath the foot, directly above the cleat. Pedals with a larger contact area may help, or you can try moving the cleat; most riders place the cleat under the ball of the foot or a centimeter or so (half an inch) behind it.

Below
Dr. Andy Pruitt checking pro rider Jens Voigts' riding position.

PROTECTING THE KNEE JOINT

All joints are lubricated by synovial fluid, the effectiveness of which deteriorates with age. So, as a large and exposed joint, the knee in particular will benefit from being kept warm. A pair of three-quarter-length bib tights in the cooler seasons will keep your knees pumping smoothly.

DIET: WHAT TO EAT

Food: it's a favorite topic of cyclists. Toward the end of a ride it can be all you think about. Which is just as well, because providing your body with all the fuel and nutrients it requires is a complex job.

Left
Protein, such as meat and fish, helps to repair the body's cells.

NEEDS

Long gone are the days when Tour de France racers, such as Jacques Anquetil, would fortify themselves with lobster and champagne; diet and nutrition are now at the center of any professional's training program. However, the average cyclist doesn't need to go so far as to weigh out food portions, and there is little to be gained from being obsessive about food. Rather than monk-like self-denial, a balanced diet should meet all of a cyclist's nutritional needs. So what are a cyclist's needs? When we ride, we burn fuel in the form of calories (stored as glycogen in the muscles and liver). This fuel needs to be replaced, and the easiest way to do that is by eating carbohydrates, which can be easily converted by the body into glucose. If we ride hard we also damage our muscles, and we need protein to repair them.

WHAT TO EAT

Protein and carbohydrate can be easily obtained from our daily diet.

Carbohydrate comes in two forms: simple and complex. Simple carbs are sugars, found in everything that tastes sweet, from jam to soft drinks and cakes. Complex carbs are mostly starches, found in grains, seeds and some fruits and vegetables. The Glycemic Index (GI) measures the effect of carbohydrates on blood sugar, and in addition to being widely used by diabetics (see p. 151), is useful for understanding the best sources of carbohydrates for cyclists.

A simple carbohydrate that breaks down easily and is rapidly absorbed into the bloodstream is said to have a high GI. These carbs – such as fruit sugars and the refined starches found in white rice, pasta and processed foods – can cause a spike in blood sugar levels. This is fine in an emergency (see bonking, p. 164), but when the energy has been burned, you will be left lower than before.

Complex carbs from a low-GI source, such as whole grain bread, brown rice, chickpeas, beans, lentils and some fruits, are absorbed more gradually into the bloodstream so take longer to burn and don't cause such peaks and valleys in blood sugars. Clearly, cyclists are better off fueled by low-GI, complex carbohydrates, leaving high-GI, simple carbs for quickly released energy boosts while on the bike. However, modern food processes mean all is not what it seems. Bread in particular poses difficulties.

Most white and whole grain breads, baked industrially, are full of sugars and refined starches, making bread a high GI food. A slice of bread can contain 15 grams of carbohydrate, so most people need only a couple of slices a day. Whole grain breads, containing soy, linseed and the like, are much better for active people. With unground

Above
Whole grains, pasta and rice are good sources of carbohydrate.

grains and seeds, good quality whole grain bread will also contain fiber, zinc, iron and vitamin E.

Protein is less confusing. Its amino acids are employed by the body to repair and build muscle. Protein is found in many animal-based foods, from meat to eggs and dairy products. But it can also be found in beans, lentils and nuts – these are called incomplete proteins, and they need to be consumed in combination with one another to give the same benefits as the complete protein found in animal products. Active people tend to need slightly more protein in their diet than the average person – about one gram of protein per kilogram (2.2 lbs) of body weight per day is standard – and protein has the added bonus of making us feel full.

Left
Peanut butter is an excellent source of protein and vitamin E.

TIP

Protein can also be used to supplement your carb intake during a long ride: it helps to level out blood sugars and is also a source of energy. A peanut butter sandwich is an example of a food that combines protein and carbohydrate.

DIET: WHAT TO EAT

Fat: many cyclists recoil at the thought of it. Yet, this third source of fuel is unfairly demonized; it is a valuable energy source and is burned on long-distance rides. Fats contain fatty acids, essential components of cell membranes and the nervous system. Some vitamins (A, D and E) are also fat soluble. Fat, like carbohydrate, comes in different forms. Monounsaturated fat (found in olive oil, avocado, nuts and seeds, for example) is the healthiest, but polyunsaturated fats, such as the omega-3 oils found in such oily fish as sardines and salmon, are also an important part of a healthy diet. The fat to watch is saturated. Animal fats and dairy products such as butter and cream are composed of saturated fat, and it is these fats that increase cholesterol and the risk of heart disease. Some can be substituted out of the diet, by using olive oil instead of butter, for example.

Above
Look out for hidden fats and sugars in breakfast cereals and bread.

Right and far right
Avocados and fish are rich in essential oils.

WHEN TO EAT

For active people, when to eat is as important as what to eat, and timing should be dictated by the nutritional requirements of their fitness routines. Training on an empty stomach in the hope of losing weight is not thought to offer any benefit; instead, ensure you have a light snack a couple of hours before exercise. Start the day with a wholesome breakfast – whole grain, unsweetened cereal with skim milk, fruit and yogurt, for example. Lunch should be a mixture of lean protein, carbohydrate (like whole grain pasta) and fresh vegetables. Although it's a myth that eating late at night causes weight gain, the evening meal should be moderate.

Snacking on healthy snacks between meals wards off low blood sugar and helps ensure that portion sizes don't become excessive.

Right
Pumpkin seeds are a superb snack food.

Left
Choose chocolate with a high cocoa content.

TREATS

Foods we may think of as being unhealthy – pizza, beer and candy, for example – are not necessarily so bad for cyclists, who can burn off 1,000Kcal in a couple of hours on the bike. In fact, some surprising foods are particularly good for you. Chocolate – the higher the cocoa content, the better – contains cholesterol-busting phenols and anti-cancer antioxidants. Salty snacks, such as peanuts or chips, can replace much-needed minerals after a sweaty ride.

A study has even suggested that a beer after exercise restores some carbohydrates, while drinking caffeine in moderation after exercise has been shown to boost the replenishment of glycogen in the body.

SNACKS

A healthy, low-fat diet does not condemn you to a bland life of fat-free foods. Tasty snacks can also be healthy and are an important way of keeping energy levels up before a short ride or between meals. The human palate craves fats and sugars, but there are natural alternatives that make great snacks:

Raisins: Rich in potassium, which helps convert glycogen into energy. Raisins, like all dried fruits, are a potent source of sugary carbs.

Pumpkin seeds: High in zinc and vitamin E, they're also a good snack food.

Almonds: High in monounsaturated fat, they're healthy and tasty. Nuts are also rich in vitamin E, which helps repair muscle tissue.

Yogurt: Calcium-rich yogurt has a mix of carbohydrate and protein. Avoid sweetened yogurts; instead add honey.

FITNESS & NUTRITION

DIET: AVOIDING THE BONK

Runners call it 'hitting the wall'. In cycling it's known as 'bonking': running out of fuel mid-ride. The French use the rather more expressive 'le fringale' or 'to meet the man with the hammer'. Whatever you call it, it's a serious state but one that can be avoided.

Cycling burns through glycogen stored in our muscles and liver (the rate depends on the amount of work being done), so while riding we need to replenish those energy stores. A standard guide is to consume one gram of carbohydrate per kilogram (2.2lbs.) of bodyweight per hour. Fail to do this and there's a chance you could bonk. It's a highly unpleasant experience, combining a sense of overwhelming fatigue and weakness with irritability and confusion. You may find you get tunnel vision and dizziness. In most cases, by the time your energy stores are this low, simply eating something sweet won't save the day.

There are several possible causes: a diet low in carbohydrates and not eating well the night before a long ride, not snacking during the ride and possibly overtraining. But, to retain some perspective, most people who do have a balanced and nutritious diet, rich in complex carbohydrates, will have enough energy stored to ride for two hours without bonking.

How can bonking be avoided? If you're planning on riding for more than an hour or two, have something to eat a couple of hours before you start. Training on an empty stomach doesn't burn fat and isn't especially useful. If you have a long ride or race planned, fill up with plenty of carbohydrates the night before ('carbo-loading' in cycling parlance). And remember that as you get fitter and stronger, your muscles will burn energy more quickly and will need more fuel to function. Your fat stores will still decrease when you're fully fueled with carbs. On a long, fast-paced ride, it's sensible to have a bite of something every 20 minutes. You won't burn as many calories at an easy pace, but for long, slow rides it's sensible to carry snacks to nibble every half hour.

Above
Top up energy levels during the ride with a gel or snack.

Right
After a ride, refill energy stores within the hour.

Left
You don't have to use
energy supplements;
real food works too.

TIP

A good practice to adopt is to make sure that you refuel
properly after exertion, ideally within half an hour of
finishing; a protein shake can help muscles rebuild and
cut down on food cravings.

ENERGY FOODS

The energy-foods market
has exploded over the
last decade. There are
shelves upon shelves of
foil-wrapped energy bars,
gels and powders in sports
shops, health food stores
and supermarkets. There are
products designed for on-
the-spot energy, post-ride
recovery and even muscle
building. How do you know
what to choose?

First, even as a serious
cyclist, you don't need
to feel obliged to use
specialist energy bars and
gels (not least when you
see their price tags), which
often have a high GI and
will deliver a burst of energy
rather than a steady flow.
Normal foods are fine, and
you can even bake your
own recipes: so long as the
food has a blend of sugars
and complex carbohydrates
(oats are a good example)
and is easily digested, it
should work. The banana is
a popular choice of energy
food because it's fat-free,
rich in natural sugars and

potassium – plus it comes in
its own disposable wrapper.
A couple will provide you
with enough energy for a
90-minute ride. Energy-rich
banana bread is a tasty snack,
just add a handful of nuts for
extra minerals and protein.

Some people find that many
energy products – gels,
powders to mix into water
and bars – are quite hard to
digest, and the flavor is not
always the most appealing;
Clif bars are one of the
exceptions, being made
from natural ingredients.
Even hydrating with water
rather than an oversweet
energy drink is fine; just add
electrolytes (*see* p. 168) if
you think you're going to
be sweating a lot.

The golden rule of energy
foods is to avoid trying a
new one for the first time on
the day of an important race
or event. It's a good idea to
have tried out various foods
to discover what works best
for you; we all have our own
preferences and tolerances.

Above and below
Gels and energy
bars from Clif are
made from natural
ingredients.

FITNESS & NUTRITION

HYDRATION

Whatever the weather, dehydration can ruin your day and your performance. Cyclists should be extra wary of not drinking sufficient fluids as they may be stranded far from home and not in a fit state to continue. That's why to drink, but there's conflicting advice about when and what to drink.

WHAT IS DEHYDRATION?

Humans are about two-thirds fluid by weight. Each of our cells is dependent on water; even blood plasma itself is 90 percent water. We're reliant on water to cushion our joints, digest our food and control our temperature. And the body is exceptionally good at regulating its water level, maintaining this delicate balance by controlling how much waste fluid passes through the kidneys. But people can still make mistakes; drinking too much water can be as deadly as not drinking enough. Mild dehydration occurs when the body's fluid level drops by just a couple of percent. Symptoms include light-headedness, dry mouth, thirst and tiredness. When 5 percent of the body's fluids are lost, moderate dehydration occurs; the symptoms include cramps, loss of strength, heat exhaustion and blackouts. A fluid deficit of 12 to 15 percent can cause the victim to go into shock, be unable to swallow and ultimately die. In a mid-sized male,

Above
Drink regularly
on long bike rides.

with about 40 liters (70 pints) of fluid, this stage can be a shortfall of just 10 to 15 liters (17.5 to 26.5 pints) of fluid. Even mild to moderate dehydration can take a couple of days to recover from, as Lance Armstrong found in the 2003 Tour de France time trial when he lost around 6 liters (10.5 pints) of fluid from his body.

DO

- Note the weather and carry extra water on hot days.
- Drink regularly; about 100ml (3.5floz) every 15–20 minutes.
- Ensure you're hydrated before going out.
- Tailor your intake to your exertion.
- Add electrolytes for long, fast rides.
- Sterilize your bottles or hydration pack occasionally.

DON'T

- Drink too much – you'll feel bloated.
- Drink sugary energy drinks.
- Forget to drink toward the end of a race.

WHAT TO DRINK

If *why* we need to drink seems obvious, *what* we need to drink is less clear cut. The body needs three things: fluid to replace that lost by sweat, electrolytes to replace those lost by sweat and fuel for more exertion. On long rides, there's nothing wrong with simply drinking water and eating a savory snack, such as a sandwich or salted nuts; contrary to the marketing hype, you don't need fancy foods to be a cyclist.

Brightly colored sports drinks can include a slew of unnecessary ingredients and be over-sweetened. When a sports drink is necessary, such as in a long, competitive event when you need hydration and quickly absorbed energy-giving fuel, look for one with the fewest ingredients (water, carbohydrate and electrolytes are all that's required). An isotonic drink (*see* p.168) is best.

Why is dehydration so debilitating, so quickly? Hydration is not just about the quantity of fluids in the body, it's about what is in those fluids: minerals. A finely balanced mixture of minerals is essential to many bodily functions. As fluids are lost, the concentration of minerals will change.

How are fluids lost? Most obviously, we lose fluid through urination. When our body realizes it's running short of fluid, it reduces the amount of urine; what little does pass is darker. This is the first hint of dehydration,

but, for cyclists, it's too late by then. We lose 1.5 liters (2.5 pints) of water per day just by being. During exercise we can lose another 1.5 liters (2.5 pints) of water an hour through sweat, the process by which the body cools itself. Sweat contains sodium (hence its salty taste), magnesium, potassium and calcium – these minerals are known as electrolytes and are essential to nerve and muscle function. As the balance of minerals shifts, so thirst is triggered. But even this signal may be too late for cyclists.

WHAT NOT TO DRINK

The list of what not to drink is straightforward: colas, coffee, tea and alcohol are all diuretics and will do more harm than good.

SWEATING

So why is it that cyclists need to take extra care? As we're whizzing along roads and trails, our sweat is evaporating in the breeze. On a dry day, it may be that we don't even notice how much we're sweating. Yet, cranking out the watts on a road bike or muscling a mountain bike down a hill, we can be sure we're sweating heavily – it's just that the sweat vanishes before it registers.

FITNESS & NUTRITION

HYDRATION

WHEN TO DRINK

On a long bike ride, simply feeling thirsty is not an adequate indication of needing to drink. By that point dehydration will have had an effect. In fact, in certain conditions dehydration can occur after just twenty minutes of exercise. When you know you will be riding or racing for a long period in the heat, be sure to hydrate thoroughly beforehand: sip some water every twenty minutes for a couple of hours before setting off. Start your exercise fully hydrated, and dehydration will be less of a concern.

Above
Mountain bikers use hydration packs to carry up to 3 liters (5.3 pints) of fluids.

When riding, it's a good habit to take a couple of sips every ten to fifteen minutes. The aim is to keep fluid levels topped off before dehydration sets in, rather than try to remedy a problem once it's begun. However, water alone won't replace lost electrolytes, although your thirst will be quenched. Marketing campaigns will have you believe that sweetened sports drinks are the answer. Invented more than fifty years ago to help prevent American football players becoming dehydrated, sports drinks are high in energy and have added salts. Avoid highly sweetened drinks and so-called vitamin waters (you're better off with real fruit juice); instead, look for isotonic drinks, which are less sweet and reflect the level of electrolytes in the bloodstream. Many of these drinks can be hard to digest, so try several to find a brand that agrees with you; you can make your own by mixing water, fruit juice and salt.

Right
Fruit and vegetables contain a lot of water, so they can play a part in keeping you hydrated.

AFTER EXERCISE

It's just as important to rehydrate after exercise; an isotonic drink will replace lost minerals and glucose after a hard ride and speed the recovery process. A protein shake (mixed with skim milk) will also deliver protein to damaged muscles. Interestingly, recent research has shown that one of the most effective recovery drinks is chocolate milk. Apparently, it has the optimum balance of both carbohydrates and protein (in a 4:1 ratio) plus essential minerals including, yes, potassium, magnesium and calcium. Another interesting study carried out by Australian university RMIT suggested that drinking caffeine after exercise helped replenish glycogen (energy) stores more effectively.

Above and left
Energy shakes and mineral-rich recovery drinks contain useful ingredients but aren't essential.

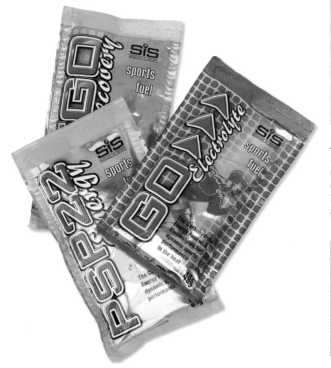

FLUIDS AND MINERALS

Foods can also replace lost fluids and minerals: vegetables such as cucumber, tomato and lettuce are mostly water, while bread replaces sodium, and bananas are a good source of potassium.

CHAPTER 5
RACING

THE TOUR

The Tour de France is more than just a bike race; it's one of the world's great sporting spectacles. You don't have to be a cycling fanatic to appreciate its drama and scale. Understanding what is going on, however, transforms it into a gripping three-week saga. The race has survived wars and doping scandals and is more popular than ever. Its heroes (and villains), from Eddy Merckx to Lance Armstrong, become household names in their quest to ride on to the Champs Elysées in the leader's yellow jersey.

THE HISTORY

Tour mythology has it that in 1910, when the Pyrenees were first added to the route, one French rider, the eventual winner Octave Lapize, had just one word for organizer Henri Desgrange as he gasped over the finish line on the Aubisque: 'Assassin!'

It's a fair point. Not since the days of Roman gladiators has so much suffering been demanded of competitors. With the whole of France as an arena, riders in a typical modern Tour are expected to race over 2,175 miles, in 20 to 22 stages, at an average speed of around 25mph.

They climb Alpine peaks in freezing weather, stream over scorched plains and push themselves – in some cases to death – to gain just seconds over their rivals. Not for nothing did Desgrange call his riders 'Giants of the Road'.

As a sporting spectacle, it is unrivaled: in no other sport can spectators get so close (for free) to their heroes and even follow in their tire tracks (see 'Sportives,' p. 214). For three weeks in July, the vast caravan of 200 vehicles, helicopters and, of course, the 180 riders, is followed by a worldwide audience of 1.5 billion. But it is the nuances of the racing that bring the event to life; understanding the tactics, alliances and hidden dramas of each day's racing reveals a compelling depth to the sport.

The first Tour de France set off in May 1903. It was a publicity scheme dreamed up by editor Henri Desgrange to promote his ailing sports newspaper *L'Auto* (although the idea actually came from young writer Géo Lefèvre). Desgrange didn't get the details right immediately. He insisted that riders raced over 250 to 310 miles in a day, that their bikes should not have derailleur gears and that the riders had to perform repairs themselves, with no outside help. So set on promoting the solo effort of the racers was Desgrange that he forbade riders drafting (slipstreaming) behind each other.

Above
Henri Desgrange, Tour de France founder, discusses the route with a competitor in 1937.

In 1910, Desgrange sent the race into the mountains for the first time, prompting Lapize's vitriolic comment. At that time, mountain roads were rough, unmade tracks, and the bikes were single-speed monstrosities weighing 45lbs or more; wheel rims were made of wood until the 1930s. Riders would have to carry spare tires and tools. No wonder many turned to doping (*see* p. 207).

THE MODERN TOUR

Times have changed a lot since then: riders no longer fuel themselves on red wine or brandy, nor do they have to fix their every mechanical problem themselves, with each team's support car (*see* p. 206) following every stage of the race. But, the principle remains the same: to test every shred of strength, willpower and courage possessed by the world's best racing cyclists along the road to the Champs Elysées in Paris.

And the crowds just keep getting larger: nowadays, up to a million people stand at the roadside of mountain stages such as Mont Ventoux or Alpe d'Huez.

Each year, the Tour takes a different route around the country. Indeed, some years it starts outside France. For example, the race began in London in 2007 and Rotterdam in 2010. Competition to host the start or finish of each stage is fierce, bringing with it prestige and the credit cards of thousands of spectators. But there are some regular features: most years there will be an individual and/or team time trial, and the Tour will usually go into the Alps and the Pyrenees. Individual climbs in these mountain stages are categorized from four (least severe) to one (hard), with Hors Catégorie (HC: unclassifiable) reserved for the very toughest.

During the race, many riders may have led the Tour and won stages, but there can be only one winner of the *maillot jaune*, the prized yellow jersey that is given to the overall winner.

Above
The 1910 Tour de France hits the mountains.

Below
Rebellious rider Octave Lapize during the 1910 Tour de France; note the spare tube wound around his shoulders.

Above
L'Auto newspaper, original sponsor of the Tour de France.

RACING

THE TOUR

Above
The jerseys of the Tour de France, left to right: the King of the Mountains, the Points winner, the General Classification and overall leader, and the leading young rider.

THE JERSEYS

The Tour is several races within a race, and the leaders of each competition wear a colored jersey. The overall leader wears a yellow jersey, the *maillot jaune*. He is the rider who has the fastest cumulative overall time in the General Classification (GC). He need not even have won many stages (Alberto Contador didn't win a single one in 2010), but he will have to avoid losing significant time on any of them, and he will have to put in at least a few quick performances to build a margin and get ahead of the competition. Points are also given out for stage victories, and subsequent placings up to 25th and at intermediate sprints (*primes*) during a stage; the rider with the most points wears the green jersey. He will usually be a sprinter capable of muscling his way across the line first on the flat stages, where 35 points are awarded to the winner. Sprinters tend to be bulkier and struggle in the mountains, so the points competition leader isn't usually an overall contender. The polka-dot jersey is worn by the King of the Mountains, the rider with the most points gained during the mountain stages. Points toward the polka-dot jersey are awarded at the summit of climbs of all categories. A white jersey is worn by the first rider under 26 years of age, in the General Classification.

Below
Alberto Contador of Spain in
the *maillot jaune* in 2010.

Below
Oscar Freire of Spain in the
points leader jersey in 2008.

Above middle
David Millar of Great
Britain wearing the
King of the Mountains
jersey in 2008.

Above
Alberto Contador
receives the best
young rider jersey
in 2007.

RACING

THE TOUR

RIDERS AND RIVALRIES

From time to time, the Tour is dominated by one exceptional individual. At the end of the 1960s that rider was Eddy Merckx. A Belgian with an uncompromising attitude to racing – he was nicknamed 'the Cannibal' for his ability to ride anyone into the ground – Merckx was a superstar and an enigma. Off the bike he was shy; on the bike it was a different story. With a solid 6-foot-high build, he was surprisingly adept in the mountains and an incomparable all-arounder.

No other rider has as varied or extensive a *palmarès* (list of achievements in cycling): five-time winner of the Tour de France; five-time winner of the Giro d'Italia (three in the same year as winning the Tour); multiple winner of the Milan–San Remo, Paris–Roubaix and Liège–Bastogne–Liège one-day races. The only rider to have won all three jerseys (General Classification, Points and King of the Mountains) in the same Tour, Merckx's style was remorseless and powerful.

Lance Armstrong is the only cyclist to have exceeded Merckx's record of Tour wins.

However, Armstrong trained for the whole year with the single objective of winning the Tour de France, while rarely entering, let alone riding to win, other major races. Few riders during Merckx's era got a chance to win anything.

Prior to Merckx, Frenchman Jacques Anquetil had also won five Tours, between 1957 and 1964. His great rival was Raymond Poulidor, and the two could not have been more different: Poulidor, dark-haired and handsome, was a working-class hero; Anquetil's preferred pre-race meal was lobster and champagne, and the public never warmed to him. The rivalry came to a head during stage 22 of the 1964 Tour, on a 6-mile climb up the Puy-de-Dôme in the Auvergne. Anquetil was a superbly stylish time trialist but not such a stellar climber. Half a million spectators watched him ride shoulder-to-shoulder with Poulidor, the better climber, up the slopes of the extinct volcano. At times, the gradient hit 13 percent. Still Anquetil clung to Poulidor, who managed to break away and gain just 42 seconds over Anquetil at

Above
Jacques Anquetil celebrates after winning the 1963 Paris–Nice stage race.

Right
Jacques Anquetil and Raymond Poulidor slug it out in the Tour de France.

the end of the day. It wasn't enough: Anquetil won the Tour in 1964, and Poulidor didn't win the race once. Years later, when dying from cancer, Anquetil told Raymond Poulidor the pain was like racing up the Puy-de-Dôme all day, every day.

After Merckx's reign, a brief interregnum was brought to an end by Frenchman Bernard Hinault, another five-time winner. Nicknamed 'the Badger' for his tenacity, Hinault was the teammate of the first American to win the Tour, Greg LeMond. The next American to win was Lance Armstrong, a rider who thrived on antagonism and rivalries. After being dumped by French team Cofidis while recuperating from cancer, Armstrong, a former world champion, was recruited by the US Postal Service's team. He won his first yellow jersey in 1999 and went on to win seven consecutive victories.

His tactics varied little: supported by a strong team, he would bide his time and deliver a knockout blow at a mountain-top finish, taking minutes out of his challengers. One of the best time trialists of the age and uniquely well organized (thanks to his team manager Johan Bruyneel), he and his team could hold off rivals until the Champs Elysées.

Armstrong's relationship with his rivals (and the press) can be characterized as abrasive. In the early years, he infuriated climber Marco Pantani, who won the Tour de France and the Giro d'Italia in 1998, by 'gifting' him a stage win in 2000. In later years, he had a fractious relationship with up-and-coming teammate Alberto Contador. But no other rider has spread the word about bike racing so far and wide as Armstrong. Even the French grew to, if not exactly love, then tolerate him.

Above top
Marco Pantani (in pink) and Lance Armstrong duel in the Alps during the 2000 Tour de France.

Above bottom
Eddy Merckx, in the middle, after the 1970 Tour de France.

Right
Greg LeMond flying ahead in a time trial.

RACING

THE TOUR

MEMORABLE MOMENTS

LeMond's time trial

By convention, the yellow jersey isn't contested on the final day's stage, which culminates on the Champs Elysées. But, in 1989's Tour, the last day of racing was a short, 15-mile time trial, and there was all to play for. Frenchman Laurent Fignon, nicknamed 'the Professor' for his university education and spectacles, had a lead of 50 seconds over the engaging young American rider Greg LeMond. Fignon was a solid time trialist, and his lead was thought impregnable.

But LeMond clipped on what was then an innovative extension to his handlebars, allowing him to assume an aerodynamic position, donned a sleek helmet and set off. It was a blistering ride, averaging 34 mph. As Fignon followed LeMond through Paris, each time check revealed he was losing second after second. By the time Fignon collapsed across the line he was almost a minute down; the American had won by the narrowest margin yet in the Tour, just eight seconds. LeMond went on to win three Tours in total but will always be remembered for this remarkable ride.

Armstrong's look

Alpe d'Huez has been the backdrop to several pivotal plot twists in the Lance Armstrong story. In 2001, during stage 10, Armstrong and his German rival Jan Ullrich were slugging it out on the run-in to the mountain. Desperate to break Armstrong, Ullrich's team, Telekom, raised the pace. Armstrong, slipping back through the pack, feigned fatigue. Telekom and Ullrich, noticing the wavering American, pressed on relentlessly. The peloton arrived at the foot of Alpe d'Huez, and Armstrong revealed his hand: dancing ahead of the spent German,

Armstrong made sure to look back into Ullrich's eyes, letting him know that he'd been bluffed.

Above left
French champion Laurent Fignon in the 1989 Tour de France, which he went on to lose by just eight seconds.

Above
German rider Jan Ullrich grits his teeth climbing the Alpe d'Huez in 2001.

Left
A popular hero of the 1960s cycling scene, Tom Simpson, in the Tour de France.

Below
Tom Simpson's memorial on Mont Ventoux, where he died during the 1967 Tour.

Simpson's death

Adored by fans and respected by his rivals, Tom Simpson was Britain's leading cyclist in the 1960s, the country's first to wear the yellow jersey and its first road-racing world champion. But, on July 13, 1967, on stage 13 of the Tour, from Marseille to Carpentras, he died a lonely death on the slopes of Mont Ventoux. It was a brutally hot day, and nothing reflects the heat more than the white rocks of that Provençal mountain. About 100 miles into the stage, and shortly after the road entered the barren and exposed upper slopes of Mont Ventoux, Simpson keeled over. The surface temperature on the day was around 120°F, and author William Fotheringham, in *Put Me Back on My Bike*, his book about the racer's death, attributes Simpson's death to heatstroke. But he also acknowledges that amphetamines, found in his jersey pocket and blood, were an important factor.

A memorial to Simpson now stands on Ventoux, and passing cyclists leave a memento. His much-publicized death changed the Tour: stages became shorter, and the race faced up to widespread doping within its ranks. What were thought to be Simpson's poignant last words, as quoted in the title of Fotheringham's book, were actually coined by a London-based journalist.

RACING

THE TOUR

SLANG MINI-GLOSSARY

To attack from the gun
To set off on an early break

Break
A solo rider (or small group) who escapes the main bunch on a breakaway

Broom wagon
The van sweeping up broken cyclists behind the race – those who have given up or failed to finish within the time limit

To be cooked
Finished, fried, unable to continue competing

GC
The General Classification, the main competition, the leader of which records the quickest cumulative time overall

Getting on
Jumping on to a train of passing cyclists for a tow

Hung out to dry
When the pack lets a breakaway rider dangle off the front of the peloton before sweeping past in the run-up to the finish line

Jump
To burst out of the main pack, either to reach a break or attack on a climb

Lead-out man or train
The powerful teammates behind whom specialist sprinters tuck, before charging for the line in the final seconds

On the rivet
To be racing at top speed; old-fashioned saddles had rivets, and the rider would be perched on the front, pounding at the pedals.

Paceline
The line formed by riders to take maximum advantage of the 'drag' effect of the cyclists in front and to protect them from the wind

Pull
To take a turn on the front of a bunch – the hardest position, with no protection from the wind and no one in front to draft

Putting the hammer down
To go 'full gas' in the hope of breaking your opponents

Road rash
The blood-soaked abrasions resulting from a slide on the tarmac

Shelled out the back
To be 'dropped' by the peloton

Sitting on
Riding at the back of a bunch without taking a 'pull'

To be dropped
To be unable to keep up with the pack's pace

Wheel sucker
A rider drafting another without taking a turn on the front

Above top
The racing life: team cars and musettes are part of the daily routine for professional cyclists.

Above
Ryder Hesjedal conquers the cobblestones – known as pavé – of stage 3 in the 2010 Tour de France.

FRENCH GLOSSARY

Arrivée
The finish line

Autobus
The last pack of riders, often containing sprinters and other exhausted riders, on a mountain stage (*gruppetto* in Italian)

Bidon
Water bottle, collected by a domestique (*see below*) from the team car and ferried forward during the race

Caravan
The publicity caravan that precedes the Tour, throwing out freebies from floats that become ever more surreal each year

Chute
A high-speed crash

Col
A mountain pass, the highest point of the road

Départ
The start

Domestique
Hard-working riders dedicated to their team leader, protecting him from headwinds, bringing food and drinks and tiring out rival team leaders

Echelon
A slanted 'paceline' of riders across the road, created for maximum protection when there's a sidewind

Flamme rouge
The red flag marking the last kilometer of the course

Grimpeur
A climber

Lanterne rouge
The last rider in the race, who carries a metaphorical red lantern

Musette
A bag containing lunch

Palmarès
A rider's list of wins

Patron
The boss of the peloton, who is not always the rider with most impressive palmarès

Pavé
Cobblestone roads through parts of northern France and Belgium

Peloton
The main pack of racing cyclists

Prime (pronounced 'preem')
A mid-race sprint that carries points toward the green jersey

Rouleur
A powerful workhorse of a rider who performs best on flat roads

Above top
The red lantern is held (figuratively) by the last rider in the Tour de France peloton.

Above
The Tour de France's publicity caravan dispenses free gifts and surrealism in equal measure.

GRAND TOURS

The Tour de France isn't the only major European stage race. Both Spain and Italy host Grand Tours, and both countries have a distinguished road-racing history. Although neither gets quite the attention of their French counterpart, the support for each remains fanatical.

Left
Riders can face freezing conditions and searing heat over the course of a stage race.

Above
Denis Menchov celebrates a win in the Giro d'Italia.

THE GIRO

Italian cycling fans are known as the '*tifosi*', and since 1909, they have turned out in force for their country's Grand Tour, the Giro d'Italia. Founded, like the Tour de France, as a promotional event for a sports newspaper, the Giro replaces the Tour leader's yellow jersey with a pink jersey (hence the race's nickname 'La Corsa Rosa') and there are also jerseys for sprinters and climbers.

As any visitor to the country knows, Italy has no shortage of spectacular scenery through which to plot a course. Distances for the three-week race typically total 2,110 miles, spread over 21 stages. Organizers make use of city landmarks, such as Rome's Colosseum, and the towering rock spires of the Dolomites in the north of Italy. In homage to Italy's most illustrious cyclist, the highest point of each year's route is called the 'Cima Coppi'.

Fausto Coppi, long-legged, narrow-shouldered and with an impossibly elegant pedaling style, began his professional career in 1940 at the age of 21 with a win at the Giro, only for it to be interrupted by the Second

THE VUELTA

World War. Regardless, he won the Giro five times, becoming an inspiring icon in an impoverished country in the process. But Coppi fell from grace in scandalous fashion after an extra-marital affair with Giulia Occhini, a married woman known as the 'White Lady' in the breathless newspaper reports of the time. He died of malaria at the age of 40.

But the Giro d'Italia goes on, testing its competitors with climbs such as the beautiful but treacherous 10½-mile climb of the Passo di Gavia and the famous Stelvio.

The Giro takes place every May, while the Vuelta a España, which celebrated its 65th edition in 2010, follows the Tour de France in September. Stretched over three weeks and covering a similar distance, the Vuelta can be seen as the poor cousin, but Spain's cycling scene is very vibrant, particularly in the Basque region and around Girona, which was once a base for Lance Armstrong. Since 2000, the race has been dominated by Spanish riders. Interestingly, Spain's most successful Tour rider, the five-time winner Miguel Indurain, never won the

Vuelta. Many Spanish riders specialize in climbing, and they have plenty of mountains in which to practice, including the Alto de l'Angliru, one of the most severe climbs in cycling.

Above
The Passo di Gavia, featured in the Giro d'Italia, tops out at 8,599 feet.

Below
Capital connection: riders stream through Madrid's Plaza de Cibeles in the Vuelta a España.

THE CLASSICS

'The Classics' is the collective name for a historic series of grueling one-day bike races that take place across northern Europe. Where once this undulating landscape of northern France and Belgium was the burial ground of tanks and soldiers during the 20th century's world wars, it is now the proving ground for the most determined and dedicated of racing cyclists.

Above
The Amstel Gold is the biggest and toughest race on the Dutch cycling calendar.

The Classics calendar can be divided into the true Spring Classics, which take place at the start of the season, and a number of other epic races, some of which are staged at the end of the season – honorary Classics if you like. The pure Classics are the Belgian and French races: the Tour of Flanders, Ghent–Wevelgem, Paris–Roubaix, La Flèche Wallonne, Liège–Bastogne–Liège and Omloop Het Nieuwsblad. The Amstel Gold race is based in the Netherlands but it is also considered to be one of the Classics.

Many of the races were founded at the turn of the 20th century. The oldest Classic is Liège–Bastogne–Liège, which became a professional race in 1894. Paris–Roubaix followed in 1896, passing through the mining towns of northern France. The intention was to promote this industrial heartland, and the first prize of 1,000 francs in 1896 was generous. However, many of these mining communities have unfortunately now fallen into disrepair as local employment in the area has plummeted.

It's arm warmers and full-length tights at the start of Milan–San Remo (strictly speaking not a Classic but treated as such), the European season's traditional opening race in March. Late March and early April sees Ghent–Wevelgem and the Tour of Flanders followed by Paris–Roubaix, usually on the first Sunday after Easter.

Paris–Roubaix is known as the Queen of the Classics, distilling the drama and triumph of bike racing down to 155 miles of suffering. The race goes over 18 cobblestone sections of road (known as pavé), each graded in difficulty from one to five stars. The five-star forest of the Arenberg is cited by most competitors as one of the toughest experiences of any bike race. The cobblestones are slippery whether they're dusty or slick with water. The 2010 race was won by a monumental performance from Fabian Cancellara and, like all winners since 1977, he received a commemorative cobblestone.

By the end of April, the pro cyclists are ready for the main season. But the Classics have one farewell to perform at the end of the racing year: the Tour of Lombardy. Known also as the 'Race of the Falling Leaves', the Tour of Lombardy is staged in October in northern Italy, covering about 150 miles around the beautiful Lake Como.

Left
While leaves fall from
the trees, riders race
the Tour of Lombardy.

Above
The Départ: Paris–
Roubaix is the start
of the European bike-
racing season.

RACING

THE CLASSICS

Left
The Cannibal: Eddy Merckx
devoured his rivals over a
13-year professional career.

Below
Eddy Merckx framed by
Joop Zoetemelk (left) and
Gösta Pettersson of Sweden.

THE SPECTATORS

The heavenly triumvirate
of beer, bikes and 'frites'
(french fried potatos)
brings out vast numbers
of spectators at the Spring
Classics. In Belgium,
cycling is the national
sport, and nowhere are the
crowds more numerous
or passionate, fired up on
the best beer in the world.
Whatever the weather,
the bleak cobblestone
roads are lined three or
four deep with supporters,
waving flags and yelling
encouragement to their
heroes. This is free,
boisterous, street-side
entertainment, and it's a
credit to cycling's working-
class roots that it has stayed
largely unchanged and
unregulated over the last
few decades.

Left
Riders find their way through
crowds in Belgium's Liège–
Bastogne–Liège one-day race.

Below
A winning time: riders race
past Big Ben during
the Tour of Britain.

SEPTEMBER & OCTOBER

Grand Prix Cycliste de Québec and Grand Prix Cycliste de Montréal
These one-day races in Canada were added to the UCI's ProTour in 2010, although that's no guarantee they will have a permanent presence.

Tour of Britain
Britain's busy roads are lined with spectators during this eight-day tour of the country in mid-September, providing the best chance for British fans to see the big names and up-and-coming pros.

Vuelta a España
Spain's three-week national Tour in September is the last of the year's Grand Tours.

Melbourne to Warrnambool Classic
This 160-mile race along Australia's south coast is the world's second-oldest one-day bike race. It was founded in 1895.

Paris–Tours
The ride from Paris to Tours is the last of France's one-day races.

Giro di Lombardia
The 'Race of the Falling Leaves' is the last big ride of the season. Typically a lap of Lake Como, in Italy, including the 14 percent gradient of the Ghisallo climb, it's a tough race. The King of Lombardy is Fausto Coppi, who won the event five times.

A winning time: riders race past Big Ben during the Tour of Britain.

Above
The British sprint champion Mark Cavendish at the Tour de Suisse.

RACING CALENDAR: OFF-ROAD

The UCI hosts the annual Mountain Bike World Championships at a single venue once a year and the World Cup series of races at around 10 venues. The disciplines covered are cross-country (XC), downhill (DH) and four-cross (4X). The World Championship is the most prestigious title in mountain biking; a new addition is the mountain bike Marathon World Championship. However, mountain bikers also have a huge range of other events to choose from at which amateurs can mix with pros.

JANUARY & FEBRUARY

Wildside MTB

Competitors race from the mountains of Tasmania to the beach in this four-day race. The total distance is 125 miles and the aim is to make the event accessible to a wide range of abilities.

MARCH & APRIL

Karapoti Classic

Places at New Zealand's number-one mountain bike race – and the longest-running mountain bike race in the Southern Hemisphere – are highly sought after. The main race is 30 miles through the Akatarawa Ranges (close to Wellington in the North Island), but there are shorter options. It takes place on the first weekend in March.

MAY & JUNE

Test of Metal

The 1,000 competitors in this Canadian epic start from Squamish and race for 42 miles over technical terrain. The winner will take just over two hours – normal people though take five or six hours.

Tour Divide

As much a test of willpower as a race, the Tour Divide covers the 2,734 miles of the Continental Divide, between Alberta in Canada and New Mexico. The ethos of self-sufficiency is at the core of the event – riders have to carry all their own gear, and support visits from friends and family mid-race are not permitted. The race is not broken down into stages; the winner will take about three weeks to complete the challenge.

Left
Cross-country racers tackle a tricky corner in the UCI Mountain Bike World Cup.

JULY & AUGUST

TransAlp
This is a 375-mile ride from southern Germany to northern Italy, across Austria and Switzerland, with around 70,000 feet of climbing. It takes the 1,100 racers in the TransAlp eight days to complete. One competitor aptly summed it up by saying: 'It's the best and worst thing I've ever done.'

TransWales
This seven-day stage race from the top to the tail of Wales is one of the UK's premier mountain bike events, taking in 'trail centers' and remote roads.

Leadville 100
Graced by the presence of Lance Armstrong, an avid mountain biker, the Leadville 100 has become America's premier mountain bike marathon. With 100 miles of riding and a maximum altitude of 13,000 feet, it's not to be underestimated.

TransRockies
The route of the TransRockies race, from Fernie in British Columbia to Canmore in Alberta, passes through some of the most spectacular scenery not only in Canada but in the world. The event was founded in 2002.

SEPTEMBER & OCTOBER

24 Hours of Moab
Competitors get to ride Utah's red rock in arguably the world's most famous 24-hour mountain bike race.

Below left
Spanish mountain biker José Antonio Ramos in the 2010 World Cup.

NOVEMBER & DECEMBER

La Ruta de los Conquistadores
Racing off-road from coast to coast in Costa Rica over four days, constitutes one of the most grueling mountain bike events in the world. It has been described by founder Roman Urbina as a 'eulogy to mountain biking in a location that hosts some of the most challenging terrain for this discipline'.

Below
Swiss Nino Schurter and Julien Absalon of France racing in the 2009 Mountain Bike World Championship in Australia.

OFF-BEAT EVENTS

Bike racing is not always just about winning; there's room for a lot of fun too. Plenty of off-beat bike races take place around the world, and this selection gives you a sample of some of the best.

EVANDALE

Evandale is a tiny town in north-east Tasmania, Australia, with a population of 1,057. One week a year, in late February, thousands of spectators and almost 100 foolhardy competitors from around the world converge on this unassuming community for one reason: the National Penny-Farthing Championships. These big-wheeled bicycles are raced in a series of fiercely contested competitions. Riders compete over 100 miles in the Century, or over 20 miles in the Clarendon road race.

The event, like the penny-farthings, has achieved a momentum of its own since its founding in the 1970s and is now recognized worldwide. All of Evandale gets involved, from the churches providing afternoon teas to the Scouts setting out the hay bales at the corners along the course, a concession to safety. There's also a degree of professionalism, with competitors enjoying a pre-race pasta party, much as their counterparts in the Tour de France do – and where the Tour de France has a cavalcade of promotional vehicles, so Evandale's National Penny-Farthing Championship has an antique Bedford truck decked out in red.

Below
Big wheels at the Evandale Penny-Farthing Championship in Tasmania.

BROMPTON WORLD CHAMPIONSHIP

On the grounds of Oxfordshire's Blenheim Palace, in the UK, another important championship takes place: the Brompton World Championship. An 8-mile course around the palace grounds determines the quickest folding-bicycle rider. The event, bathed in October's autumnal light, celebrated its fifth anniversary in 2010; the 2009 BWC was won by Roberto Heras, Spanish ex-pro and Lance Armstrong's wheelman in the mountain stages of the Tour de France. But even he had to adhere to the occasion's strict dress code: a suit, tie and a collared shirt must be worn.

CYCLE MESSENGER WORLD CHAMPIONSHIPS

The Cycle Messenger World Championships pre-date the Brompton World Championships by more than a decade. Since 1993, the world's fastest and most fearless bicycle messengers have fought for the title in cities around the world. First staged in Berlin, the Championships have visited Tokyo, Dublin, London, San Francisco, Sydney, Budapest and New York among other cities. The main race, which takes place in September, involves competing for more than three hours and picking up or dropping off up to 100 packages while reaching multiple checkpoints.

THE RACER

Are great bike racers born or made? What do you need to become a world-class cyclist? And how do you take the first steps towards fulfilling your ambition? The life of a pro cyclist is a hard one, but, for some people, getting paid to ride a bicycle is the dream of a lifetime.

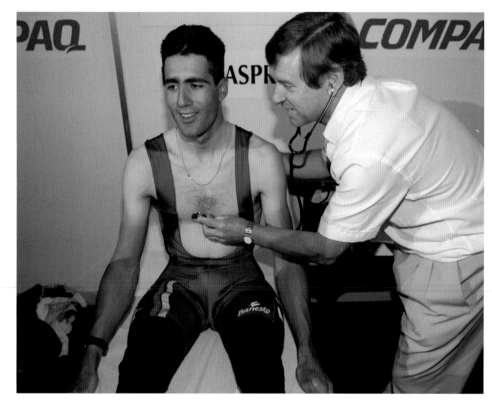

THE BODY

Cyclists come in all shapes and sizes. Even within the same discipline – road racing, for example – there are significant variations according to the specialty of the rider. A climber will tend to have a slight frame – Marco Pantani weighed around 125lbs at his peak – with a high power-to-weight ratio. All-arounders, such as Lance Armstrong, who tipped the scales at around 165lbs, will have a bulkier build, enabling them to produce more power on the flat but also keep up with lighter climbers in the mountains. A sprinter, on the other hand – for example Thor Hushovd, weighing around 180lbs – is more likely to be packed with muscle for the high-speed efforts at the end of a stage.

Size and weight aren't the only factors determining whether you will succeed as a bike racer. Many champion cyclists, from Eddy Merckx to Jan Ullrich, have struggled with their weight yet still managed to haul themselves up and down hills. Numbers other than the readout on a scale

Above
Spanish champion Miguel Indurain has a huge lung capacity.

Right
Physiology of a racer and an average cyclist.

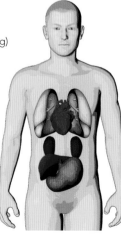

	Racer		Average cyclist
		Lung capacity	
		7 liters / 6 liters	
		Heart rate	
		32 bpm (resting) / 60–70 bpm (resting)	
		200 bpm (max) / 180 bpm (max)	
		VO_2 max	
		85ml/kg/min / 45 ml/kg/min	
		Power output	
		6 watts/kg/hr / 3 watts/kg/hr	
		Body fat	
		5 percent / 15 percent	

are important. Chief among these is the VO$_2$ max (*see* p. 133) and max heart rate, which govern how much oxygen and blood the heart and lungs can move around the human body. Athletes such as Miguel Indurain and Lance Armstrong have exceptionally high readings in these areas thanks to certain genetic gifts (a huge lung capacity in Indurain's case; an over-sized heart that can beat 200 times a minute in Armstrong's). You can't make your heart or lungs larger, but through improving cardiovascular fitness you can make them more efficient. Another important measurement is power (in watts) per kilogram of bodyweight – the greater this ratio, the more able a cyclist is to climb mountains. A professional of Tour de France quality may produce up to seven watts per kilogram of bodyweight; an amateur will develop around half that.

For the greatest riders, however, what lies beyond the bare numbers is the mental strength to push through the pain barrier without a backward glance and a willingness to dedicate years of their life to training and racing. Cyclists go through extremely grueling training regimens, pounding out mile after mile on the road. Professionals have routines tailored to their exact requirements, and the dedication required to stick to such a painful and monotonous lifestyle weeds out many more aspiring cyclists.

National programs, such as British Cycling's Go-Ride scheme, aim to uncover talented youngsters who have the right physical attributes, but from then on the battle to succeed becomes as much psychological as physical.

Above left
Lance Armstrong's physiological statistics are above average, even among professional cyclists.

Above
God-like: the Norwegian sprinter Thor Hushovd's powerful body enables him to win sprints against the best in the world.

THE RACER

THE MIND

While all successful racing cyclists must have the physical foundations on which to build a winning career, only a few have the mental attributes to get to the top. The sacrifices required – socially, physically, emotionally – mean that plenty of potential champions never reach the top step of the podium. Champions such as Lance Armstrong and Nicole Cooke are totally single-minded in their pursuit of success.

Once a rider gets to the top, their successes may depend more on riding a wave of confidence than their purely physical readouts. Confident cyclists focus on the positives from each experience and are unafraid to work on their weaknesses. It's no surprise that teams often go through a run of good or bad results.

This is where experience plays a part: with the maturity of several years in the saddle, even veterans such as sprinter Erik Zabel could continue winning races over younger, quicker riders. But good mental skills – concentration, positivity, confidence – take as much learning as physical skills. The battle for many races is won or lost in the head. Many professional teams now employ a 'mind' coach who uses psychological techniques, such as visualizing a victory sprint, and setting failures and disappointment aside. Veteran winners, such as Erik Zabel, who mentored Mark Cavendish during his record-breaking 2009 and 2010 seasons, are often hired by cyclists to pass on their secrets.

Above
Hungry for victory: British sprint champion Mark Cavendish.

Left
World and Olympic champion: Britain's Nicole Cooke (center).

Below
Nicole Cooke leads the peloton in the 2008 Women's Road Race World Championship.

WOMEN'S RACING

Despite being such a female-friendly activity, as with much professional women's sport, women's bike racing has struggled on the international stage. Women have a World Cup and World Championship to contest at the same time as the men in all disciplines from track and road to mountain bike.

But the women's versions of the Grand Tours and the Classics (the Grand Boucle is the Tour de France for women) have struggled for sponsorship and coverage. However, at a national and local level, women's racing is thriving in the USA, Australia and Britain. For example, from 2008 to 2009, female membership of British Cycling (the governing body for cycle racing in the UK) grew by 25 percent, and women are the fastest-growing category for new racing licenses in the country.

The career path of female pro racers is as varied as that of the men: Nicole Cooke, 10-times British National Champion, won her first national road race title at 16, but other women arrive at the sport much later.

Above
Promoting women's racing: Britain's Emma Pooley (center) with Judith Arndt of Germany (left), and Linda Villumsen of New Zealand (right) at the 2010 UCI World Championship.

RACING

THE TEAM

In road racing, the team is all-important, whatever goal is set. Unlike mountain biking, cyclo-cross and track cycling, where events are generally determined by individual effort, a road-racing team is designed around supporting not only the team leader but also specific objectives, such as winning stage races, one-day races or even just contesting sprint stages.

A road-racing team is a complex organization comprising the racers and the backroom support staff. A well-organized team of average individuals can often beat a lone-star cyclist on a poor team. A good team led by a great cyclist can be almost unbeatable, as Lance Armstrong proved during his years at US Postal. That's not to say that there's no space for mavericks in the peloton; some highly skilled cyclists ride without the support of a strong team but are clever enough to make the most of their opportunities.

However, it speaks volumes that the winners always share their prize money with the rest of the team – this represents a fundamental acknowledgment of the important role the team plays in achieving the win.

Right
Domestiques play an important role in the team by ferrying water bottles forward to teammates.

Above
Leaders such as Mark Cavendish are sheltered from the wind by teammates.

Right
Lance Armstrong, leading Team Radio Shack.

ON THE ROAD

At the start of each season, a road-racing team will identify certain objectives. For some it will be to win a major Tour; for others it will be to dominate single-day races such as the Classics. Each objective requires the team to be composed of a certain set of characteristics.

A team wanting to win a Grand Tour will need to include a group of strong climbers, as these races are more often than not decided in the mountains. However, a team out simply to win stages without contesting the overall race might build a team based around powerful sprinters.

At the top of each will be the leader; typically, the rider most able to meet the team's specific objectives. Supporting the leader are the 'domestiques'. Originally an insult coined by Tour de France founder Henri Desgrange, who banned riders helping each other, domestique refers to an essential member of any major team. They work exceptionally hard for their leader, sacrificing their own places in the standings for the team's overarching goal. They fetch food and water from following team cars, riding up and down the length of the peloton several times on a long race. They also shield their leader from headwinds – by riding directly behind a few teammates, or 'drafting', a cyclist can save 30 percent of their energy. If the leader falls behind, punctures or crashes, the domestique will wait with them and coax them back to the main field. They make attack after attack that rival teams have to chase down, expending valuable energy in the process. And, at sprint finishes, the fastest team members will ride at top speed at the front of the peloton, sheltering their top sprinter until the very last moment. It's a hard life, but it's a rite of passage for many young cyclists.

Above
Strong leaders inspire, or demand, teamwork.

RACING

THE TEAM

TACTICS

Great teams are made up of a mixture of talent. In each race, that team's tactics and how the available talent is employed will depend on the specific goal.

Sprinting

The job of a sprinter's team is to deliver him to the front of the peloton with just a few hundred meters to go before the line. This will often involve some high-speed maneuvering in the last few kilometers before the line, as every team strives to drive the race. In the final kilometers, the sprinter's team will form a train, with the sprinter sitting four, five or six

teammates from the front. As each teammate does their turn at the front, at maximum effort, and then drops off to be replaced at the front by the next in the train, the sprinter stays sheltered by his team. In the closing few hundred meters, the sprinter will rely on his strongest teammate, his lead-out man, to crank up the pace. Bearing in mind that there can be four or five teams competing for a sprint finish, the front of the race can be a very dangerous place. With the line in sight, the sprinter will jump out from behind the lead-out rider, put his head down and power toward

the line. The great Italian sprinter Mario Cipollini was recorded hitting 46mph in the last 200m of a sprint. An opportunist sprinter without team support will latch on to the train of a rival sprinter. The train will try to shake him off, which is why you sometimes see lines of cyclists snaking back and forth across the road in the lead-up to a sprint finish.

Above
Sprinters use every trick in the book to get an inch ahead of their rivals.

Left
How a team sets up the lead-up to the sprint.

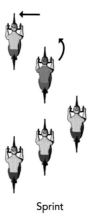

Train

Lead-out

Sprint

Climbing

A line in Tim Krabbé's novella *The Rider* (*see* p. 342) sums up cycling perfectly: 'Winning is licking your opponent's plate clean before starting on your own.' The idea is true for climbing. A climber will ask his team to exhaust any opponents by repeatedly attacking on a climb.

Each time the opponents surge forward to catch the climber's teammate, they grow a little more tired. The climber's teammates don't have to worry about winning the race, so they can pedal at a harder rate than the prospective victors – more often than not, they will finish the ride at the back of the pack, exhausted but satisfied that their job was done. Finally, when the team's climber senses the weakness of his rivals, he'll make an attack, often on a particularly hard stretch of the climb, such as a steep turn. With his opponents softened up, there's a much better chance that he'll escape to victory.

For the non-climbers in the peloton – and the rest of us – climbing real mountains is a matter of survival. Certain tactics can ease the way up. While pure climbers have a slight build and will regularly stand up out of the saddle, larger riders will benefit from sitting and spinning wherever possible. Where the gradient eases off, they'll turn an easy gear to give their legs a momentary rest. Each mountain is different: racers may attack at the start of a climb with a blistering acceleration or wait until a steeper section higher up the hill; but they will all use the terrain and the conditions to their advantage, while keeping a watchful eye on their rivals.

Above
Climbers such as Marco Pantani made it look easy, but for cyclists of all levels there's nowhere to hide on the mountain, even if you're having a bad day.

Left
Climbers stand up out of the saddle or sit depending on their build.

THE TEAM

ONE-DAY RACES

The goal of a team during a one-day race is to conserve their leader's strength for the final section. This means that the leader will rarely take a turn at the front of the peloton, preferring to draft teammates by riding an inch or two from their rear wheel. Riding so closely behind another cyclist is an essential skill for all racing cyclists, as the vital energy conserved can be used in that all-important winning attack, or, on a basic level, simply help them to keep up with everyone else who is doing the same.

GROUPS

Taking turns at the front of a group of cyclists, and leaving the energy-conserving protection of riding behind other riders for a while, is standard in most races (and training rides). The idea is to maintain a steady, high speed by riding at a high tempo for a few minutes. When you can't continue, you move to one side and the rider behind you takes

Above
Riders draft (slipstream behind) teammates to conserve energy.

HAND SIGNALS

Racing cyclists have a repertoire of hand signals to communicate their intentions.

1. **Hazard ahead:** such as a pothole (left or right): point at the ground, to the left or right.

2. **Large obstacle ahead:** requiring a significant change in position on the road, such as a traffic island or parked car (left or right): point away from the obstacle, across your back.

3. **I'm slowing down:** palm facing the ground, move your hand up and down.

4. **Let's form a paceline:** rotate your finger.

5. **I'm done: Take a turn at the front:** twitch your outer elbow.

CROSSWINDS AND COBBLES

the lead; as the group circles in this way, effort is shared. Some riders, nicknamed wheelsuckers, avoid their time at the front. Not only will they get a hard time from other riders but they may find others less inclined to help them later in the race.

Where there's a crosswind rather than a headwind, teammates will often form an echelon, a paceline (a line of riders normally drafting each other), this time angled across the road, to shelter their leader from the wind. Where there are strong crosswinds and corners, it's important to stay near the front of the race, as breaks can easily form where riders can't keep contact with the cyclist in front after a corner.

The same tactic is key for riding on cobblestones for different reasons: crashes are common on cobbles, and no potential winner wants to be stuck behind a pile-up.

Right, top
Extra vigilance is called for on cobblestones.

Right
A crosswind causes riders to form a diagonal line.

THE TEAM

Right
Team managers decide tactics from the team car, which follows the peloton.

Below right
Soigneurs ease riders' aches and pains at the end of the race.

BEHIND THE SCENES

Behind a successful bike-racing team stands an army of support staff. At a tactical level, big decisions about the structure of the team will be made by the directeur sportif. Often a former racer, such as Johan Bruyneel and Bjarne Riis, the directeur sportif is responsible for team management and will typically decide upon goals before the season, following the course of each race from a car and remaining in contact with the racers through small radios with earpieces (introduced by the Motorola team during the 1990s).

Many cycling aficionados complain about the presence of these team radios, claiming they take away spontaneity and decision-making by the cyclists, and organizers have experimented with banning race radios during certain stages.

Teams also have coaches who work with riders on fitness and tactics. After a race, the racers will visit the team soigneur who will massage their legs, kneading the lactic acid out of overworked muscles. In French, *soigner* means to 'tend to' or 'care for', and the team soigneur (often male but occasionally a soigneuse) prepares the musettes (feed bags) for each day's racing and looks after the riders' wellbeing. While the racers are being massaged, the team mechanics will take their bikes for a thorough service.

After the massage, racers will want to eat as soon as possible to refill their glycogen stores. On larger teams, this is the responsibility of the team chef. Chefs such as Willy Balmat, who has cooked for several of the top teams and riders, including Lance Armstrong at US Postal, prepare healthy, energy-rich meals that deliver up to 8,000 calories per day.

Finally, a potentially more controversial role is played by the team doctor. Since the arrest of Festina's team physiotherapist, Willy Voet, in 1998, with a car full of performance-enhancing drugs, cycling's authorities have been aware of doping programs organized by team doctors. But, more conventionally, the team doctor will patch the riders up after crashes and ensure they recover from illnesses and exhaustion.

Above
Racer-turned-manager Johan Bruyneel.

CHEATING

Doping is not a new phenomenon in cycling, or indeed in sports in general. Since the outset, riders have used stimulants simply to survive hard races. Before the advent of advanced pharmaceuticals, this would include brandy and cocaine. In the post-war period, riders would use amphetamines, sometimes to fatal effect, as in the case of Tom Simpson (see p. 179).

It was Fausto Coppi who had the infamous exchange with a journalist about doping in cycling: 'Did you take drugs?' Coppi was asked. 'Only when necessary,' he replied. And how often was that? 'Practically all the time.' More sophisticated doping programs arrived with the drug erythropoietin (EPO) in the 1990s, a blood-boosting drug given to cancer patients to boost the quantity of red blood cells. The more red blood cells, the more oxygen can be carried around the body – a dose of EPO can improve performance significantly,

especially for climbers. Until a reliable test was developed, EPO was the most abused drug in cycling. Its side effect of thickening the blood is thought to have caused the deaths of several cyclists in their sleep.

Cycling's darkest days were in the late 1990s and early 2000s, when many well-known cyclists were found to have been doping. It wasn't just EPO; some used hormones, such as testosterone, while others were even injecting extra blood before a race. But cycling, unlike some other sports, has long admitted it has a problem and is addressing it in a determined manner. A recent initiative is the introduction of 'blood passports', which will show testers if there are marked changes in a cyclist's blood during the year. At times, doping is said to have been so widespread in the peloton that clean riders didn't stand a chance; hopefully, that is changing.

Above top
The race leader has to undergo a drug check after each day's race.

Above
Anti-doping feelings are strong, especially in France, where many feel their national racers have lost out to cheats.

RACING

THE RACE

Road racing comes in several formats, from short, sharp crits to epic three-week stage races. In between those extremes, there is a competitive cycling event to suit everybody. The main types of road racing are widely recognized within any cycling nation.

ROAD RACING

Cycling's core event is the road race. A mass start sees riders set off to race over a distance of around 60 to 120 miles at a professional level, although shorter races are widespread. Roads may be closed to traffic during major events, such as the Tour de France. Races can be completed in a single day (such as the Classics, *see* p. 184) or may be spread over several stages that can take from one to three weeks to complete.

At a professional level, teams will be entered, but at an amateur level, it is common for local clubs and individuals to make up the field.

TIME TRIALING

Road racing had outlaw status in the UK in the first half of the 20th century. Mass starts were forbidden by the National Cyclists' Union for 50 years from the 1890s. In response, cycling clubs organized clandestine time trials – solo rides against the clock on set courses – because, after all, cyclists can't be racing if they're alone on the road. Time trials would take place early in the morning on quiet roads; courses were given coded names, and the riders would wear black.

Today, time trialing is an established form of the sport, and one in which the British specialize. The discipline has been formalized, with distances set of 10 miles, 25 miles, 30 miles and up to 50 and 100 miles. Riders strive to beat their personal best and the times of other time trialists.

Courses tend to be flat, and, with less need for maneuverability, time trialists will adopt an aerodynamic postion: bar extensions stretch the body so the rider's back is low and flat, while the saddle is high and typically tilted forward.

Serious time trialists will also wear aerodynamic helmets, and their bicycles may have a limited number of gears. The benchmark 25-mile time trial is known as the 'race of truth'. Michael Hutchinson, many times a British national time trial champion, can complete the course in less than 50 minutes, averaging over 30mph.

Right
The mass start of a road race, the most lucrative form of cycling competition.

Left
Time trialing cyclists wear streamlined helmets and use aerodynamic bikes. Riders can compete individually against the clock or as a team.

CRITERIUMS

A criterium (crit) is a race over a certain number of laps of a compact circuit, for example, around a town center. Typically, riders will race for one hour plus two laps; because the total distance is less than that of a road race and the tempo is much higher, it's exciting for spectators. A night-time criterium is called a 'nocturne' and is just as thrilling for spectators and competitors.

Crits have been described as chess at 25mph: you have to be fit but clever too. Tactics differ from road racing because the speeds are so high and there are

frequent intervals of maximum effort to keep up (for example, accelerating around a corner). Courses will have minimal climbing, so attacks can come at any point; it's up to the racers to decide which to respond to. With such close-quarter racing, experience counts for a lot, as the wiser riders have learned how to read the pack.

Left
Criteriums are staged on short circuits around the heart of a city or town.

SO YOU WANT TO RACE?

The simplest form of bicycle racing is a group of friends racing to the next traffic sign while out riding. But, to participate in more carefully organized events, you may need to get a racing license and insurance. With that in place, you will be ready to enter races and move up the national rankings.

LICENSES

You don't need a racing license to compete in many cycling events, but if you wish to enter nationally recognized events, such as national race series conducted by the sport's national governing body, you may require one. This license, requiring an annual membership or subscription, will also often include some form of public liability and accident insurance, so check with the organization.

CATEGORIES

Racing licenses are typically broken down into ascending categories. A novice racer will be in category three or four. Once racers have accrued a certain number of points during the season they can move up to the next category for the following season.

Above and right
You don't have to join a local cycling club to enter and compete in races but it helps.

GOVERNING BODIES

In most countries, a national federation is responsible for promoting the sport, accrediting coaches and administering racing licenses. If you wish to find a local cycling club, discover more about cycling as a sport in your country or compete at a certain level, contact the national governing body:

USA:
USA Cycling (www.usacycling.org)

UK:
British Cycling (www.britishcycling.org.uk)

Australia:
Cycling Australia (www.cycling.org.au)

New Zealand:
Cycling New Zealand (www.cyclingnz.com)

Canada:
Canadian Cycling Assocation (www.canadian-cycling.com)

France:
Fédération Française de Cyclisme (www.ffc.fr)

Spain:
Real Federación Española de Ciclismo (www.rfec.com)

Germany:
Bund Deutscher Radfahrer (www.rad-net.de)

Italy:
Federazione Ciclistica Italiana (www.federciclismo.it)

The Netherlands:
Koninklijke Nederlandsche Wielren Unie (www.knwu.nl)

More national federations can be found on the websites of European cycling confederations.

THE BIKE

Although many find that entering a race is a good excuse to buy a new machine, you can race on any bike. There are several low-cost tweaks that you can make to an existing bike to improve performance. Most critical are the wheels – since rotating weight has a disproportionate effect on performance, an upgraded, lighter wheelset should take priority. If that's not an option, simply fitting the best and lightest tires you can afford will improve performance. Keep your old wheels and use them for training; lightweight wheels are not as durable and should be reserved for race day.

**Right
1 & 2.**
A cycle computer will measure power, cadence, speed, time and distance.
3 & 4.
A lightweight saddle and racing wheels are good investments.

SO YOU WANT TO RACE?

FIRST RACE

You've entered a race. You've trained as well as you can, but you're still apprehensive. What next?

The night before
Get your bike ready: Clean and lube the chain, make sure the gears change smoothly, the brake pads aren't worn, the pedals and cleats are clear of grit or mud, the handlebar and saddle bolts are secure and the quick releases are tight.

Eat well: Have a low-fat, carbohydrate-rich meal and an early night.

Prepare your race food and drink: Make sure you choose things that are easy to consume on the bike. Energy drinks, gels and bars are convenient, or you can prepare natural, home-made, bite-sized snacks, such as rice balls, wrapped in foil.

Be warned: You might not sleep well due to nerves and anticipation.

To shave or not: Racing cyclists shave their legs not for aerodynamics but to make it easier to clean wounds and massage in liniment. It's also the mark of having joined the tribe.

Race-day preparation
Get to the race venue early and check out the course. What's the weather? Will there be a headwind or crosswind? Where are the big hills? Consider your goals and tactics. Are you confident about attacking on an uphill stretch?

Have something to eat an hour before the race; ideally, about 50g (2oz) of carbohydrate.

Warm yourself up with some exercises (*see* p. 152) and a short ride.

Above
The night before race day (top) have a carbohydrate-rich meal such as pasta (bottom).

CLOTHING

Stick to your favorite clothing and avoid trying new shorts or gloves. Take a spare set of clothes for changing into after the race. The weather forecast will suggest whether you need to carry a shell, arm or leg warmers, or just a vest.

Checklist

Sign in and collect your race number.

Pump your tires to the maximum recommended pressure, unless you need a bit more grip in slippery conditions when a lower pressure may help.

Plan your food and drink schedule, and make it all as convenient to consume as possible: cut the tops off energy bars to make them easier to open mid-race.

The start line

Get a space at the front if you want to be in contention. The leaders will disappear up the road as their rivals get stuck behind others.

Get ready to put the chain on the big ring: the first few minutes of a race are very rapid as riders jostle for a crucial position.

Once the pace has settled, find a rhythm.

During the race

Eat before you're hungry; drink before you're thirsty.

Don't worry about bad patches; they will pass.

Don't give up. Focus on the next 100m, then the 100m after that to keep yourself going.

Watch your rivals, and strike when they seem to be struggling. Make the attack count; commit to it. Sprint for the finish when others are hesitating.

Watch out for attacks at the bottoms of hills, around steep turns and on corners.

Don't waste energy chasing down every attack; let the novices do that.

At the top of a hill, shift into a bigger gear immediately and don't let off.

Pace yourself.

Most importantly, enjoy yourself. Take in the scenery. Have fun.

RACING

'SPORTIVES'

'Sportives,' known here in the United States as challenge rides, are long-distance, timed events for amateur cyclists, typically held over closed roads. Sportives have rocketed in popularity and these days are as close as many cyclists get to riding a major road race. This is a list of the world's best.

Above
Etape Caledonia in Scotland.

EUROPE

Gran Fondo Felice Gimondi, Italy
Choose from three routes around Bergamo, Lombardy, in April, in honor of this Italian pro cyclist. www.felicegimondi.it

Etape Caledonia, Scotland
The rolling hills of Perthshire are the setting for the Etape Caledonia, a popular British sportive with about 4,000 riders. The event is held in May on closed roads. www.etapecaledonia.co.uk.

Paris–Roubaix Cyclosportive, France
The biennial Paris–Roubaix sportive follows the full route of the cobblestone Spring Classic but takes place in June rather than April. Shorter options are also available. www.vc-roubaix-cyclo.fr

L'Ardèchoise, France
Explore the Ardèche over a variety of distances on closed roads. One of France's largest cycling events, with about 15,000 riders, L'Ardèchoise takes place in June. www.ardechoise.com

Gran Fondo Sportful, Italy
Once known as the GF Campagnolo, the Sportful is held in June and is one of Italy's largest sportives. www.gfsportful.it

The Dragon Ride, Wales
Venture into the hills and valleys of South Wales in June's Dragon Ride, the UK's premier sportive. Distances range from 25 miles to 118 miles. www.verentidragonride.com

La Marmotte, France
Perhaps the toughest challenge on the calendar, La Marmotte takes in the Col du Glandon, the Col de Télégraphe and the Col du Galibier before finishing at the top of Alpe d'Huez. With 16,400 feet of climbing in the Alps, a medical certificate is mandatory. Entries open in December for the July event, and it's best to sign up with a tour operator as space fills up quickly. www.sportcommunication.com/

Gran Fondo Pinarello, Italy
The first edition of this event was staged in 1997. The format has changed slightly, but it still takes place in July. Two routes, 80 miles and 125 miles, are offered. www.lapinarello.com

L'Eroica, Italy
L'Eroica is a ride with a difference: all bikes ridden on this excursion around the *strade bianche* (white gravel roads) of Tuscany must date from before 1987. You won't find a tastier selection of vintage bikes in one place. Scheduled for October. www.eroica-ciclismo.it

Above
L'Eroica in Chianti, Tuscany.

Left
The Iron Horse Bicycle Classic in Colorado can be a muddy affair.

USA

Tour de Palm Springs, California
This is a well-established charity bike ride, taking place in February, with up to 8,500 cyclists riding routes of 5 to 100 miles in length. www.tourdepalmsprings.com

Gran Fondo Colnago San Diego, California
Starting from San Diego's Little Italy neighbourhood, riders complete courses of 50km, 50 miles or 100 miles, in March. http://granfondosandiego.com

Hell's Gate Hundred, California
Ride a century (100 miles) through Death Valley, in March. www.adventurecorps.com

Iron Horse Bicycle Classic, Colorado
A fixture since 1972, the Iron Horse has grown into a weekend-long festival. www.ironhorsebicycleclassic.com

El Tour de Tucson, Arizona
Up to 9,000 cyclists ride over a range of distances in arguably America's largest mass bike ride. www.pbaa.com

Univest Cyclosportif, Pennsylvania
September's Univest Cyclosportif covers the 60 miles of the Univest Grand Prix pro cycling race. www.univestgrandprix.com

Levi's Gran Fondo, California
Founded by US pro Levi Leipheimer, this Gran Fondo, in October, has space for 6,000 riders who set off from Santa Rosa. www.levisgranfondo.com

TIP
Note that sponsors, events and schedules can change.

Right
Death Valley, scene of the Hell's Gate Hundred century.

'SPORTIVES'

AUSTRALIA & NEW ZEALAND

Three Peaks Challenge, Victoria
A testing 145-mile course through the Alpine Region of the state of Victoria in March. The route starts at Falls Creek and the peaks include Mount Hotham.
www.bv.com.au

The Great WA Bike Ride, Western Australia
A 350-mile, eight-day tour of WA's beautiful forests, wine-growing regions and beaches.
www.bv.com.au

Gran Fondo Masterton, New Zealand's North Island
A new event in the Wairarapa region, with distances of 50km, 50 miles and 200km (125 miles), taking place in September.
www.gran-fondo.co.nz

Around the Bay in a Day, Victoria
An annual ride for 16,000 cyclists around Melbourne's bay area, taking place in October.
www.bv.com.au

Great Victorian Bike Ride, Victoria
Held since 1984, today 5,000 participants ride 375 miles, through rural Victoria in five days. The route changes annually, but it usually takes place in November or December.
www.bv.com.au

Right
First held in 1993, Around the Bay in a Day in Melbourne has grown enormously in popularity.

L'ETAPE DU TOUR

Each July, amateur cyclists have a shot at riding a stage of the Tour de France a few days before the professionals compete. The event is called L'Etape du Tour, and it's the cycling equivalent of playing a game of football in a World Cup stadium just before the final. The amateur cyclists, who come from all over the world, enjoy the same conditions as the professionals: closed roads, crowds and split-second timing. Few cycling experiences compare with lining up at dawn among 8,000 other avid cyclists, in a French town somewhere, knowing that around 125 miles of hard riding lies ahead. There are nerves but there's also the huge thrill of speeding through the countryside as part of a massive peloton.

One thing is certain, the organizers will select a mountain stage. In recent years, Etappers have tackled Mont Ventoux, Alpe d'Huez and the steepest Pyrenean climbs. Training for the ride begins as soon as your application is accepted (a doctor's letter is required) in January. Pedaling across the finish line of a stage of the Tour de France is a serious challenge, but it's a sobering thought that the pros will complete the same course a few days later in half the time of an average amateur, and as just one part of three weeks' worth of racing.

Above left and right
The amateur L'Etape du Tour winds through the Alps.

HOW TO ENTER

Application forms are published in *Vélo Magazine* early in the year, but applicants outside France are encouraged to sign up with one of the tour operators approved by the organizers ASO. Details of the route are posted online at www.letapedutour.com in late autumn.

RIDING IN A PACK

- Keep a steady speed.

- Ride within a couple of inches of the person in front but don't overlap wheels.

- Don't weave or change direction without warning.

- Use hand signals to indicate your intention (*see* p. 205).

- If you take a turn at the front, don't speed up, simply maintain the same speed.

- When moving over to let another rider take over, don't sit up – this will slow you down dangerously.

MOUNTAIN BIKE RACING

Mountain bike racing differs from road racing, not only in the surfaces and bikes involved but also in the formats and tactics. For such a young sport, which developed in the 1970s and came of age in the 1990s, an exciting array of events has evolved rapidly. These events fall into three distinct categories: cross-country (XC), endurance and downhill (DH).

PROFESSIONAL RACING

Racing at a professional level revolves around each country's national championship and the UCI's World Cup and World Championship competitions. The first World Championship was held in 1990 in Durango, Colorado; by 2009, there were 14 nations represented by male and female racers. There are far fewer professional mountain bikers than road racers, they're paid less, and sponsors tend to be bike manufacturers rather than the banks and other big businesses that sponsor road teams. However, the racing is no less competitive and no less serious.

Above and right
Cross-country racers cover all sorts of terrain, requiring advanced bike-handling skills.

CROSS-COUNTRY

Cross-country races, usually abbreviated to XC, are fast-paced, two-hour efforts over a wide spectrum of terrain, from rocky, technical trails to easier, faster courses. Elite races range from 25 to 30 miles in length, over five or six laps of a circuit. Racers have to have good aerobic fitness, the power to muscle the bike up short, steep slopes and solid technique. Unlike road racing, cross-country mountain bikers need to put in repeated out-of-the-saddle efforts, so they often exceed their body's oxygen capacity ('go into the red'), but a high level of skill and a smooth riding style can enable racers to conserve their energy.

CLIMBING

All good cross-country courses have a tough climb. To avoid walking it, prepare for it in advance. Get into your lowest gear, crouch over the top tube to keep weight spread between the front and rear wheels, and keep your arms relaxed. Don't lock out the suspension; it will help the wheels roll over small roots and rocks without stalling the bike. On loose ground, stay seated and keep the pedals spinning quickly.

Courses consist of a mix of singletrack – narrow ribbons of trail just wide enough for one bike – and wider tracks. Occasionally, there will be a choice of routes around an obstacle, with the more technically difficult choice being quicker, and the safer route (known as the 'chicken run') taking longer.

Cross-country racing is more about the individual than the team; at most there will be two or three racers in the same team, and there's little they can do to work together. Many top mountain bike racers cross over into road racing, which is more lucrative and offers greater career development opportunities, while the bike-handling skills learned through mountain biking are invaluable on the road. A prime example is 2010 world road racing champion Cadel Evans.

Depending on the course, riders will either use a full-suspension bike for rougher circuits or a hardtail on smoother ones. They will want to keep the weight down as much as possible but will carry minimal tools to keep going after a flat tire or minor mechanical failure.

Above right
Powering up a short climb: cross-country racing demands physical strength and stamina.

Left
A mass start: races have lots of changes of pace, but the start is always all-out.

TACTICS

- Start at the front; there's often a bottleneck as the race enters singletrack.

- Races start fast; try to pace yourself to avoid blowing up.

- Overtake on the wider tracks, sprinting if necessary.

- Know your strengths (and weaknesses) and use them to make up places.

- Take extra care later in the race when fatigue can cause painful mistakes.

- Research the course, fitting the right tires for the terrain.

MOUNTAIN BIKE RACING

24-HOUR RACES

It's the fastest-growing form of mountain bike racing: all-night, all-day events with names such as Sleepless in the Saddle and the 24 Hours of Adrenalin, raced by teams of friends or even, for the truly brave, solo. The 24 Hours of Adrenalin series started in the USA in 1995, and since then the format has boomed in Britain, America and around the world.

Its appeal lies in the camaraderie between the competitors. Being up at two o'clock in the morning riding a mountain bike around the middle of nowhere is a fundamentally absurd thing to do, so it breeds a shared sense of fun, good humor and achievement. These events are social occasions, providing an opportunity for mountain bike lovers to get together, ride their bikes, share experiences and compete against each other. Another factor is that weekend-long 24-hour races and enduros (see pp. 222–223), with on-site camping and entertainment, are regarded as offering better value for money

than an afternoon of cross-country racing. Courses vary enormously. But, as they're designed to be ridden at night as well as in daylight, they tend not to be too technically difficult. Riders will use expensive, high-powered off-road lights, typically powered by lithium-ion cells that give two to three hours of bright light.

A 24-hour race will often include shorter options of 6 or 12 hours. The event is designed to be raced by a team, typically of four or more, but pairs and solo riders are welcome. Men and women can form mixed teams. Each team member will take a turn riding a lap of the course. Since the circuit will be based close to the team area, you won't be too far from help if you have a mechanical problem – many racers carry two-way radios or mobile phones.

After each lap, you tag a teammate and relax until it's your turn again. One idea is to ride a couple of laps at a time, so you have a chance to get warmed up and into a rhythm.

After several hours in the saddle, much of the battle takes place in the mind; the field will be strung out after just a few laps of the course, so it's hard to work out where you are in relation to others, and you'll often be riding alone. However, the exhilaration (or relief) at finishing the full 24 hours is incomparable.

Above
Riders in a 24-hour race may spend more time riding alone.

WHAT TO PACK

- Tent, with an air mattress or roll mat and sleeping bag.
- Table, chairs, blankets.
- Sunshade or canopy.
- Stove and a cooler.
- Enough food and drinks for 24 hours for everyone in your group.

TOP 24-HOUR EVENTS

24 Hours of Moab, USA

Sleepless in the Saddle, UK

Mountain Mayhem, UK

Kona 24 Hour, Australia

24h Finale Ligure, Italy

EXTRA EQUIPMENT

- Powerful lights of up to 1,000 lumens, typically with lithium-ion batteries.

- Recharger for lights or spare charged batteries.

- Spare brake pads, tires and tubes.

Above top
A hard day's night: races go on into the darkness.

Above
24-hour races often have a Le Mans–style running start.

MOUNTAIN BIKE RACING

MARATHONS AND ENDUROS

Britain's first National Marathon Championship took place in 2006, but these endurance (enduro) events now outnumber all other entries in the mountain biking calendar. In many places, there's an enduro every weekend, from spring to late summer and that's not including multi-day monsters like the annual TransRockies race, in August, and the TransAlp (*see* p. 193).

Enduros are races of six hours or more, raced by teams or solo riders, and they can continue overnight for 24 hours. A marathon mountain bike race is usually 30 to 60 miles in distance, from point to point rather than laps of a course. They tend to attract the same sort of people, who love pushing their bodies and their bikes to their limits. The races are sustained efforts and can require special preparation, but as Oli Beckinsale, British Olympic mountain biker, explains, they're accessible to all (see box below).

Below
British National Champion Oli Beckinsale in action.

ENDURO EXPERT

Oli Beckinsale, Olympian and twice British National Champion, is an experienced enduro rider. Before his racing season, he will train for 370 to 435 miles per week on the road, and is capable of finishing a 60-mile marathon in 3 hours and 30 minutes.

But he explains how anyone can compete in an enduro: 'Three months is enough training time to be able to ride for 4½ hours. Add about half an hour per weekend to your rides. After six weeks, you will be able to do a four-hour ride at your own pace. Try to stay flexible and don't lose motivation if you break your schedule.

'A bad back will come out on an enduro, so build core stability in the abdomen and back [*see* p. 136]. Power is channeled by the back and hips.

'Forty-eight hours before the event, fill up with carbohydrates. Graze on things during the preceding days so you don't use your body's glycogen stores. The day before, have a substantial evening meal, a snack before bed and then a big breakfast in the morning.

'On race day, you'll surprise yourself with what your body can do; adrenaline is amazing stuff.'
www.olibeck.com

Right
Racers in the Ten Under the Ben ride for ten hours in the shadow of Ben Nevis, Scotland.

Below right
Crossing a mountain range is all in a week's work for riders in Canada's TransRockies race.

Experience counts for a lot in an enduro; you will have few reference points, so the more you compete, the better you will understand how fatigue cramps your performance (literally) and what food and drink works best for you.

Races are usually advertised in magazines, on the internet and by word of mouth. Places at the most popular events fill up rapidly, so enter online. As a team event, they're a great introduction to competitive mountain biking, with friends along to share the pain as well as the triumphs.

Set your goals before the race: do you want to race against your friends, against other teams, or go for a place on the podium? Your goals will govern your tactics and keep you going when it gets hard. As with 24-hour races, the battle is also psychological: when you're suffering from fatigue, aches, pains and doubts, break the race down into manageable chunks. Use your favorite parts of the course – the singletrack, the downhills – as a reward for riding the toughest parts.

Above
Pack cereal bars for an energy burst.

ENDURO FOOD

The standard requirement is of one gram of carbohydrate per kilogram (2.2 lbs) of body weight per hour of exercise. An 80-kg (176-lb) man will need 80g of carbs every hour.

Don't underestimate how much this is: a banana is less than 20g of carbs, a muesli bar not much more than 20g. Carry foods you enjoy eating. Avoid energy drinks if they disagree with your digestive system; many experienced enduro riders have their own preferred drinks, such as lightly sugared tea or watered-down cola. What works for you is best. After the ride, remember to recharge and refuel fully.

MOUNTAIN BIKE RACING

DOWNHILL

Unlike cross-country and marathon events, downhill races are races by solo riders against the clock. Riders will start at 30-second intervals at the top of the course and, after a qualifying run, the rider with the quickest time in the final is the winner.

Fort William's World Championship Downhill course is 1¾ miles long, has a vertical drop of 1,821 feet and will take a professional downhiller about four-and-a-half minutes to complete (and an average rider twice that). Downhill courses are renowned for frightening first-timers; they will often include very large jumps, drops and highly technical sections. Practice thoroughly before entering a race.

Downhillers use specially adapted bikes with reinforced tubing, up to eight inches of suspension travel, extra-strong wheels, heavy 2.5-inch-wide tires and slack angles (see p. 34).

TOP DOWNHILL COURSES

Fort William, Scotland: Rocky top section with big jumps at the base

Maribor, Slovenia: Fast, open track with a rock garden

Downieville, USA: 14 miles of downhill through Californian forest

Schladming, Austria: Longest downhill course in the country

Mont Saint Anne, Canada: Fearsome jumps and rock gardens

Top left
Downhill all the way: racers race against the clock rather than each other.

Left
Downhill racers wear a full-face helmet, goggles and body armor for protection as they speed down rough trails.

4X

In an attempt to make mountain biking more television-friendly, the UCI has introduced '4X'. Four riders race together over a short downhill course of jumps and berms (banked corners); races take a matter of minutes, and there's a degree of body contact. It's an exciting addition to the sport, although one that few everyday riders will experience, as courses and races remain limited.

BMX

Counterculture no longer: in 2008 BMX – bicycle motocross – became an Olympic sport. Such a thought would have been inconceivable to the inventors of BMX in the early 1970s, when the sport played on its anti-establishment credentials.

Above
BMX racing in full flight.

Right
BMX is now an Olympic sport.

RACING

As a way into cycling, BMX has been incredibly important. Indeed, before the sport was welcomed into the Olympics, former world BMX champion Jamie Staff had already competed in track cycling (see p. 230) for Britain. BMX started when young cyclists took their bicycles – in particular, according to BMX folklore, the Schwinn Stingray – on to motocross courses. Within a few years, small-wheeled bikes designed specifically for dirt jumps and berms had evolved.

In its original form, BMX racing takes place on a short, manmade course of jumps and corners. Up to eight racers, wearing full-face helmets, line up in the start gates before flying around the course in a blur of color. The BMX bikes used for racing often have slightly larger wheels, at 20 inches in diameter, than freestyle BMX bikes.

Courses, typically 350m (380 yards) in length, vary in difficulty, with the hardest having large double jumps

Below right
Ramps and half-pipes
allow BMXers to perform
aerial tricks.

Below
BMXers often use
skateparks to practice.

FREESTYLE

many meters across. All BMXs have a single gear, and the riders don't sit down; this is a sprint event demanding explosive power and excellent bike-handling skills. National governing bodies group racers with others of similar ability and age, from novice to veteran. The winner is the first across the line.

While some BMXers enjoy racing others around a course, many prefer to express themselves performing tricks and stunts on their bikes. This is called freestyle BMX, and it comes in several flavors, including vert, street, park and dirt jumping. Each has their style and code, and in competitions such as the X-Games, the riders' tricks are rated for difficulty and execution. Tricks can be strung together for extra kudos, and flair added with bar spins, tail whips and 180s.

Vert BMX uses a half-pipe that is up to 16 feet high at the edges. With the momentum gained by riding down one side, riders perform mid-air moves and tricks along the lip of the half-pipe.

Skateparks are used by BMXers as a venue for performing fluid tricks and moves. Street riding uses urban furniture, such as walls, railings and staircases, as a springboard for BMX tricks. Out in the woods, BMXers also build dirt

jumps so they can pull tricks, such as superman seat grabs, in mid air. BMXs for each specialty will differ slightly (for example, being fitted with pegs on the wheels for street riding), but ultimately the sport is about the fun and freedom of riding a bicycle anywhere.

CYCLO-CROSS

Foggy mornings, muddy fields and falling leaves: cyclo-cross is a sport that revels in autumn and winter. Devised about a century ago as a way for road cyclists to stay in shape during the off-season, it is enjoying a renaissance, especially in North America. However, the spiritual home of cyclo-cross is Belgium, where its star riders are worshipped.

Above
Thrills and spills: slippery cobblestones and mud often result in cyclo-crossers hitting the ground.

Cyclo-cross is raced off-road on a short circuit (often no more than a couple of kilometers in length), over grass, gravel, small obstacles and steep slopes. Mud is a common feature and something the bikes have evolved to deal with: the road-style bikes will have narrow knobby tires, wider clearances and a more upright position.

Left
Victory is all the sweeter in the cold and rain of a northern European winter.

The original cyclo-crosser is thought to have been a French soldier, Daniel Gousseau, who rode his bicycle around his local woods before organizing the first French National Cyclo-cross Championship in 1902. But Belgium leads the cyclo-cross world, hosting the major annual competitions such as the GVA Trofee and the Super Prestige series.

Top Belgian 'crossers earn thousands of euros. Belgian star Bart Wellens has even had a reality-TV crew following him. Previously, top cyclo-cross racers, such as Roger De Vlaeminck, would cross over to road racing. That happens less commonly today, although British racer Roger Hammond has managed to carve a career in both road and cyclo-cross.

Racers love cyclo-cross because it's an exciting way to get an intensive cardiovascular workout during the winter. The races are short, the pace is breakneck and riders will be flat out the whole time. Tactics are largely redundant since there is no need to draft another rider, although bike-handling skills are very important. Riders may have to bunny hop logs, dodge opponents and control the bike on slippery surfaces.

Events are also popular with spectators, where, fueled up on beer and 'frites,' they can view the action over most of the course from one place. At big races, the atmosphere is as lively as that of a mountaintop finish in the Tour de France. As well as the Belgians, the Dutch, Czechs and Swiss are also big on cyclo-cross. In the UK and especially the USA, the sport is growing strongly. In 2013, the USA will be hosting the Cyclo-cross World Championship for the first time ever (in Louisville, Kentucky).

Above
Racers use cyclo-cross to sharpen their bike-handling skills.

Right
Running up short, steep slopes is often quicker than riding.

TOP CYCLO-CROSS RACES

Super Prestige: Series of races across Belgium and the Netherlands

The Three Peaks: The toughest race in the UK, held in the Yorkshire Dales, founded in 1962

CrossVegas: America's biggest 'cross race is held in Nevada, in September

TRACK CYCLING

To outsiders, track cycling can often seem impenetrable, with obscurely named competitions, strange bicycles and freakishly muscled riders. Yet, of all cycling disciplines, track is perhaps the most accessible and spectator-friendly. And, after a lull in popularity, it is enjoying a renaissance.

VENUES

Track cyclists perform in a velodrome, which can be covered or outdoors. Indoor tracks are constructed from wood, while outdoor velodromes are usually asphalt or concrete. With space for spectators and the competition taking place in a contained area, track cycling has an almost gladiatorial appeal.

HISTORY

The sport has a long history. In the USA, velodromes were extremely popular. In the late 19th and early 20th centuries, track racing was more popular than baseball in North America. Racers like Major Taylor and Iver Lawson were national celebrities and world champions. In the 1920s, velodromes in cities such as Indianapolis and Milwaukee attracted 20,000 spectators to bike races. Riders were heroes and counted Ernest Hemingway among their fans. The Great Depression and the Second World War put a stick in the spokes of the sport, however, and today only a handful of tracks remain as evidence of those heady days.

But thanks to an open-door policy at many velodromes, and lively events such as the twilight series at Kissena Park Velodrome near New York City, the sport is regaining its popularity.

Below
Track cycling can come close to being a contact sport.

Bottom
A motorcycle can be used to pace riders up to speed.

DISCIPLINES

To be initiated into the sport, you will have to understand all its complex permutations. Competitions are either sprints or endurance races.

Sprints

- The kilo – the benchmark speed test over a kilometer, which is ridden from a standing start.

- The match sprint – a head-to-head sprint over three laps, this is a knockout competition with the quarter-finals, semi-finals and finals being the best of three sprints.

- The team sprint – three-rider teams do three laps of the track against the clock, drafting each other in a line to save energy. After each lap, the first rider in the line peels off and plays no further part until lap three, when it's the last rider in the team to cross the finish line whose time is recorded as the team's finishing time.

- The keirin – a more confrontational sprint event, originating in Japan, in which competitors do laps of the track behind a derny (a low-powered motorbike) and build up speed. With two-and-a-half laps to go, the derny pulls off the track and the riders sprint for the finish line.

Endurance races

- The pursuit – the leading event in the endurance category, raced solo or as a team. In the individual pursuit, riders start at opposite sides of the track and ride for 4,000m around the velodrome trying to catch each other.

- The points race – this sees up to 30 riders on the track, racing over 20, 30 or 40km. Points are allocated to the highest placed riders at intervals during the race (for example at 10 or 20 laps) and at the finish. Competing riders can work together, until these short-term alliances break down in the white heat of competition. Winners tend to be those riders who can monitor what their rivals are doing while at the limits of their physical endurance.

- The Madison – a more complicated version of the points race: teams compete in pairs, but only one of each pair is racing at any one time. They exchange turns by slingshotting each other around the track. The event is named after Madison Square Garden, where it originated in the 19th century.

WORLD-CLASS VELODROMES

Darebin International Sports Center, Melbourne, Australia: A 250-m track, opened in 2005

National Cycling Center, Manchester, UK: A state-of-the-art 250-m velodrome

Palma Arena, Mallorca, Spain: A 250-m track, with space for 4,500 spectators

RACING

TRACK CYCLING

DESIGN

Many of the world's best indoor tracks are laid with Siberian Pine. This is because it is a smooth wood, and so, in the event of a high-speed crash, it is less likely to splinter, although impact with it will still hurt. Tracks used in Olympic and UCI-sanctioned competition are 250m in length. The corners are banked at an angle of 42 or 43 degrees at their steepest; the faster you go, the more you adhere to the track. If you slow down, you will automatically swerve down the slope to the center of the velodrome.

First-time track cyclists may want to start on a track with a slope that is less steep: some outdoor tracks, such as the Kissena Park Velodrome in New York, are less intimidating and offer more space for beginners. Ask your local cycling association or club for suggestions.

Top
Fast-paced track cycling is an exciting sport to watch.

Above
Winning can come down to a matter of inches.

TECHNIQUE

Novices are advised to visit a local velodrome for a sample session. The majority are eager to welcome newcomers and will hold sessions for beginners and children throughout the year. Coaching is also often available. The coaches will familiarize the rider with the track bike, which is a machine with unusual features. It will have just one gear and it will be a fixed-wheel bike, meaning that you can't stop pedaling and freewheel. The pedals may have toeclips or use a clipless system – either way, you will be firmly attached to them. Track bikes don't have brakes and they are not suitable for everyday use.

On a track, however, they're perfect: fast, aerodynamic and very light. All this adds up to a considerable top speed. In a velodrome, an Olympic champion at top speed can cover a kilometer in about a minute. Beginners are encouraged to start gradually. The banked corners can be intimidating, so just move up a meter at a time. Keeping an even pressure on the pedals – pedaling in a fluid, circular style – can reduce the risk of the wheels slipping. Look ahead and keep an eye on what other riders are doing. When riding around the track in a group of novices, head up the slope to slow down slightly.

Above
The high-tech, lightweight track bicycles have no brakes and just one gear.

CHAPTER 6
CYCLING DESTINATIONS

THE COLS: THE ALPS

The high passes of the Alps, the cols, are les lieux sacré (sacred places) for cyclists, confirming Europe's status as the spiritual home of road riding. Names such as Col du Galibier and Alpe d'Huez have a resonance for any rider who follows the Tour de France; this is where the fortunes of the greats rise or fall. Many recreational cyclists make a pilgrimage to the Alps to ride the same mountains as their heroes.

THE HISTORY

Sitting on the eastern border of France (with Switzerland and Italy), the Alps became part of the Tour when the Col du Galibier was included in the 1911 race. At 2,645m (8,678 feet), the mountain is one of the monsters of the Tour, with the steeper, harder approach coming from the north. It is one of a cluster of famous cycling peaks in the High Alps (Haute-Alpes) to the east of Grenoble, including the Col du Lautaret to the south of the Galibier, the Col du Télégraphe north of the Galiber and Alpe d'Huez.

The 21 numbered hairpin bends of Alpe d'Huez have been the scene of many of the Tour's most memorable moments, not least Fausto Coppi's win when the peak was first added to the Tour in 1952. Another Italian, Marco Pantani, holds the record for the fastest ascent of the Alpe, at a blistering 37 minutes 35 seconds, set in 1997. He may have

been urged upward by the half-million cycling fans that regularly congregate on the roadside during the Tour, many of whom are Dutch, giving the mountain a distinctly orange flavor.

To the south of these mountains, in Provence-Alpes-Côte d'Azur, lies a second group of Alpine peaks that includes the Col d'Izoard, a steady climb at a gradient which averages 7 percent up to 2,361m (7,746 feet). The Izoard was first used in the Tour in 1922.

Above
Cycling up the Alps is a tough challenge.

Right
The column marking the Col d'Izoard.

THE RIDING

Many riders tackle the Alps as part of an organized ride, for example, by riding the Etape (*see* p. 217) when it is scheduled for the Alps or by entering La Marmotte, which starts from Bourg d'Oisans, the town at the foot of Alpe d'Huez and ascends the Télégraphe and Galibier. Riding the Alps with a group means you get the practical and moral support that can help you up even the most testing roads. This leaves you more time to enjoy the postcard-perfect scenery of snow-capped mountains and flower-filled meadows. But you can also ride these peaks alone: a four-day, 152-mile loop from Grenoble takes in the five biggest Cols in the region: the Lautaret, Galibier, Télégraphe, Croix de Fer and Alpe d'Huez (it's probably best not to emulate Armstrong's 'look' at his rival Jan Ullrich at turn 16, *see* p. 178).

The Col d'Izoard can be ridden by taking the D902 from Briançon to Guillestre.

PRACTICALITIES

When to go: Bad weather can strike at any time in the Alps; plan on visiting from June to September, but be prepared to reschedule.

Further information: National tourist office www.franceguide.com; regional tourist office www.hautes-alpes.net

Above top
The road up to L'Alpe d'Huez has 21 hairpin bends.

Above
The world's top professional riders take on the Alps every July.

THE COLS: THE PYRENEES

The Pyrenees tower over southwest France, as well as the Tour de France. Wreathed in mist and mythology, their peaks have as much appeal as the Alps for many. They extend for 270 miles from the Atlantic to the Mediterranean.

THE HISTORY

In 2010, the famous Col du Tourmalet, the highest pass in the Pyrenees, celebrated the 100th anniversary of its first appearance in the Tour de France. In its early days, the route was no more than a goat-herding track, but it is now one of the race's seminal climbs, the road winding up from the valley for 10½ miles at a gradient averaging 7.5 percent, although the final few meters ramp up steeply.

The Tourmalet is in the heart of the Pyrenees, and there are several other peaks nearby, such as the Col d'Aspin – an appetizer that also lies on the D918 road – that typically form part of a day's riding. Other giants of the Pyrenees lie to the east: the Peyresourde, the Portet d'Aspet and the Col de Portillon. And, to the west stand the Col d'Aubisque and Luz Ardiden.

Look out for the red, green and white flag of the Basque Country. This region, which is wedged between France and Spain, in the western corner of the Pyrenees, is fanatical about bike racing and has produced several fine climbers.

Below
Basque fans are among the most passionate cycling fans in the world and crowd the Pyrenean mountaintops.

THE RIDING

Unlike the Alps, there are few big ski resorts in the Pyrenees, so the range remains relatively undeveloped. This means that the mountain roads tend to be steep, narrow and twisty, sometimes with a loose or broken surface, slicked with fallen leaves. The surroundings – rural villages in which the houses are decorated with drying red peppers, fields full of cows and sheep producing milk for local cheeses such as Ossau-Iraty – feel much more remote and tranquil than those of the Alps. All this makes cycling in the Pyrenees as challenging as it is rewarding, even if their final altitude isn't as lofty.

THE RAID

The Raid Pyrénéen is a challenge for even the toughest cyclist: riders have to complete a full traverse of the range in just ten days, ensuring their *brevet* (authorization card) is stamped at every checkpoint, according to the rules of the Cyclo Club Béarnais, which manages the challenge. The route, more than 435 miles in length, is from Cerbère (on the east coast) to Hendaye on the lovely surf-pounded west coast (you can do it the other way around) and is open from the start of June to the end of September. You'll have to register in advance, although you can ride the route in your own time – you just won't receive a medal.

Above left
The road zigzags up the Col de Peyresourde.

Above top
Coast to coast: the Raid Pyrénéen.

Above bottom
The Géant du Tourmalet statue greets cyclists on the Tourmalet.

PRACTICALITIES

When to go: There can be snow throughout the year, although the Pyrenees tend to be warmer and wetter than the Alps. June and September are often good months for cycling.

Where to stay: The attractive town of Pau is the gateway to the Pyrenees, lying in the foothills.

Further information: Cyclo Club Béarnais www.ccb-cyclo.fr

CYCLING DESTINATIONS

MONT VENTOUX

The Tour's most iconic mountain is a bit of an oddity: it sits neither in the Alps nor the Pyrenees, France's two great mountain ranges. Instead, the extinct volcano squats over the lavender fields of Provence in the south of the country, where it acts as a magnet for cyclists hoping to prove themselves against its pitiless slopes.

Below
Sleeping giant: Mont Ventoux looms over the surrounding countryside of Provence.

Right and below right
Mont Ventoux's rocky terrain is bleak and exposed to the wind and sun.

THE MOUNTAIN

The 'Giant of Provence' has an altitude of 6,273 feet, and the road runs all the way up to the weather station at the top. It's an appropriate site for the station, as the weather has a huge influence on the ride up: British cyclist Tom Simpson, who died on the road (see p. 179), described it as 'another world up there, among the bare rocks and the glaring sun'. Its name also refers to the powerful wind – the Mistral – that swirls around its summit (in French *venteux* means 'windy'). The mountain is one of France's great extinct volcanos (more are in the Auvergne to the north, including the Puy de Dôme), which is why the upper slopes of white limestone, seared by the Provençal sunlight, seem so barren – neither the longest nor the steepest climb in France, it is one of the most feared. Nevertheless, a steady stream of cyclists can be seen pedaling up, many to pay tribute to Simpson's memorial beside the road.

THE RIDE

There are several different ways to approach Mont Ventoux but the most usual is via Bédoin. From here it is just over 13 miles to the summit; the final six being around the edge of the rounded peak, exposed to the sun and wind. Through the trees at the foot of the climb, the gradient is a relentless 8 to 10 percent, with no hairpins for respite. As you break out of the shelter of the trees, the gradient slackens off, before the final kilometer at 10 percent. A professional rider will take less than an hour (Charly Gaul did it in 1 hour 2 minutes from Bédoin in 1958, although Ventoux was first included in the Tour in 1951). A good amateur can expect to do it in 1 hour 30 minutes or more, depending on the weather. The descent to Sault, however, makes the agony worthwhile.

PRACTICALITIES

When to go: Ventoux is swelteringly hot in the middle of summer; May, June, September and October are good months to attempt it.

Where to stay: You can see Ventoux from Avignon, the closest city. There are several villages close to Ventoux that offer accommodation; book via the tourist office.

Further information: Tourist information www.provenceguide.com, www.etape-ventoux.com

CYCLING DESTINATIONS

WHERE THE PROS TRAIN: MALLORCA

In January and February, professional cyclists in Europe and North America fly south. Some travel as far as Australia for the Tour Down Under, but many teams will stop at Mallorca, a sunny Mediterranean island that offers some of the best riding in Europe.

Mallorca, one of the Balearic Islands off the east coast of Spain, has carved a niche for itself as a haven for wintering cyclists. Pro teams doing pre-season training are a common sight; snaking lines of cyclists in team kit, hissing along lanes through groves of olives, oranges and lemons. But, in addition, more than 90,000 recreational cyclists also visit Mallorca each year, typically before the sun-seeking tourists arrive; time a visit for when the almond trees blossom in late January and February and white drifts of petals blow across the rural roads.

THE HISTORY

Mallorca's history reaches back to 5,000 BC, with Romans and Moors paying extended visits. However, its cycling history began in 1913 with an annual five-day race around the island. Today there's a busy calendar of events organized by Federació de Ciclisme de les Illes Balears. The world-class Palma Velodrome opened in 2006 to host the Track Cycling World Championships.

Left
The mountain roads of the Serra de Tramuntana mountains often have beautiful views of the Mediterranean.

Right
Mallorca is used as a training ground by many professional cyclists.

THE RIDING

The island, which measures 45 miles north to south and 60 miles east to west, has terrain for every cyclist: on the west coast, the Serra de Tramuntana mountain range lures riders with pine-lined climbs and descents past monasteries, while the heart of the island is a flat plain (Es Pla) punctuated by vineyards, and on the east coast there are coves, beaches and low-lying hills. In a week you can explore every corner of the island by bicycle, although most cyclists base themselves within reach of the Tramuntana mountains, in towns such as Port de Pollença and Sóller. From here, long loops through the mountains can be plotted, for example, from Pollença up to the monastery at Lluc, along the spine of the Tramuntana to Sóller, and back via Castell d'Alaró along meandering back roads.

Alternatively, ride from Sóller to Deià, Valldemossa and the southern end of the Tramuntana. Even the island's capital, Palma, has a seafront bike path.

Expect your senses to be delighted: herbs grow wild on the mountains, and the villages are built from a photogenic shade of golden stone. But don't be fooled; there are some serious climbs, including Sa Calobra, an impossibly steep ribbon of road that turns in on itself as it rises from the sea, and the climb over the Coll de Sóller will test your fitness. Few places can rival Mallorca for sun, scenery, fantastic roads and a bike-friendly infrastructure.

Above
Climbing the Coll de Sóller is a rite of passage for cyclists.

Right
In spring, Mallorca's roads are filled with avid amateur cyclists.

CYCLING CITIES: COPENHAGEN

First-time visitors to Copenhagen can feel like they've arrived in a parallel universe, in which bicycles rule the roads, and cyclists – unhurried but purposeful – glide like schools of fish through the city. Laid out over a series of islands, the Danish capital is one of the greenest cities in the world.

Left
Copenhagen cycling chic: crossing one of the city's many bridges.

> ## TIP
>
> The entire city can be navigated by bicycle: the central commercial district is called City; to the east lies the island of Christianshavn, to the north Østerbro, to the south Vesterbro and to the west Nørrebro and Frederiksberg. Maps of bicycle routes are available from the tourist office and bike shops.

Copenhagen's cycle culture infuses the whole city. Neighbourhoods, from affluent Østerbro in the north, to the former industrial quarter of Vesterbro in the south, are connected by bike paths threading their way through the city like blood vessels. But it's not just commuters who benefit – although half a million of them take to the 215 miles of bike lanes every day – every aspect of the city is transformed by the Danish love of cycling.

'Nobody rushes around,' says Ken Bødiker, the founder of Velorbis, a bicycle company based in the fashionable Frederiksberg district.

The city's bicycle revolution began during the fuel crisis of the 1970s when oil prices forced cars off the road. Danes dusted off their bicycles and haven't looked back. Today, bicycles are widely available to rent from 125 city bike-parking racks, and, once you've grasped a couple of points of etiquette – slower cyclists keep right, always stop for a red light – it's easy to be a Copenhagener for a day. Here, cycling is transport not sport. Traffic signals and road layouts are all in the cyclist's favor. And forget Lycra (spandex), Danes pedal with panache on upright town bikes: women wear heels and skirts; men sport suits.

INFRASTRUCTURE

On major roads, cyclists ride in a separate, raised lane protected from vehicles by a curb and have their own traffic light signals. Measures introduced by Copenhagen's city council and its pro-bike mayor include relocating stop lines for cars to 16 feet behind the cyclists' stop line at intersections. At busy intersections, cyclists also get a 4- to 12-second head start. Copenhagen's commuting cyclists are ushered in and out of the city with the Green Wave, a sequence of favorable traffic light signals during rush hour. But it's the detail and consistency that most impress out-of-town cyclists. Cobbled pavements run over T-junctions so it is the car driver that feels out of place and is extra alert when turning; railings and barricades against which cyclists could be crushed are absent; bikes can be wheeled up and down steps on stone slopes or metal troughs; and there are racks and dropped curbs outside shops, cafés and stations.

PRACTICALITIES

When to go: The maritime climate is unpredictable but mild. Summers begin in May, with daylight hours stretching way past bedtime during June. September temperatures range from 52°F to 64°F and fall to 35°F on average over January and February. March and April are the driest months.

Bike rental: There are 2,000 city bikes available for a deposit of 20 dkr. Bikes can also be rented from Rent-A-Bike (www .rentabike.dk) at the Central and Østerport stations.

Tourist information: www.visitdenmark.com and the city's own tourist office, www.visitcopenhagen.com

Above
Bike lanes in Copenhagen are wide and separated from vehicles, making them safe and appealing for all types of cyclist.

CYCLING CITIES: PARIS

In France, the bicycle is known as la petite reine (the little queen), and while it doesn't quite rule Paris, it's a great way of getting around the French capital. The city's wide avenues and narrow streets open up to cyclists, and with the advent of the Vélib bike rental service, the infrastructure is catching up.

VELIB

Vélib is a contraction of *vélo liberté* – bicycle freedom – and that's exactly what it enables. Once registered on the system (which requires a credit card), visitors can rent one of the sturdy Vélib bikes by the hour; the first 30 minutes are free, and the rates jump up when you go over five hours. The idea is to encourage short-term use of the bikes, which can be picked up and dropped off at more than 1,500 streetside stations.

There are more than 20,000 Vélib bikes, but almost half have had to be replaced due to theft or vandalism since the scheme started in 2007.

Certain locations are more popular than others, especially in the sightseeing heart of the city, making it occasionally hard to find a free docking station at which to leave the bike, but the bikes are constantly being shuffled around to areas of greatest need.

Left
The back streets of Paris are often quieter than the main roads.

Above
Collect a Vélib bicycle from the many stations around the city.

GETTING AROUND

Vélib isn't the only cycling initiative the mayor of Paris has undertaken. In 2010, proposals to close stretches of the main roads alongside the Left Bank of the Seine in central Paris (from the Musée d'Orsay to the Eiffel Tower) were aired. It's an extension of the 'Paris Respire' scheme that closes the roads along the Seine (and elsewhere in the city, such as Montmartre and the Marais) every Sunday from 9am to 5pm. These roads, past Parisian icons, become playgrounds for cyclists, *flâneurs* (leisurely walkers) and roller-bladers. What better way to get to the Louvre and Le Jardin des Tuileries? And since 2002, the banks of the Seine have become a riverside beach (Paris Plage) in the summer.

It takes a certain daredevil attitude to brave some Parisian roads; the traffic swirling around the Arc de Triomphe, into which 12 tributary roads flow, can terrify most cyclists. But there are more than 125 miles of marked bicycle lanes in Paris, some being separate two-way paths, others running the length of major shopping streets such as Rue de Rivoli. Back streets are often quieter than the main roads, but the usual urban precautions still apply.

Alternatively, make your way to Paris's two great green lungs: the Bois de Boulogne to the west and the Bois de Vincennes to the east.

Above
In this compact city all the famous sights, such as Notre Dame, pictured above, can be reached by bicycle.

PRACTICALITIES

When to go: Paris can be ridden all year round, but spring (April to May) and autumn (September to October) are the most pleasant times of year.

Bike rental: www.velib.paris.fr

Further information: City authority www.paris.fr; tourist information www.parisinfo.com

CYCLING CITIES: LONDON

London can scarcely claim to be a cycling nirvana. It's big, busy and dirty. But Britain's capital is changing fast – and it has to, with more cyclists than ever before on its roads. Not all of them are commuters; even in this concrete jungle, there are some traffic-free routes for recreational rides.

Above top
London's skyline.

Above
The British capital has its own bike-share scheme.

INFRASTRUCTURE

London is not designed for the bicycle (you could argue it's not designed for the car either), which is why Transport for London is spending more than £100 million on improving the city's cycling network from 2010. The work includes creating the capital's bike-share scheme (modeled on Paris's Vélib), marking bike routes, plus training for cyclists. The number of journeys by bicycle in London doubled over the decade from 2000, and many new cyclists means new hazards. From 2010, 6,000 bikes have been made available for rent from 400 docking locations in central London; the first 30 minutes are free (after an access fee payable by the day, week or year), but the price increases steeply the longer you retain the bike. The first two so-called 'superhighways' – painted bike routes leading from Barking to Tower Gateway and Merton to the City – were launched in summer 2010. Ten more are planned to be ready by 2015, radiating out from central London. London's existing bike lanes, often interrupted by parked cars and poor road layouts, are much maligned, but there are several excellent traffic-free routes, and many of London's own signed bicycle routes avoid the busiest roads and take to the backstreets, making them a great way to explore otherwise unseen areas of the city.

PRACTICALITIES

When to go: London, like Paris, can be ridden all year round, but it's most pleasant when the sun is shining, so avoiding the winter months is best.

Bike rental: www.tfl.gov.uk/BarclaysCycleHire

Further information: Tourist information www.visitlondon.com; Transport for London www.tfl.gov.uk; routes www.sustrans.org.uk; free maps available to download from the London Cycling Campaign: www.londoncyclenetwork.org.uk

ROUTES

Despite the traffic, nothing beats a bicycle for creating a connection with your city: you become part of it, experiencing sights, sounds and smells inaccessible to drivers. Sustainable transport crusaders Sustrans (www.sustrans.org.uk) plot routes to rouse the inner explorer: try National Route 4, which follows the Thames from Hampton Court through Richmond Park and along the South Bank to Greenwich. This is London at its finest: regal, urban, historical and leafy. Or head south of the Thames on the Wandle Trail from Wandsworth to Carshalton. Richmond Park, home to herds of deer, also has a circuit for cyclists, and many of London's canals offer flat, traffic-free cycling.

SURVIVE CYCLING IN LONDON WITH THESE SAFETY TIPS

Don't pass trucks or buses in stationary or slow-moving traffic; vehicles may be turning left. This is the most common cause of accidents in the capital.

At intersections, use the advance stop line for cyclists if there is one available. Position yourself to ensure that truck drivers can see you.

Use bike paths and lanes wherever possible. Maps can be downloaded for free from both Sustrans and the London Cycle Campaign.

Always stop at red lights and make eye contact with drivers at intersections.

Use your arm to indicate when turning left or right.

Be wary of doors on parked cars opening unexpectedly.

Don't ride in the gutter; give yourself about a meter's space from the curb.

Be visible: use lights when appropriate and wear brightly colored or reflective clothing.

Below
You can escape the rat race with a bike ride through parks and alongside rivers in London.

CYCLING DESTINATIONS

CYCLING CITIES: PORTLAND

Recently, Portland, Oregon, has established itself as the most cyclist-friendly city in the USA. In part, this is because of enlightened leadership from the city's council, which in turn has attracted bike-loving, green-living newcomers to a city, population 575,000, that was already pretty progressive.

THE CITY

In February 2010, the city council of Portland voted unanimously to implement the 'Portland Bicycle Plan for 2030'. The plan calls for bicycle boulevards, more bike parking facilities, a denser network of bike routes and measures to entice drivers out of their cars and on to bicycles for short journeys. Its official policy is to increase cyclists from 8 percent of the population (the highest in the USA) to 25 percent, a European-style level. It's what you'd expect from a city that is home to the Bicycle Transportation Alliance, a nationwide lobbying group.

This would perhaps be of less interest to the cycling tourist if Portland was a bland urban jungle with cookie cutter streets and big-box chain stores. But it's not. Few cities in the USA can rank more highly for sustainability or eclecticism. Portland's heart beats strongly to an independent rhythm;

downtown is suffused with great restaurants, and the city is famous for its micro-breweries. Farmers' markets, bike lanes (more than 185 miles of them), and cafés with great coffee proliferate. What more could a cyclist want? There are more than 200 parks, including Forest Park – at 5,000 acres, one of the largest urban parks in the USA – which has miles

of trails linking it to the southeast of Portland and the Willamette Valley.

In Portland, the emphasis is always on buying locally, whether that's food or bicycle frames: the city is home to some of the most skilled bike builders in the world, such as Sacha White of Vanilla Bicycles.

Above
Portland's residents and visitors enjoy the benefits of being in a cyclist-friendly city.

PRACTICALITIES

When to go: The driest months are from June to September.

Bike rental: About a dozen places, from bike shops to tour operators, offer bikes to rent.

Further information: Bike-route maps can be downloaded from the City of Portland Bureau of Transportation www .portlandonline/transportation; maps of the Historic Columbia River Highway cycle routes can be downloaded from www.columbiariverhighway.com; tourist information www.traveloregon.com

THE RIDES

Portland makes a great base for exploring the region by bicycle. There are around 4,000 cycling events during the year, such as the rather flat and featureless Seattle to Portland (STP) ride in July, but the best idea is to get on your bike and head out into the countryside. The 125-mile Willamette Valley Scenic Bikeway starts just south of the city and ventures into Oregon's world-class wine-making country along a marked route.

The Historic Columbia River Highway can form an 50-mile loop up to the Multnomah Falls. But, be prepared: it's no accident that the Pacific Northwest is as green as the sprinter's jersey in the Tour de France, because the region is persistently wet, with rain falling throughout the year.

Above
Waterfalls cascade down green mountains just a short ride out of town.

Right
Use Portland's many bike lanes to explore the city and its parks.

CYCLING CITIES: NEW YORK

For cyclists, New York's report card might read 'most improved city'. The metropolis – as teeming, vibrant and ambitious as ever – has joined the likes of Seattle, Chicago and Portland as a place that has embraced cycling. Indeed, it is home to some of the most forward-looking initiatives in the land. Cyclists can approach Manhattan with confidence, although it remains wise to watch out for cabs.

A large amount of the credit for this remarkable transformation can be given to the Department of Transportation, which between 2007 and 2010 built 200 miles of bike lanes across the city's five boroughs, taking the total to more than 620 miles of bike paths, lanes and routes. The first protected on-street bike lanes were laid along 8th and 9th Avenues and Broadway.

Life in the Big Apple is now much easier for those on two wheels: parking places have been replaced by bike lanes, and bikes are permitted on subway trains at all times (although the advice is to avoid rush hour). The CityRacks scheme introduced 5,000 bike racks to the city. Times Square and Herald Square on Broadway have been closed to motor vehicles. The result of these changes? In the three years to 2009, bicycle commuting increased by 45 percent. And the League of American Bicyclists now ranks NY as a 'bike-friendly community'.

Mayor Michael Bloomberg's PlaNYC 2030 sustainability plan calls for over 500 miles of segregated bike lanes, and at least 50 miles of bike lanes will be installed annually until the network is complete. New York also has natural advantages for cyclists: flat terrain, rivers and parks, and the grid layout makes navigation a cinch.

Above right
Stopping for refreshment at Williamsburg.

Right
Biking on Brooklyn bridge, the gateway to Manhattan.

Below
Cyclists taking part in Bike New York.

WHERE TO RIDE

The Hudson River Greenway (www.hudsongreenway.state.ny.us) is the most-used bike path in the USA, covering the 12 miles from near the Bronx (the Little Red Lighthouse) to Battery Park at Manhattan's southern tip. All the lower bridges of Manhattan (Williamsburg, Manhattan and Brooklyn) have designated bike lanes. Brooklyn, in particular, has a green-striped forest of bike lanes making it easy to divert to neighborhoods such as hip Williamsburg, which is sprinkled with cafés and vintage shops. Along with the East River and Harlem River Greenways, it forms a pleasant 30-mile circumnavigation of Manhattan Island.

In deepest Manhattan, cycle south from Times Square, through Madison Square Park, past the Flatiron Building and Union Square, before reaching Washington Square Park in Greenwich Village.

For cycling sightseers, the Metropolitan Museum of Art has free bike parking in the underground parking lot (entry on the south side of the building) and the Museum of Modern Art has bike racks on 53rd and 54th Streets. Central Park can be explored by bike so long as you don't ride on pedestrian paths; take the 6-mile loop road and jump off to see the Great Lawn and the Mall.

CYCLING CITIES: MELBOURNE

Melbourne is a city that looks better from a bicycle. Victoria's state capital has improved bicycle access, closed roads to cars and created a strong local cycling scene. A bicycle is now the best way to explore the city's hip neighborhoods, riverside trails and oceanfront.

While Australia may not have the most hospitable roads for those on two wheels, Melbourne is attempting to change that with a concerted pro-cycling campaign. In 2009, a total of A$115m was committed to improving Melbourne's cycling network; bike lanes are being built and the city rolled out a bike-share scheme in July 2010, with 600 robust blue bikes to be available from 50 stations. Unlike bike-share schemes in other cities, Melbourne's system is hampered somewhat by Victoria's state-wide compulsory helmet laws – a bring-your-own policy is in operation.

Danish urban design guru Jan Gehl spent a whole decade advising Melbourne (from 1994 to 2004) how best to emulate the success of Copenhagen's cycling infrastructure. 'Compared to other investments in society, not least expenses for health and traffic infrastructure, the cost of moving people about in a city is modest,' Mr. Gehl says.

Gehl recommended promoting the city's café culture, improving the waterfront area, opening up the historic 'laneways' to pedestrians and adding more urban plazas. After a decade of work, there were 275 percent more cafés and 71 percent more people-oriented spaces. Once a classic doughnut-shaped modern city, when the CBD empties at night as workers return to the suburbs, Melbourne is now regularly rated as one of the most liveable cities in the world.

Below
Melbourne's bike-share scheme and bike-friendly culture have been based on the successes achieved in Copenhagen.

THE RIDING

The 18-mile Capital City Trail heads south via Merri Creek and Yarra Bend Park from Flinders Street. It passes through Fitzroy North and Royal Park.

The Bay Trail swoops toward Melbourne from Seaford, 30 miles south of Melbourne, all the way through Sandringham, St Kilda and Albert Park. The riverside Yarra Trail starts from Southbank and follows

Above
The Yarra River flows through central Melbourne, flanked by the Yarra Trail.

Melbourne's iconic river to Eltham via the Royal Botanic Gardens, Yarra Bend Park and Heidelberg School Artists' Trail.

West of the city, follow the Hobson's Bay Coastal Trail, which hugs the coast from West Gate Bridge and joins the Skeleton Creek Trail, taking in Jawbone Conservation Reserve and Altona Coastal Park.

Pack a picnic (and a compulsory helmet), rent a bike from Rent-A-Bike in Federation Square and explore Australia's most liveable city.

OUT OF TOWN

There's great cycling through two of Australia's leading wine-growing regions: the Mornington Peninsula and the Yarra Valley. The Great Ocean Road west of Geelong has hosted the Cycling World Championship, and there's some of the country's best mountain biking in Forrest, a couple of hours beyond Geelong.

PRACTICALITIES

When to go: Winter, June to August, can be cold and wet; September to December and February to April are best for avoiding the high-season heat.

Bike rental: www.melbournebikeshare.com.au

Further information: Tourist information www.visitmelbourne.com and www.visitvictoria.com; take a bike tour with Real Melbourne www.rentabike.net.au/biketours.

MOUNTAIN BIKE MECCA: CALIFORNIA

When a group of Californians fitted old cruiser bikes with fat tires and took them up to the top of their local hills before riding the dirt trails down, did they foresee that they would be sparking the fastest-growing cycle sport in the 20th century?

HISTORY

Of course, people have been riding off-road ever since the invention of the bicycle. It was unavoidable in early Tours de France, when mountain routes were no more than goat tracks. But it is to 1970s California, Marin County in particular, that mountain biking can be traced. Pioneers such as Charlie Kelly, Joe Breeze and Gary Fisher determined not only the shape and style of the first 'mountain bikes' (a phrase coined by Kelly and Fisher) but also the freewheeling spirit of the riders. No spandex, please, denim jeans and a checked shirt were just fine.

The first bikes, christened 'clunkers', had steel frames, drum brakes and motorcycle-style brake levers. Their 26-inch wheels wore fat, knobby tires to grip the dusty trails of California. The advantages of these proto-mountain bikes were obvious: they could take you farther and faster into wilderness inaccessible to road bikes and cars.

It wasn't very long before mountain biking started to become competitive. The earliest races took place in the mid-1970s on Mount Tamalpais in Marin County,

north of San Francisco, and were nicknamed 'repack', because the brake drums needed to be repacked with grease after each downhill run was completed.

In the years to follow, mountain biking was adopted by cyclists across the USA. California's landscapes, from the shady redwood forests of the north to the mountains of the Sierra Nevada, were perfect for off-road cyclists.

Downieville in California's Gold Country, north of Nevada City, has dusty downhill trails lasting

more than 12 miles. South Yuba, also north of Nevada City, is home to some heavenly singletrack.

Below left
Mountain bike pioneers (left to right) Joe Breeze, Vince Carlton, Fred Wolf, Gary Fisher, Charlie Kelly and Eric Fletcher at the top of Mount Barnabe, west Marin County, in 1977.

Below
Rob Stewart, Charlie Kelly and Roy Rivers pushing their 'clunkers' up Pine Mountain in Marin during an early cross-country race in 1977.

Below
Nowadays, mountain bikers can ride on purpose-built trails.

STATE PARKS

Some state parks in California welcome mountain bikers and have some fantastic trails:

Annadel State Park in Sonoma County

Henry Coe State Park, near Morgan Hill

Wilder Ranch State Park, near Santa Cruz

Further information: California State Parks www.parks.ca.gov

PRACTICALITIES

When to go: April to October is generally the best time of year, but in the south of the state there can be good weather all year round. Beware of the intense heat in mid-summer, though. Higher regions have winter snowfall, and fog is common on the coast. Dust can be a problem toward the end of summer.

Safety: Wildlife large and small can potentially be dangerous, but you're more likely to encounter ticks or poison oak than a mountain lion or a snake.

Further information: International Mountain Biking Association: www.imba.com

MOUNTAIN BIKE MECCA: COLORADO

Colorado has been blessed with out-of-this-world mountain biking trails through the Rocky Mountains and bike-friendly towns such as Boulder, Durango and Crested Butte. This is wilderness biking at its best.

The Rocky Mountains sound like the perfect setting for mountain biking – and they are, with one caveat: the altitude is such that lowland-dwelling cyclists may struggle for breath. Colorado is the eighth largest state, but much of the best biking is located several hours west of Denver and Colorado Springs around Gunnison National Forest (Crested Butte, Leadville, Snowmass) and Rio Grande National Forest (Durango, Telluride). Other hotspots are Vail, Breckenridge and Steamboat Springs, closer to Boulder.

The landscape, which is snow-covered in winter when these places are top ski resorts, is one of forest, alpine meadows and box canyons. Riding here entails taking precautions that are perhaps overlooked at more populated spots: telling someone where you are going, when you expect to return, being diligent with navigation, carrying spares, and extra food, water and clothing. The trails roll on for epic distances, and you

can be miles from help. Crested Butte is one of the hubs of mountain biking, and it has embraced fat tires with affection: it's the home of the Mountain Biking Hall of Fame, and access to the trails – which are numbered – is managed responsibly. Maps, rental bikes and valuable advice are available from shops. The 403 and 401 loops are very popular.

Fruita, a town on the border with Utah, shares that state's rock formations, around

which dusty ribbons of singletrack wind: head for the Book Cliffs area and Mary's Loop for a taste of what's available.

FAT TIRE BIKE WEEK

Fat Tire Bike Week in Crested Butte, Colorado, lays claim to being the world's oldest mountain bike festival. The week-long celebration of all things fat-tired is still going strong, with an eclectic line-up of action sports photography, workshops, open-air yoga and music concerts. But the core of the festival is the racing – the Mountain States Cup and a 37-mile cross-country race on alpine singletrack – and group rides open to all.

Further information: www.ftbw.com

Below
Catch your breath: Looking out over Colorado's spectacular landscape.

PRACTICALITIES

When to go: The higher the altitude, the shorter the peak season – June to September is prime riding time in the mountains. In the lowlands, you can extend to April and October. Watch out for changeable weather, strong sunshine, and rifle-toting hunters (later in the year).

Further information: tourist information www.colorado.com; trail information www.visitcrestedbutte.com

UTAH

Colorado and California aren't the only US states where mountain bikes are part of the fabric: Utah, Colorado's western neighbor, has some of the country's most revered trails. Some of the best roll over the red, super-grippy rock around Moab: the Slickrock Trail and the Porcupine Rim Trail are once-in-a-lifetime experiences thanks to the desert scenery and rollercoaster riding.
Further information: www.utah.com

RESORTS

Colorado's resorts may have been slow to embrace lift-accessed mountain biking, but more are opening their gondolas in the summer. Colorado's best resorts for biking include Telluride, Winter Park, Keystone, Snowmass and, of course, Crested Butte Mountain Resort, where a mountain bike school takes residence in the summer. The resorts can still have snow cover as late as June.

Above left and left
Be prepared: Colorado's singletrack threads its way through remote wilderness where getting lost or injured can have serious consequences. Always tell somebody where you are going and when you expect to return.

CYCLING DESTINATIONS

MOUNTAIN BIKE MECCA: BRITISH COLUMBIA

The North Shore of Vancouver is a magnet for mountain bikers, who test themselves and their bikes on the world's toughest trails. Pick up the skills required at nearby purpose-built mountain bike parks.

Above
The mountains around Vancouver and Whistler are the cradle of freeriding, mountain biking's most extreme expression.

The bike racks on buses and the numerous bike lanes are just two of the clues that suggest Vancouver, the gateway to the province of British Columbia, is a bike-mad city. But they don't convey how central the place is to mountain biking; the sport was born in California, but it came of age in British Columbia. Many of the world's most technically challenging trails lurk in the dark forests of Vancouver's North Shore mountains, spawning a new style of mountain biking – known as freeriding – and some of the sport's most photographed stars.

For this reason, Vancouver is a place of pilgrimage for mountain bikers. From the airport, you can see the 4,000-foot high mountains of Vancouver's North Shore lying just 30 minutes north of Downtown. Over the years, local riders, organized by the North Shore

Mountain Bike Association, have built trails that twist across the steep, wooded slopes of Mount Seymour, Fromme and Cypress. Using log ladders to cross impassable areas, they created a network of more than 125 man-made trails where rocks and roots are

TIP

Trail maps are available in many of Vancouver's bike shops, including Cove Bike Shop on the North Shore, and are essential for finding many of the trails, which often lie unmarked off logging roads. A local guide (ask at Cove Bike Shop) is even better.

Cove Bike Shop: 1389 Main Street, North Vancouver, 604 929 2222, www.covebike.com

the least of the obstacles facing riders. As local pro Richie Schley says: 'Without question, this is the most difficult riding in the world.'

Luckily, Vancouver is within easy reach of three of the best places for learning the skills required to tackle the North Shore. Mountain bike parks are a recent invention. Originally a way for out-of-season ski resorts to stay open during the summer months, they have boomed as bikers have discovered the delights of lift-accessed off-road trails. The largest bike park that is in British Columbia is at Whistler, the Olympic ski resort located just two hours from Vancouver via the Sea to Sky Highway. Here, experienced mountain bikers can take the gondola or chair lifts to the top of Whistler mountain and ride all the way down to the resort on world-famous trails such as the A-line. For bikers who prefer to work for their thrills, there are several tough cross-country routes, including A River Runs Through It – complete with a 40-foot log across a river.

Tuition is available from Whistler's own guides, and the bike park provides full-suspension rental bikes and protective gear. At the end of a weekend at Whistler, most mountain bikers will find that their confidence levels have increased, and they've begun to acclimatize to the standard of British Columbia's mountain biking.

Above right
Easygoing rides can be found in British Columbia.

DIAMOND RATINGS

Trails in British Columbia, from the North Shore to the bike parks, are rated for difficulty with colored diamonds that help visitors ride within their limit.

Green: Limited experience of off-road riding, can control bike speed and direction

Blue: Two years' experience, can control speed and direction on moderately steep trails

Black: Confident rider, comfortable on steep terrain and taking on moderate obstacles

Double-black: Experienced freerider, confident riding large jumps and elevated trail sections

BIKE PARKS IN BRITISH COLUMBIA

Whistler Mountain Bike Park: www.whistlerbike.com
World-class facilities and man-made trails on Whistler Mountain, ranging from easy-going to extreme. There's plentiful accommodation for all budgets.

Sun Peaks Resort: www.sunpeaksresort.com
There are 27 trails served by lifts at Sun Peaks near Kamloops, four and a half hours northeast of Vancouver. Rated as a top-five bike park in North America, it offers rentals, guides and tuition.

Silver Star: www.skisilverstar.com
At the north end of the Okanagan Valley, near Kelowna, Silver Star has 490m (1,600 feet) of descent and 16 man-made trails, from beginner to advanced.

PRACTICALITIES

When to go: April to September

What to bring: Waterproof outer layer, full-face helmet if available, chunky tires

Rentals: Bikes are available in Vancouver (www.endlessbiking.com) and Whistler (www.whistlerbike.com) and other bike parks.

Contacts: North Shore Mountain Bike Association www.nsmba.ca

Further information: www.tourismvancouver.com; www.hellobc.com

MOUNTAIN BIKE MECCA: NEW ZEALAND

Above
New Zealand's pristine landscapes are slowly being opened up to mountain bikers.

'The Land of the Long White Cloud' – Aotearoa to Polynesians – inspires superlatives. As an adventure sports destination, New Zealand has few rivals, and none that are quite so clean, green and easy-going.

Unsurprisingly, the famously practical nation was quick to adopt the mountain bike. The Kennett brothers (Simon, Jonathan and Paul) have pioneered off-road biking in New Zealand, managing one of the oldest mountain bike races in the world (the Karapoti Classic, *see* p. 192) and now working as trail advocates. After the financial crash of 2008, the government also recognized the value of biking to the country and committed NZ$50m to creating a network of bicycle routes linking existing trails the length of the nation. New Zealand is not a litigious society, and riders are expected to bear personal responsibility for the risks they take.

TRAILS

From March to the end of November (i.e. from autumn to spring), one of the most beautiful walking routes in New Zealand is open to bikers: the Queen Charlotte Track along the shore of Marlborough Sound in the South Island. The full 45-mile journey can be done in a day or two, but why not savor it? In the North Island, the 42 Traverse in Tongariro Forest, which is 28½ miles long, takes a day to complete. Trails also radiate out from Waimate in South Canterbury. In the mountain ranges around Wanaka and Queenstown, tour operators take riders heli-biking, for example dropping bikes and riders at the Coronet Peak ski area in the Remarkables. Although much of the land in New Zealand is privately owned – in the form of sheep ranches and farms – you can always ask land owners for permission to ride on their property.

NATIONAL PARKS

New Zealand's Department of Conservation (DOC) has always been fiercely protective of the country's national parks, which boast many of the world's most unspoiled walking trails. Mountain bikes are restricted to roads in all the national parks. In 2007, the DOC began a three-year trial, located in Arthur's Pass National Park, to permit greater access to mountain bikers, who were allowed to ride up Poulter Valley. Check with individual parks about the access available to cyclists; however tempting, cyclists caught riding where they shouldn't can be fined.

MOUNTAIN BIKE PARKS

Although bikes are restricted in national parks, a growing number of mountain bike parks have sprung up to meet the demand for technical, challenging trails. Makara Peak, just minutes from downtown Wellington (you can see the South Island from the top on a clear day) welcomes 100,000 riders a year. Farther north, near the bubbling mud and hot springs of Rotorua, the Whakarewarewa Forest has 43½ miles of trails through pines, eucalyptus and silver ferns, the national emblem.

Above and below
Bicycle tourists can explore New Zealand on quiet roads and dirt trails.

MOUNTAIN BIKE MECCA: SCOTLAND

Scotland has all the ingredients of a world-class mountain biking destination: enlightened access laws, rugged mountains and a friendly welcome. From the mountain bike centers of the Borders to the wilderness of the Highlands, nowhere else in Britain offers such enticing riding.

Above
Many Scottish forests have purpose-built mountain biking trails.

Right
Take note of the signs: they indicate the severity of the trail.

Scotland's transformation into mountain biking heaven began in 2000 with the construction of the Glentress trails, less than an hour south of Edinburgh. But the raw materials were already in place: an ancient network of paths over low-lying hills and mountains, plus a temperate climate for much of the year. It's the perfect combination: new bikers can practice at the groomed trails of Glentress and other mountain bike parks before venturing on to northern Scotland's wilder routes.

CODE OF CONDUCT

- Leave gates as you find them.

- Carry all your trash home.

- Give way to horse riders and walkers.

- Avoid riding on wet or muddy ground; follow tracks where possible.

PRACTICALITIES

Watch out: Midges (small biting insects) plague some locations in the summer.

Bike rental: Bikes are available to rent at many of the 7Stanes centers, including Glentress (www.thehubintheforest.co.uk) and Kirroughtree (www.thebreakpad.com).

Further information: www.7stanes.gov.uk; www.visitscotland.com

MAN-MADE

The 7Stanes ('stanes' being Scottish for stones) is a necklace of seven mountain biking parks or 'centers' on Forestry Commission land, strung east to west across the Borders. From Kirroughtree overlooking the Irish Sea to Glentress and Innerleithen, a 40-minute drive south of Edinburgh, via Glentrool, Mabie, Dalbeattie, Ae and Newcastleton, the 7Stanes have earned a worldwide reputation for high-quality, man-made, all-weather trails. Each trail is graded for difficulty, like a ski run, from green to blue to red to black, according to the fitness and expertise required to complete it.

As Emma Guy of Glentress mountain biking center says: 'We cater for all types here, from families with children to serious racers, and the centers are great places to learn new skills in a safe environment.'

There are now centers across Scotland, with some, such as Laggan Wolftrax, on the doorstep of the Cairngorms. The country has also hosted the downhill and cross-country World Championship at Fort William, the only lift-accessed mountain bike trail in Britain.

NATURAL

The Land Reform (Scotland) Act opened all Scottish countryside to responsible users, to the envy of their neighbors south of the border. It meant that Britain's wildest landscapes, from the high mountains of the Cairngorms to the lochs of the Western Highlands and the bucolic Speyside, could be freely explored by bicycle on historic routes through the glens, deer trails and 4WD tracks. Scotland's natural riding is very different from its trail centers: there are few signs, so navigation skills with a map or GPS are essential, and riders will have to take the rough with the smooth on the trails.

Long-distance routes include the West Highland Way and the Sligachan Loop on the Isle of Skye, but detailed route planning is required for most off-road trips outside the trail centers.

Below left and below right
Access all areas: Scotland's mountains and lochs are open to mountain bikers, as long as riders behave responsibly.

CYCLING DESTINATIONS

MOUNTAIN BIKE MECCA: WALES

Wales squeezes a lot of riding into a small space. With man-made trails at mountain bike parks and natural routes through green valleys and mountains, there's something for every mountain biker.

Readily accessible from many of Britain's biggest cities, Wales has become a popular weekend choice for British mountain bikers. Riders can let off steam on the rollercoaster berms and jumps of the trail centers' tracks or take on long-distance rambles over the Welsh hills. You're never far from the coast – Pembrokeshire's Preseli Hills, rich in Neolithic settlements and bike trails, overlook white-sand beaches – or windswept granite mountains.

Left
Welsh singletrack tests riders' skills with roots and rocks.

TRAIL CENTERS

There are five mountain bike trail centers in Wales. From north to south they are:

Coed Llandegla
A small park with a variety of trails suitable for beginners.
Facilities: Bike rental, shop, car parking

Coed y Brenin
The original trail center in Wales, Coed y Brenin has six demanding trails and a beginner-level trail, Yr Afon.
Facilities: Bike rental, shop, showers, café

Nant yr Arian
There are three trails at this remote base in central Wales.
Facilities: Parking, café

Afan Forest Park
More than 60 miles of man-made cross-country trails spread across two parks – Penhydd and the Wall are the easier options.
Facilities: Camping, accommodation, secure bike storage, bike rental, café, shop

Cwm Carn
There are two trails: the Twrch cross-country route begins with a long climb, and there's a downhill-only track.
Facilities: Café, parking, bike rental (nearby)

Above
Cyclists riding over the southern Welsh mountains.

In addition to the many trail centers (see opposite), Wales has also welcomed bikers to its hills, valleys and unpronounceable towns since the pioneering days of the Man vs Bike vs Horse race at Llanwrtyd Wells in the 1980s.

Several areas have evolved as bases for exploring the Welsh countryside by mountain bike: Betws y Coed and the Clwyds in the north, Machynlleth and the Elan Valley in the middle, and the Brecon Beacons and Brechfa toward the south. Many natural routes are marked from these starting points, but an Ordnance Survey map will reveal many more. As you venture north, the terrain changes from the rounded hills of the Brecon Beacons National Park to the rocky mountains of Snowdonia. But one constant is the changeable weather; rain is a regular feature.

Below
Sharpen your skills on man-made boardwalks at Welsh trail centers.

TOP TRAILS

Highly rated trails at Welsh trail centers include:

White's Level at Afan Forest Park: A 9-mile trail, starting from the Glyncorrwg Mountain Bike Centre, with fast, technical descents

Skyline at Afan Forest Park: The longest man-made trail in Wales at 29 miles, incorporating the descents of White's Level linked by long stretches of forest road

Beast of Brenin at Coed y Brenin: A long-distance route of 24 miles with technical, rocky sections

RIGHTS OF WAY

While riders in Scotland enjoy unprecedented access to the countryside, England and Wales have a much more arcane system of rights of way. Mountain bikers are permitted to ride on horse tracks and roads but not footpaths.

PRACTICALITIES

When to go: Winters in Wales are cold and wet; summer (May to September) can be warm and sunny.

Further information: Trail information www.mbwales.com; tourist information www.visitwales.co.uk

MOUNTAIN BIKE MECCA: THE ALPS

The hills are alive with the sound of brakes squealing: Europe's largest mountain range opens its lifts to mountain bikes during the summer and becomes an adrenalin-charged playground.

Big mountain scenery, Alpine chalets and local food draw mountain bikers from all over the world during three frenetic summer months. Within the Alps, there's every flavor of riding from World Cup downhill trails requiring a full-face helmet to gripping cross-country trails. Many resorts open bike parks – areas with man-made stunts, such as jumps, drops and wall-rides – during the summer, while others, such as the quaint Swiss village of Champéry, offer a less intense experience. Wherever you are, the advantage of resort riding is that rental bikes, guides, maps and essential services are all within easy reach.

THE RESORTS

Les Arcs

Les Arcs is home to a wide variety of trails from cross-country to downhill; some of the singletrack downhills unravel down the mountain side for 6 miles or more. There's a greater choice of natural trails than at the Portes du Soleil resort. Lifts close at the end of August.

For further information, visit www.bikepark-lesarcs.com.

Below
Alpine singletrack draws riders from all over the world.

Chamonix

The terrain at Chamonix, like that of Verbier, tends to be steeper and more technical than the flowing downhill trails of Les Gets. The singletrack riding, such as the downhill route to Trient (take the train back to Chamonix) or on the slopes of Brévent, is astonishingly good, with vertical descents of up to 5,000 feet. At Chamonix, hikers generally take priority, with restrictions on bikers during July and August; other resorts, such as Morzine and Les Gets, focus more on bikers. Long-distance rides from Chamonix to Zermatt or Verbier are possible.

For further information, visit www.chamonix.com.

Les Gets and Morzine

Part of the vast Portes du Soleil area, with three of the area's 25 lifts, Les Gets is a very mountain bike-oriented resort during the summer, with cross-country and downhill trails. The jump park and freeride zone called The Bike Park is 30 miles from Geneva; lifts open from mid-June to mid-September. Morzine was one of the first French ski resorts to open its lifts to mountain bikers in the summer, and consequently many mountain bikers have a soft spot for it.

For further information, visit www.lesgets.com or www.paradisvtt.fr.

PRACTICALITIES

When to go: June to August is the busiest period; lifts close to bikers in September. Snow is possible at the highest levels all year round.

Where to stay: Groups of bikers tend to rent chalets in the resorts.

THE PASS'PORTES DU SOLEIL MTB FESTIVAL

Want to race in the Alps but put off by the thought of climbing? The Pass'portes du Soleil is the event for you. Each June, 4,000 mountain bikers race for 75km (47 miles) through some of the Continent's most thrilling scenery – but they take lifts uphill with the help of seven participating ski resorts in France and Switzerland (including Les Gets, Morzine-Avoriaz and other resorts in the Portes du Soleil region). There's just 3,200 feet of climbing and 4½ miles of downhill; the descent to Morgins and Champéry is a highlight. The weekend is part of a bike festival, with local food and drink provided by surrounding villages. The ideal bike to use is a full-suspension bike with 125–150mm (5 or 6 inches) of travel, but it's possible to ride the route on a hardtail, if slightly more uncomfortable. Many riders wear elbow and knee pads. For further information, visit www.passportesdusoleil.com.

Above
Resorts' ski lifts are used by bikers to access downhill trails in the summer months.

Left
The scenic Pass'portes du Soleil.

CYCLING DESTINATIONS

EASY RIDES: EUROPE

Cycling in Europe doesn't have to mean pounding up and down Alpine mountains. The Continent, spiritual home of the bicycle, has easy-going rides from top to bottom, if you know where to look.

Above top
The Camel trail, near Padstow, England follows the route of an old railway line.

Above
The coastline of Northern Ireland provides some dramatic scenery for cyclists to savor.

BRITAIN

You don't need giant thighs to ride to the Giant's Causeway in Northern Ireland, but the 23-mile Causeway Coast Cycle Route has a couple of long climbs that might test your muscle power. The route, part of Sustrans' National Cycle Network 93, starts in Castlerock and hugs the coast until you reach the geometric geology of the Causeway. The Bushmills Irish Whiskey Distillery in County Antrim provides a welcome diversion.

The Camel Trail, perennial favorite of vacationers, follows an old railway line through the North Cornish countryside from Padstow to Wadebridge. Beyond Wadebridge, the trail divides, leading riders to either Poley's Bridge or Bodmin; the total distance is 18 miles. Bicycles can be rented at Wadebridge and Padstow.

East Sussex's Cuckoo Trail is a deservedly popular slice of family cycling, following

an old railway line for the 11 miles from Polegate to Heathfield. It's quiet, mostly flat and free from traffic, making it perfect for youngsters ready to practice riding longer distances. There are plenty of spots for stops, plus sculptures along the route.

In the north of the country, the Solway Firth to Wallsend section of the Hadrian's Cycleway (National Route 72 in its 175-mile totality) takes in history and scenery as you cross the neck of England. Much of the route is on lightly trafficked roads making it suitable for extended family rides.

SPAIN

The Camino de Santiago de Compostela in France and Spain is filed under 'easy' because the route can be divided into 31 stages of 12 to 18 miles from Saint-Jean-Pied-de-Port to Santiago de Compostela, each with a hot meal and an affordable bed at the end. Taking a donkey may be authentic, but a bicycle is a much more practical companion on this pilgrimage, the Way of St. James.

There are multiple routes, but finishing your trip in northwest Spain allows you to explore the green Picos de Europa mountains before you leave. The Picos are perfect for cycle touring, being little traveled – although waterproof shells are required due to the sometimes wet and wild Atlantic weather.

Above right
Two cyclists enjoy a flat stretch of road in northern Spain.

Right
Take a well deserved rest in Santiago de Compostela.

EASY RIDES: EUROPE

Above top
Cycling past Berlin's cathedral.

Above
The Rhine, Germany.

GERMANY

Arguably the most popular long-distance bicycle route in the world, the Danube Cycleway ushers riders from southwest Germany to Budapest. The entire 845-mile route can be broken into smaller stints easily. Like the river, the trail meanders through wild gorges and pockets of civilization.

Germany's cities have also embraced the bicycle, with bike-share schemes and bikeways: the Mauerweg trail, completed in 2006, snakes around Berlin for 100 miles, following the route of the Berliner Mauer, the Berlin Wall.

Elsewhere in Germany, well maintained and extensive bike lanes are common, with more than 43,500 miles of marked bikeways and more than 50 long-distance routes so far. Allgemeiner Deutscher Fahrrad-Club (ADFC) rates Germany's planned cycling routes for useability (accommodation, traffic and access are all considered). In addition to the Danube, the river Rhine is also the focus for many of Germany's best routes, such as the RheinRadWeg. Rivers or mountains, cities or castles, for cycle tourists of all abilities, Germany is one of the world's best cycling destinations.

INFO

www.berlin.de
www.germany-tourism.co.uk
www.adfc.de

SCANDINAVIA

The compact country of Denmark is well known for its bike-friendly cities, but even in the countryside bicycles are an established and respected form of transport and have the luxury of 6,000 miles of paths to themselves. Cross the Øresund bridge to southern Sweden, and it's the same story: a flat landscape and bike-friendly attitudes. Routes wind around the lakes and waterways of the southern half of the country (which freeze over in winter to the joy of long-distance ice skaters). There are plenty of easy-going themed routes suitable for families, such as the Astrid Lindgren (author of *Pippi Longstocking*) ride with accommodation stops. Bikes are also welcome on boats, enabling cyclists to explore the 30,000 islands of Sweden's archipelago.

As you go farther north, the distances between towns and villages increase, and the landscapes become higher and wilder; the top two thirds of Sweden offer the prospect of genuinely adventurous cycle touring where preparation matters.

Norway shares the more remote landscapes of the mountainous plateau, with many of the best rides involving a train ride into the interior of the country and a largely downhill ride back to the coast. Popular routes in Norway include cycling between the two top adventure sports towns Voss and Bergen (73 miles, on quiet roads, best attempted between May and September), and island-hopping on the long-distance Vestfjord route.

INFO

www.visitdenmark.com
www.visitsweden.com
www.visitnorway.com

NETHERLANDS

Famously flat (the highest point is just a fraction over 1,000 feet above sea level) the Netherlands has long suited relaxed cyclists. From laidback Amsterdam, the 12-mile route to Haarlem is a short ride that takes you out to sand dunes; other routes pass through sleepy villages and along rivers and canals. Traffic-free cycle lanes and considerate drivers elsewhere add to the appeal of the Netherlands. Indeed, the town of Giethoorn – the Venice of the North – was car-free for years.

INFO

www.holland.com

Above top
Relaxing in Bergen, Norway.

Above
Bike-loving Amsterdam, Holland.

EASY RIDES: EUROPE

FRANCE

With the pounding surf in your eardrums and a pine-laden scent in your nostrils, riding the bike paths behind the Atlantic coast's beaches is one of life's great pleasures. France is full of such simple joys, and the variety of its countryside attracts all kinds of cycle tourists, from those intent on conquering mountain passes to others more interested in wine and cheese. The second group is spoiled: cycle touring is a fantastic way of seeing grape-growing regions such as Burgundy, Bordeaux and the Vaucluse in Provence, and local specialities make the end-of-day refueling all the more enjoyable.

In Burgundy, Dijon is a good base for an 80-mile tour of the Côte d'Or; head toward Nuits-Saint-Georges and pick up the Routes des Grands Crus.

Those who possess a bicycle and prefer cabernet sauvignon to pinot noir should visit Bordeaux: the region is laced with bike-friendly roads (although few bike lanes), including the flat roads running along the banks of the Garonne. Pauillac makes a convenient base, although the scale

of the region lends itself to moving day by day rather than looped rides. Continue along the Garonne to reach the Dordogne, a deservedly popular holiday location, thanks to charming villages, châteaux and pretty but undemanding scenery.

Head south to Provence and Languedoc-Roussillon for sunshine and vivid fields of lavender. In central Provence, you can ride past Roman antiquities in Orange, fields of lavender, grapes and melons, and up the grueling climb of Mont Ventoux (see p. 240). The Alps have a toehold in Provence, so expect some serious inclines in places:

the Luberon rewards cyclists with picturesque villages and gorges. Avoid the Côte d'Azur itself in peak season; the roads are suffocatingly busy with tourist traffic.

Go west to the limestone hills of the Languedoc or farther, to the Cévennes, setting for Tim Krabbé's seminal book *The Rider*, to truly escape the crowds. The riding is tougher here, with lots of up and downs.

One of the most unsung yet rewarding parts of France for cyclists is also one of its least crowded: the Jura. Stretching between Burgundy and the Alps, this region's gorges and

plateaus make for some demanding days in the saddle but compensate with quiet roads, local cheese and wine, and the sense that you're off the beaten track. The riverside town of Besançon is a good base, accessible from Paris on a new TGV train.

Above
Lavender fields and vineyards: cycling in France is a sensory journey.

INFO

www.franceguide.com

ITALY

While Italian driving may have a reputation for a certain flamboyance, drivers are generally courteous toward cyclists. Once you've braved the sometimes frenetic traffic, getting out into the countryside on a bicycle opens up regions rich in art, architecture and food, such as Tuscany, Umbria and Piedmont. Piedmont, in northeast Italy, is where some of the country's best food and wine is produced: Barolo's back roads are perfect for cycle touring. Moving south, the region of Emilia Romagna, long overshadowed by its glamorous neighbors, has set itself up as a cycle-touring destination, with bike hotels in Riccione, close to the birthplace of Italian cyclist Marco Pantani, dedicated to serving cyclists.

In Umbria and Tuscany, the rolling hills and vineyards are best explored outside the heat of mid-summer; the cooling breezes and quieter roads of spring and autumn are perfect for comfortable cycling.

Above
Emilia Romagna, Italy, was the birthplace and training ground of Italian champion Marco Pantani.

INFO

www.italiantourism.com
www.bikeemiliaromagna.com

TIPS FOR TRAVELING CYCLISTS

Several thin layers of clothing are better than one thick layer.

Keep maps in a plastic folder to protect them from rain.

Cover the saddle in a plastic bag when leaving the bike in rain.

Check that your hotel has secure bike storage or keep your bike in your room.

Leave room for spontaneity in your schedule.

EASY RIDES: NEW ZEALAND & AUSTRALIA

With a fast-developing network of cycleways, Australia and New Zealand are fast becoming must-visit cycling destinations. Investment has brought access and amenities to what were already breathtaking landscapes.

In both Australia and New Zealand, retired railways have been turned into bike trails. Rail Trails have the advantage of being largely flat and traffic-free, making them well suited to family bike rides. Many are just a few miles long at the moment, but several figurehead projects stand out: 12,000 people a year ride the 90-mile Central Otago Rail Trail in New Zealand, through breathtaking scenery and past pinot noir wineries.

NEW ZEALAND

New Zealand is set to become one of the world's great cycling destinations with a NZ$50 million project to build a network of linked bike routes, totaling 1,860 miles, from the top down to the bottom of the country. Famous for its 'Great Walks' in the National Parks, New Zealand is now hoping to match their worldwide appeal with a series of 'Great Rides'. Although mountain biking is severely restricted in the National Parks, cycling is permitted on roads. But you don't have to enter the parks for a memorable bike ride: this is a surreally beautiful country of bubbling mud, steaming springs and wind-sculpted trees. The east side of the North Island boasts the easiest riding, with the mountain scenery of the rainswept west coast of the South Island being better suited to hardy tourers.

AUSTRALIA & TASMANIA

Australia is not to be outdone: Brisbane, Queensland, has a 90-mile Rail Trail running from Ipswich to Blackbutt, while Victoria has a Rail Trail deep in the Yarra Valley's wine country (from Lilydale to Warburton), and the Murray to the Mountains trail runs for almost 60 miles into Australia's highest mountains and past historic towns such as Beechworth and Bright.

But you don't have to stick to the tourist hotspots in a country as vast as Australia. Out west, follow the signed 560-mile Munda Biddi Trail through Western Australia's eucalyptus forests for a life-changing taste of the outback without the need for search-and-rescue. Funding has been secured to complete the route in the next couple of years; the first half from Mundaring is already complete.

In Tasmania, the riding tends to be more extreme. The Tasmanian Trail, for example, runs from the north of the island to the south, and is 300 miles long, on dirt roads. However, there is also the rather less daunting 9-mile waterfront bike path in the state capital Hobart.

Left
Explore Australia's wine country on two wheels.

Right
Mountain bikers tackle the shore of New Zealand's South Island.

Below
Watch out for the indigenous wildlife in Australia.

Food and wine have been joined with pedal power for regional projects such as Pedal to Produce in Rutherglen, and the 20-mile Clare Valley Riesling Trail in South Australia, which passes vineyards and cellar doors via Auburn, Watervale and Clare. Hotels and restaurants increasingly cater to cyclists in these areas, and local tourist offices usually have maps.

CONTACTS

New Zealand tourism: www.newzealand.com

New Zealand cycle touring guides: www.paradise-press.co.nz

Central Otago Rail Trail: www.otagocentralrailtrail.co.nz

Victoria: www.visitvictoria.com

South Australia: www.southaustralia.com

Western Australia: www.westernaustralia.com

Munda Biddi Trail: www.mundabiddi.org.au

Pedal to Produce: www.pedaltoproduce.com.au

EASY RIDES: USA

Singling out the best rides in the Americas is an impossible task. But some generalizations can be useful: the monotonous, flat, headwind-plagued Corn Belt states, such as Iowa and Nebraska, won't excite most cyclists. The densely developed coastal states are well suited to touring expeditions, while the mountain states, such as Montana and Wyoming, offer significant challenges to adventurous riders. Alphabetically, by select states these are some of the USA's cycling highlights:

Left
Off the beaten track: travel through California's vineyards on two wheels.

CALIFORNIA

Stay off the freeways and focus on California's wine country: the state has world-class vineyards in and around Napa and Sonoma, north of San Francisco, and around Santa Barbara on the central coast north of Los Angeles. Cycling is a well-established way of touring the wineries. While mountain bikers head inland to the hillsides of Gold Country, road riders benefit from cool sea breezes and mists off the coast. Santa Cruz is a bike-friendly town, while to the south San Luis Obispo County has some of the state's most scenic rides, with ocean views, vineyards and quiet back roads. At the southern tip of California, San Diego is a hotbed for triathletes, but for many touring cyclists, the cooler roads through the redwood forests at the top of the state are preferable.

INFO
www.visitcalifornia.com

Below
Off-road in Gunnison, Colorado.

Below
Acadia National Park in Maine.

COLORADO

Many of this mountain state's 25 designated historic and scenic byways are perfect for touring, although remember that the altitude and ascents will ratchet up the challenge.

INFO
www.colorado.com

GEORGIA

Georgia has jumped on the rail trails bandwagon and has some great rides, which include the 60-mile Silver Comet Trail (the western end is quite remote) that will be part of a longer trail between Atlanta and Alabama.

INFO
www.exploregeorgia.org

MAINE

Up on the northeast coast, Maine shares both a city name with Oregon (Portland) and a pro-cycling attitude. The state offers rides for every ability, from century loops through the mountains of Franklin County and the 37-mile loop of Acadia National Park to the shorter coastal rides that form part of the East Coast Greenway. The Bicycle Coalition of Maine lists signed trails, such as the 12-mile Heritage Trail along the St. John River.

INFO
www.exploremaine.org
www.bikemaine.org

MASSACHUSETTS

College towns, from Amherst to Boston, abound in Massachusetts, and where there are colleges, there are cyclists. The roads around Amherst tend to be quiet, but at the end of the ride you return to a lively (and youthful) community. There are numerous short rail trails as well as longer trails, such as the 11-mile, traffic-free Nashua River Rail Trail, which heads toward New Hampshire. On the New England coast, Martha's Vineyard and Cape Cod are fantastic places to explore by bike.

INFO
www.visit-massachusetts. com

Right
Wheels and waterways: see Martha's Vineyard by bike.

EASY RIDES: USA

OREGON

Oregon and its northern neighbor Washington are two of the most bike-friendly states in America. Portland is the unofficial bicycle capital of the country, and the Willamette Valley Scenic Bikeway, which is the state's first designated bikeway, starts 30 miles south of the city, in Champoeg State Park, and finishes 130 miles later, in Armitage State Park near Eugene.

INFO
www.oregon.gov
www.rideoregonride.com

PENNSYLVANIA

One of the best-kept cycling secrets in the USA, Pennsylvania has quietly developed a network of rail trails such as the 250-mile Great Allegheny Passage from Cumberland to Pittsburgh, along the beautiful Youghiogheny River Gorge. There are already more than 1,050 miles of rail trails in Pennsylvania, and even the busy city of Pittsburgh offers signed bike routes today.

INFO
www.visitpa.com
www.atatrail.org

NEW YORK

New York City may have embraced the bike recently (*see* p. 252), but the state has always welcomed riders; after all, it is home to champion cyclist George Hincapie. Plenty of New Yorkers head up state to the Catskills and Adirondacks, but there are more than a dozen rail trails in the state, plus 500 miles of canalside cycle paths, including the Erie Canal Heritage Trail. At 455 miles, the Seaway Trail in New York state is one of the longest recreational trails in the country.

INFO
www.iloveny.com
www.bikeadirondacks.org
www.seawaytrail.com

Above
The Willamette Valley, Oregon.

Right
The Seaway Trail through New York and Pennsylvania.

VERMONT

Cycling through this New England state offers a unique way of appreciating the beautiful scenery, particularly the changing colors of the leaves in the fall and the scent of its flowers in the spring. Towns such as Burlington and Brattleboro are surrounded by a maze of quiet rural roads and car-free trails, such as the 25-mile South Burlington Recreation Path to Champion Lake, while the Green Mountains in the south of the state have loops over 4,000 feet high, plus mountains for cyclists wanting a workout. Shorter, easier routes can be plotted around Woodstock and Pomfret in Windsor County (east Vermont), through rural farmland. In western Vermont there are exceptional routes on quiet roads through Champlain Valley, circling lakes, waterways and country towns of classic white-washed Vermont architecture. The college town of Middlebury makes a good base.

WISCONSIN

Up near the Great Lakes, Wisconsin is carving a niche for itself as a cycling hotspot. The university cities of Madison (with 120 miles of bike routes) and Milwaukee are among the most cycling-friendly communities in the USA, but the quiet roads through the farmlands of 'Cheese Country' and Dane County in southern Wisconsin are also to be recommended. Bicycles are a good way of exploring West Central Wisconsin's Amish Coulee Country, while in the north, a good example of Wisconsin's rail trails is the 17-mile Bearskin-Hiawatha State Trail, which passes through beautiful fields full of flowers in the spring.

> ### INFO
> www.travelwisconsin.com

> ### INFO
> www.visit-vermont.com

Right top
Watch the seasons change in Vermont.

Right
Bike-friendly Milwaukee.

CYCLING DESTINATIONS

EPIC RIDES: ASIA

From the high passes of India and Nepal to the jungles of Thailand, Laos and Vietnam, Asia offers some of the most rewarding and challenging cycling in the world. And on a bicycle you're uniquely positioned to absorb as much of this intoxicating continent as possible.

Right
On top of the world: riding through Ladakh, India.

The bicycle has long been an essential mode of transport in much of Asia, so cycle tourists are welcomed with warmth. But that won't insulate many visitors against the culture shock of riding in such hectic traffic. Whether it's dodging sacred cows in India or mopeds in Ho Chi Minh City, riding in Asia can be an adrenalin-charged experience, but you can also readily find serenity, once-in-a-lifetime moments and priceless sights.

INDEPENDENT OR ORGANIZED?

Riding independently in many Asian countries requires a high degree of planning, almost to the point of preparing for a round-the-world expedition. You'll need to work out whether to take water purification equipment, how you will navigate with limited mapping and technological coverage and what sort of spares you will carry when a Shimano-stocked bike shop could be some distance away. This is why, in recent years, tour operators such as Exodus (www.exodus.co.uk) in the UK and Backroads in the USA (www.backroads.com) have been very successful in running trips in Asia: if you're short on time, joining an organized tour simplifies the experience (not least in getting the paperwork completed). Typically, bags will be carried by vehicle from stop to stop, which will leave you free to ride unencumbered, while the guides will provide some refreshments, commentary on what you're cycling past and a vague guarantee that you won't get lost during the day. Such tours are typically priced at the top end of the market, but companies such as Exodus and Backroads have built solid reputations on their expertise.

Independent cycle tourers can consider basing themselves in two or three locations and doing day rides in the vicinity, then journeying to the next base by train or bus.

TIP

Avoid cycling on major roads and highways, such as Highway 1 in Vietnam. The traffic and road conditions are dangerous. Seek out backroads, local advice or use an experienced guide. Even recent maps may contain mistakes.

HIGHLIGHTS

In such a diverse continent cyclists have much to choose from: there are ancient temple complexes, from Angkor Wat in Cambodia to Polunnaruwa in Sri Lanka that are easily explored by bike; there are cool highlands, such as the tea plantations of Darjeeling; and there are tropical jungles and islands.

But some places have emerged as must-do biking destinations. Riding the length of Vietnam, a long sickle-shaped country, has become a classic cycling trip, taking in dramatic coastal views, small villages and famous cities. The total distance, from Halong Bay to Ho Chi Minh City is about 1,050 miles but with use of transfers and trains it can be condensed to 430 miles. Neighboring Laos offers an altogether quieter and more beguiling experience.

In Thailand, the area around the northern cities of Chiang Mai and Chiang Rai has become an established destination for mountain bikers. Cooler than the south, the landscape of rice paddies, plantations, and teak forests is punctuated by small tribal villages.

Nepal, northern India, and even Tibet (through a tour operator), can all be discovered by bicycle. It's a harsher environment with rugged scenery and will require sturdy equipment, but the satisfaction of overcoming its many difficulties shouldn't be underestimated. Some places, such as Sri Lanka, blend a variety of elements in a compact space and are ideal for bike touring (the island is also much more laid-back than mainland India). Ultimately, the most rewarding aspect of cycling in Asia is the immersion in the local culture and traditions.

Right top
Tour Sri Lanka's temples at Polunnaruwa.

Right
Island-hop in Thailand with a bicycle.

EPIC RIDES: EUROPE

Nowhere else in the world is there such an expanse of cycle paths and routes as there is in Europe. And nowhere is the history and culture attached to some of these long-distance routes so rich. Europe can offer cycle tourists lifelong enjoyment on the road.

FRANCE

In France epic rides are known as *grande randonnées*. Sometimes they are organized as mass participation events (such as the Marmotte, *see* p. 214), but there is nothing stopping riders from following the route of a *randonnée* in their own time. One of the most famous is Bayonne to Luchon, which usually takes place in June and follows the 202½-mile route of a stage in the 1910 Tour de France; the riders in 1910 finished in 14 hours.

The *randonnée* dives into the Pyrenees, climbing the Tourmalet and Peyresourde (*see* p. 241). If it's a more in-depth Pyrenean adventure you're after, the Raid Pyrénéen (*see* p. 239), criss-crosses the range from Atlantic to Mediterranean.

One of the longest rides in France is Paris–Brest–Paris, a historic *brevet* (timed ride) of 1,200km (745 miles), dating from the 19th century.

Above
Cyclists gather at Land's End, Cornwall, England.

CONTACTS

Audax UK, the leading long-distance cycling organization in the UK: www.aukweb.net

Sustrans designs and maps cycle routes in the UK: www.sustrans.org.uk

European Cyclists Federation, planners of the EuroVelo project: www.ecf.com

Association Française de développement des Véloroutes et Voies Vertes (France): www.af3v.org

Fundacion de los Ferrocarriles (Spain): www.viasverdes.com

VeloLand Schweiz (Switzerland): www.veloland.ch

Below
Cycle routes in Tallinn, Estonia, eastern Europe; the EuroVelo project plans to join up cycle routes across Europe.

Bottom
Sustrans cycle route signs are increasingly common in the UK.

UK

While the whole Land's End to John o'Groats route, the length of the UK, is a week-long commitment, cherry-picking the tastiest roads through the Scottish glens is very appealing. National Route 7, plotted by Sustrans from Glasgow to Inverness, is a 214-mile highlight, passing through some of Britain's most breathtaking scenery in the Cairngorms and the Trossachs. The full Land's End to John o'Groats route is more than 800 miles long.

Lon Las Cymru, the Welsh National Route, covers 250 miles from Anglesey to Cardiff. One of the best stretches is from Dolgellau to Machynlleth, a 30-mile spin through Snowdonia. This may be mountain biking country, but the route is entirely on quiet paved roads.

To the north, the Sea to Sea (C2C) ride from Whitehaven to Newcastle or Sunderland is Britain's classic coast-to-coast bike ride, although there are plenty of other routes to choose from. The C2C covers 140 miles and entails crossing the Pennines on some of the highest cycle paths in the country.

An alternative to the northern challenge, the Devon version is oriented north to south, starting from Ilfracombe and finishing in Plymouth, after 150 miles via retired Victorian railway lines. The ride incorporates parts of Sustrans' National Cycle Routes 27 and 3.

EUROVELO

EuroVelo is a project to plot long-distance bike routes across mainland Europe – it is more than two-thirds of the way toward its target of 66,000km (41,000 miles) of signed cycle paths over 12 routes. Routes can be found across Europe, from Scandinavia to southern and eastern Europe.

CYCLING DESTINATIONS

EPIC RIDES: USA & CANADA

Europe doesn't have a monopoly on long-distance cycling challenges. With vast landscapes, varied climates, modern amenities and welcoming people, the USA and Canada have some superlative long-distance bike routes, whether you're going north to south or east to west.

COASTAL

Since 2008, spending on cycling has increased significantly, so there are more chances for cyclists to explore the USA, such as the East Coast Greenway, a key part of the proposed US Bicycle Route System. It's in its early stages, with 25 percent of the route currently on car-free paths, but if it progresses, the East Coast Greenway would be an epic ride of 3,000 miles from Florida to Maine.

On the west coast, the 1,700-mile Pacific Coast Route runs through Washington and Oregon and down the length of California, from the redwood forests to the desert. From San Francisco, the Western Express takes cyclists to the start of the TransAmerica Bicycle Trail in Pueblo, Colorado, the most popular route for crossing the country. You can also compete with other ultra-cyclists in the Race Across America (RAAM).

Right
The Race Across America is a test of cyclists' steely determination.

RURAL

A more leisurely pace is required to enjoy cycling in beautiful rural areas such as Vermont, stopping at inns and savoring the changing seasons. Certain communities in the USA – typically university towns such as Madison, Wisconsin, and Austin, Texas – are very supportive of cycling and have a network of long and short routes radiating out. Communities also play a role in hosting events: the Cycle Zydeco 220-mile ride is organized by locals in south Lousiana, and there are many more tours like it.

As well as being a great way to meet people, epic bike rides take you into unforgettable scenery, and this is where the USA excels. The off-road, 2,500-mile Great Divide route follows the great mountain ranges of the Midwest from Canada to Mexico, through some true wilderness. If you're not ready for the high country (there's 200,000 feet of elevation along the Great Divide), warm up with the 1,240-mile Great Rivers route through Mississippi, Missouri and Lousiana. North of the border, in Quebec, Canada, the Route Verte is a famous 2,500-mile long cycle ride through mountains and great rivers.

To plan a long-distance bicycle ride in the USA, talk to those who've done it and learn from their experiences; there isn't cycling infrastructure as extensive as Europe's, but that may be about to change.

Above left
Acadia National Park in Maine.

Above right, top
The Great Divide Mountain Bike Route in southern New Mexico.

Above right, bottom
A map of the major long-distance bike routes in the USA.

CONTACTS

Advice, maps and itineraries from the Adventure Cycling Association: www.adventurecycling.org

Advocacy and contacts from the League of American Bicyclists: www.bikeleague.org

EPIC RIDES: AROUND THE WORLD

Some cyclists just don't know when to stop. Around-the-world cycling adventures are becoming less unusual, with more and more cyclists packing up and taking off on the bike ride of a lifetime.

Above
James Bowthorpe completes his circumnavigation by bicycle, pedaling into Hyde Park in 2009.

In 2008, the Scottish cyclist Mark Beaumont broke the world record for cycling around the world, completing the circumnavigation in 195 days. His solo feat was followed, in September 2009, by that of James Bowthorpe, who raised the bar to 176 days, averaging 100 miles a day.

The following year Vin Cox managed to break the record again, taking just 163 days to complete the circumnavigation.

To qualify as a record attempt, round-the-world cyclists must pedal more than 18,000 miles in a single, continuous loop in one direction; the total distance traveled must exceed 40,000km (24,900 miles), the length of the equator. With the fastest circumnavigation now taking less than six months, and several professionally supported attempts, we could one day see the record tumble to 80 days!

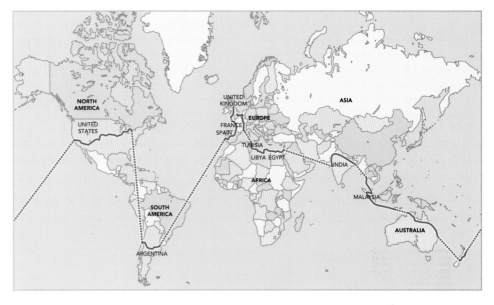

Difficulties encountered on the route are often more challenging than asking for a puncture repair kit in Japanese. Beaumont's close shaves included being knocked off his bike in Louisiana, food poisoning in Lahore and setting fire to his hotel room in Calcutta. Bowthorpe was ambushed by kidnappers in Iran, collided with a wombat in Australia and suffered food poisoning in India. And don't forget the daily task of pedaling a 176-lb bike 100 to 150 miles a day, through all weather.

Planning – applying for documentation, sending gear such as spare tires ahead and scheduling the journey to avoid the worst of an area's weather – is the key to a successful around-the-world trip. But not everyone is in a hurry; adventurer Alastair Humphreys spent more than four years riding 46,000 miles before returning to Britain in 2005.

Above
Vin Cox's record-breaking around-the-world route in 2010.

Below left
Mark Beaumont cycled 18,296 miles in 195 days.

BIKE FESTIVALS

Timing your visit to coincide with a bike festival adds another dimension to your biking trip.

Sea Otter Classic, Monterey, California
The cycling community descends on the Pacific coast of California in April for the Sea Otter Classic, a festival, show and race all wrapped in one tasty package. Despite frequently dubious weather, the event is always a hit.
www.seaotterclassic.com

Riva del Garda Bike Festival, Italy
Europe's best mountain bike festival is hosted by Riva del Garda, at the north tip of Lake Garda. With the spectacular Dolomites as a playground, the festival includes a night ride plus a 60-mile off-road marathon.
www.gardatrentino.it

Melbourne Cycling Festival, Australia
A week of bike-related activities is held in October, as Victoria's state capital embraces the bike. The three-day festival incorporates National Ride to Work Day and Around the Bay in a Day (see p. 216).
www.bv.com.au

PLANNING A CYCLE TOURING TRIP

Cycle touring of any kind is a great way to experience a country, at a pace that really allows you to immerse yourself in the sights, smells, sounds and culture of a place while getting out on your bike in the fresh air. The level of physical challenge is up to you, but the success of any extended trip may be decided before you leave by what you take – or don't take. Planning and packing for cycle touring is a very personal task, but there are several guidelines that can simplify the process.

Above
A bicycle is the key to free travel and independence.

Where you are going, for how long and with what budget will determine what you pack for the trip. A three-month cycle tour across Africa will require very different gear from a week-long riding vacation in the south of France staying in hotels. Be sure about what you want to do before making big decisions about what to take.

TIME AND DISTANCE

When cycle touring, how far you will ride in a day will depend on several factors: the terrain and weather, your bicycle and its load and simply your own comfort levels. Cumulative days in the saddle are not to be underestimated, and you may want to allow some spontaneity in your riding plan. But it's a good idea to work out an approximate daily mileage so that you know how far you can go between accommodation stops. Remember that you will become fitter as the tour continues so you may average 30 miles per day in the first week and 45 miles per day in subsequent weeks. On a fully laden touring bike, you will also find your average speed is much slower. Be honest with yourself; it's better to underestimate your daily distance than struggle to get to each stop.

TIP

Insurance: Before departing, check whether your travel insurance policy covers bicycling and the bicycle in transit or places restrictions and maximum limits on what can be claimed in the event of an incident.

Right and far right
Cycle tourists can camp or stay in hotels – the only difference lies in how much gear needs to be carried.

STAYING OVERNIGHT

Where you plan to stop each night will determine a large portion of the luggage you will carry. A fully self-sufficient trip, camping at night and cooking for yourself, will require a tent, a sleeping pad and bag, a stove, cutlery and pans. But if you plan to stay in hostels, hotels, inns or with friends, you will require much less equipment and will therefore be able to travel farther faster. For lightweight tourists, a credit card may be all you need to carry.

WHAT TO TAKE

Strip weight ruthlessly wherever you can. When you've planned the distance and duration of your trip and researched the likely terrain and weather, you will have a better idea of what you'll need to carry.

Camping

In recent years there has been an arms race in lightweight camping equipment. Everything from minimalist stoves, such as those by Jetboil, to titanium pans has been designed to cut down on the pounds and ounces.

Clothing

Personal preferences and weather conditions play a large part in determining what clothes to pack. The pleasure of putting on a fresh set of dry clothes after a day on the bike is not to be underestimated. Similarly, staying warm and dry on the bike is important; if rain is likely – for example, if you're riding in Ireland or the Pacific

Northwest – pack a lightweight waterproof layer. Cold air rushing through damp clothes can cause chills. At the very least, a multi-purpose windproof top is strongly recommended.

A warm underlayer is also very useful; merino wool base layers are excellent for their long-term odor-repelling properties and for being very comfortable. Pack a couple of pairs of the best cycling shorts you can afford; it will save having to wash a pair every night and hoping it dries in time. Another good investment is in cycling shoes that suit your feet.

Whether you wear a helmet or not, a sunhat or visor can be helpful in keeping the sun off your face.

Remember that unless you are venturing into the middle of nowhere, you can usually buy clothing (such as underwear or T-shirts) along the route.

For the bike

You will also need to make space for an assortment of spares and tools for the trip. Again, this depends on how far away from civilization you are going. If your bike has parts, such as disc brakes, that require particular spares, don't forget to pack them. A small roll of duct tape and a length of strong cord are useful for repairs on the road. A bottle of durable lube, a type that stands up to rain, is also essential.

PLANNING A CYCLE TOURING TRIP

Below
Wet weather gear will need to be packed.

RACKS AND PANNIERS

A bike suitable for touring will have rack mounts into which the rear rack can be bolted. Racks are typically made from steel for resilience; steel racks can also be easily repaired in out-of-the-way places. A specialist touring bicycle will have mounts on the seat stays and at the rear hub. For longer tours, a front rack, mounted on the forks, may be necessary. With racks front and rear, you will be able to carry four panniers (each pair offering a maximum capacity of around 40 liters), plus a handlebar bag. You can also strap extra gear on to the top of the rear panniers for an expedition.

Below
Pack your panniers with the essentials.

There's a vast range of panniers on the market. They can be made from a variety of fabrics, from rip-proof polyester to canvas and Cordura. Each has its advantages. Waterproof panniers may be a good idea, but you can pack your luggage into waterproof bags or use a waterproof liner, before stowing it in the panniers. When buying panniers, check the seams, which are often the weakest point for waterproofing.

Typically, panniers clip or hook on to the rack and are then secured with a strap. Some panniers are easier to remove than others, and it's worth testing some different designs in the shop. The most important point is that they stay attached on a rough road.

INSTALLING A RACK

Above
1 & 2. Use an Allen (hex) key to attach the rack to the frame's rack mounts at the seat and hub.

3. Racks can also be attached to front forks.
4. Panniers fit over the rack.

CHECKLISTS

Clothing: Cycling shorts, windproof top, waterproof top and pants if required, merino wool base layer, gloves, socks, shoes, jersey, off-the-bike clothing including warm top, sunglasses, sunhat

Toiletries: Toothpaste, shampoo, sunblock, small towel, medical kit

Camping gear: Tent, stove and fuel, sleeping bag and pad, cutlery, pots and pans, water purification system if required, sterilizing tablets, dishwashing kit, matches

Useful items: Insect repellent, ear plugs, sewing kit, elastic cord, small quantity of detergent, headlamp, plug adaptors for rechargers, waterproof pouch for documents

Tools: Multi-tool with Allen (hex) keys, adjustable wrench, Phillips screwdriver, multi-tool with pliers (such as a Leatherman), pump, puncture repair kit, tire boot, spare inner tubes, zip ties

Bike equipment: Lubricant, brake pads, spokes, cables, lights in case you end up cycling at night, recharger, water bottles, lock (if required)

Left
Families can enjoy cycle touring with careful preparation.

PLANNING A CYCLE TOURING TRIP

Above and above right
Using a map and compass is a useful skill for cycle tourists in remote places.

MAPPING

The accuracy and availability of mapping is an important consideration if setting out on a bicycling adventure. For the most part, using route maps designed for cyclists and distributed through bicycle shops, cycling organizations and local tourist offices is the best idea for most cyclists – but don't take their accuracy for granted. Having a topographic map at hand when riding a plotted but unsigned route is helpful, so you can match up landmarks to trace your progress. When venturing on to smaller roads (or

off-road) in an unfamiliar place, a topographic map is essential. Each country has its own agency in charge of maintaining national mapping: in the USA it is the US Geological Survey, in the UK it is Ordnance Survey (OS) and in Australia it is the National Mapping Agency. Some outstanding mapping may be produced by individual national automobile associations, such as the Automobile Association (AA) in the UK and the Algemene Nederlandse Wielrijders Bond (ANWB) in the Netherlands. Typically, maps

will be available in varying degrees of detail (see Map Scales, opposite). Maps intended for recreational use, such as the Explorer and Landranger series from Ordnance Survey, will be the most useful for cyclists. Many agencies, including OS and USGS, offer maps for sale by mail order or download from their websites.

MAP SCALES

A large-scale map covers a small area in great detail, while a small-scale map does the reverse. A scale of 1:50,000 means that the area covered on the map – a county, for example – is one fifty-thousandth life size. So, a centimeter on the map represents 50,000 centimeters on the ground. In practice, this means that on a 1:50,000-scale map, 1¼ inches equates to 1 mile. For road cyclists, the most useful scale is probably 1:100,000, although 1:75,000 and 1:50,000 are fine. Any greater detail and you may have to carry several maps for one long ride. For mountain bikers, a larger scale may be useful.

Right
Unlike a GPS, a map will never struggle to find a signal or run out of battery power.

Below
An analog watch can aid navigation in an emergency.

SO, WHAT IF YOU GET LOST IN THE SOUTHERN HEMISPHERE?

Your GPS has run out of juice and you forgot your compass – but you need to find north and south?

Finding north
You don't have to have a compass to find north but an analogue watch is essential. Point the 12 on your watch in the direction of the sun. Draw an imaginary line toward the middle of the watch face then divide the angle created by that imaginary line and the actual hour it is. The midpoint is north, more or less. For example, if it's 8 a.m. and you point the 12 at the sun, north will be about 10 o'clock.

Finding south
After sunset, and on a clear night, you can find south. First, locate the Southern Cross. Draw an imaginary line extending from the lower end of the long axis of the cross, four and a half times the length of the long axis. From that line's end, draw a line straight down to earth. Where that line meets the ground is, near enough, south.

PLANNING A CYCLE TOURING TRIP

LOADING TIPS

Loading a bicycle affects its handling negatively, which is why the geometry of touring bikes is designed to give as stable and predictable handling as possible. Depending on the quantity of luggage you need to carry, there are certain things you can do to keep the bike stable.

Pack the weight low: the higher heavy items are packed, the less stable the bike will be.

Distribute the weight evenly: putting all the weight in the rear panniers and just having a handlebar bag will cause the steering to feel light.

If using front panniers, put about 60 percent of the weight in the rear panniers and 40 percent in the front. This will make braking safer.

Have a bag mounted on your handlebars in which you can store things you'll need frequently, such as snacks, sunblock, maps, money and a camera.

For convenience, have a predictable packing routine: keep food-related gear in one place, sleeping gear in another. This will save you having to dig through each pannier in the hunt for an item.

Compartmentalize your luggage and use waterproof bags; if something leaks it won't ruin the whole cargo.

Right
Cycle tourists can travel light by leaving gear in a hotel or sending it on ahead.

Below
Fully loaded touring bikes will have panniers front and rear plus a handlebar bag.

TRAILERS

Trailers, such as those made by BOB, are an increasingly popular cargo-carrying alternative to panniers. The appeal of a trailer is that it can be unhitched at the end of the day, leaving you free to enjoy riding your bike unencumbered. Modern trailers are compatible with a variety of bikes, can carry up to 70lbs and can be used off-road. They can weigh around 13–14lbs.

Right and below
A trailer is a convenient way of carrying gear over smooth terrain; the trailer can be left somewhere safe while you explore unencumbered.

SECURITY

This can be a major consideration, depending on your location. Store your valuables (phone, money, passport and ID) in a removable handlebar bag that you can carry with you when leaving the bike anywhere. Good locks tend to be heavy; you will have to weigh the pros and cons of taking one with you and what size and strength you choose if you do; this will depend on where you are cycling. It's always worth checking the bike storage options when booking accommodation or traveling by overnight train.

TRANSPORTING YOUR BICYCLE

When packing a bicycle for a journey by airplane or bus, the objective is to protect it from by being damaged when handled and from damaging itself. Airlines usually require that a bike is packed in a box or bag, but how that is done is up to you.

There are three main bike-packing options. In order of cost these are: a specialized, hard-shell bike box for ultimate protection; a soft but padded bag; and a cardboard bike box – ask your local bike shop to put one aside after a delivery. Each has its advantages, but if you need to watch its weight, depending on your airline's luggage policy, the cardboard box or bike bag are the most practical options.

YOU'LL NEED:

- A bike box or bag
- Wheel bags, if possible
- Zip ties
- Fork brace
- Allen (hex) keys
- Padding

Above
Once the bike is partially dismantled it can be padded to prevent damage.

Right
Brace the drop-outs of the rear chain stays and front fork.

TIP

Separate your wheels and frame with panels of cardboard and secure everything in place with zip ties to reduce the risk of damage caused by continuous rubbing on a long journey.

Right
Airlines have different rules about bicycle transport: check before you go.

PACKING A BIKE

To fit your bike into a box or bag, you will need to remove its pedals, remembering that the left, non-drive-side pedal has a reverse thread. Store the pedals somewhere safe, in a soft bag, for example. Remove the wheels (stow them in wheel bags if you have them, or wrap them in newspaper) and the seatpost. Put them to one side.

With an Allen (hex) key, remove the handlebars from the stem and loosen the stem's bolts. Turn the stem 180 degrees. You can hold it in place with a zip tie.

To prevent your forks or seat stays being squashed together (if something heavy is placed on the bag) brace them with an old hub or a piece of dowling cut to size. Bike frames and forks delivered to shops will often come with a plastic brace, so ask your local shop.

Secure the derailleur out of the way with a zip tie. Put the frame in the box or bag. You can protect the tubing with pipe lagging or cardboard if you wish. Fit the handlebars (still attached by the cables) around the frame and

secure with a zip tie or two. Put the pedals and seatpost in the box or bag – you can wrap the seatpost in bubble wrap to prevent its scratching the frame. Slide a wheel on either side of the frame. You can wedge them in place to prevent any movement.

Check that there's little or no movement in the whole arrangement; what happens from here on is in the hands of the baggage handlers.

TIPS WHEN FLYING

Different airlines have different luggage restrictions when it comes to transporting a bike. For some, a bicycle is classed as sports equipment and attracts a surcharge, while others will include it in your overall weight limit, and some may not charge at all. Check carefully with each airline. Also check the maximum dimensions permitted.

Note that some low-cost airlines may not be contractually obliged to carry your bike even if it is booked in advance.

Right
1. Bicycle wheels can be stowed in individual bags.
2. A structured bicycle bag has padding.
3. Use the shoulder strap to carry the bag.

CHAPTER 7
MAINTENANCE

MAINTENANCE

TOOLS: BASIC & ADVANCED

As modern cars, gadgets and appliances become more technologically impenetrable, the bicycle stands alone in not hiding its engineering away. With the right tools and a bit of experience, almost any problem with your bicycle can be fixed at home.

Professional bike mechanics have a golden rule: ten minutes of maintenance can save an hour of repairs. Clean gears and tuned brakes will last longer and be less likely to fail. This chapter covers the most minimal maintenance required to keep your bicycle on the road before introducing some of the more advanced tasks and repairs a home mechanic could attempt.

Bicycle maintenance isn't just about preventing problems. Cyclists who know the basics benefit in other ways: it's cheaper to do a simple job yourself than pay a shop to do it, and you'll be better prepared to fix a problem on a ride. It can also be enormously satisfying figuring out how a bicycle works and keeping it in peak condition. Cycling is a lot more fun without squeaks, creaks or rattles.

Right
Basic bicycle maintenance can be done at home or by a shop.

ESSENTIAL TOOLS

To keep a bicycle running smoothly from day to day, you will need just a handful of essential tools (see list on right). To attempt more complex jobs, you may have to invest in a few advanced tools or a friendly local bike shop may be persuaded to lend them to you. Wear a pair of thin latex gloves to prevent fingers becoming grimy, and carry a pair with you when you are out and about.

- Allen (hex) keys or wrenches
- Screwdrivers
- Pliers
- Wrenches
- Chain breaker
- Lubrication, grease and degreaser
- Puncture repair kit
- Pump

Below
1. Pliers.
2. Wrenches.
3. Chain breaker.
4. Multi-tool including Allen (hex) keys.
5. Bottom bracket tool.
6. Allen/hex keys.
7. Screwdrivers.
8. Chain whip.

ALLEN (HEX) KEYS OR WRENCHES

Many bike parts are secured by bolts that have a hexagonal socket in the head, and so a full set of Allen keys, also known as hex keys or wrenches, is worth its weight in gold. Ball end ones are especially useful. Buy the highest quality set you can afford; cheap Allen keys are more likely to round off a bolt, potentially ruining an expensive component. Weight is a good guide to quality; heavier wrenches are of a poorer quality. Sizes required (in mm) are: 1.5, 2, 2.5, 3, 4, 5, 6, 8 and 10.

SCREWDRIVERS

Both crosshead, also known as Phillips, and flathead screwdrivers are useful. The Phillips, required in a small size, will be used for several adjustments on the bike (for example, adjusting derailleurs), while the flathead, preferably a medium, can be useful for prying parts off.

PLIERS

Needlenose pliers are useful for delicately picking out small bolts or bearings. Some will have a built-in cable cutter, although a dedicated cable cutter will do a cleaner job. Locking pliers, can hold parts in place while you work on them.

WRENCHES

A selection of open-end metric wrenches, in sizes 7mm to 17mm, are required for tightening pedals and other parts. A spoke key or wrench is needed for tensioning wheels.

CHAIN BREAKER

A good chain-breaking tool is worth the expense, although you can get away with using the chain breaker on a multi-tool.

OTHER EQUIPMENT

Use a thread-locking adhesive, such as Loctite, for bolts you don't want to come undone, and a dab of grease for those you do want to be able to undo. Keep rags for wiping chains, and a chain bath for cleaning the chain, or a toothbrush and spare jar for doing it by hand.

TOOLS : BASIC & ADVANCED

Vulcanizing glue | Rubber patch | Sandpaper

Above
Puncture repair kit.

ADVANCED TOOLS

If you plan on doing jobs a step beyond basic maintenance, having your own tools can be a money-saving investment.

- Chain measurer, chain whip and cassette lockring remover.

- Bottom bracket remover and crank puller (if required; many modern types of cranks, such as Shimano's Hollowtech are simply attached by Allen bolts).

- Torque wrench, particularly if you have carbon-fiber components that could be damaged by over-tightened bolts.

- Plastic-headed hammer.

- Vise and a fine-toothed hacksaw for trimming handlebars.

- Headset press.

- Truing stand if you want to build your own wheels.

PUNCTURE REPAIR KIT

To patch up an inner tube puncture, your kit needs to contain tire levers, patches and some vulcanizing rubber solution.

PUMP

To inflate your tires at home, a floor pump does the job quickly and saves aching arms. A mini-pump can be carried on rides, and a finely calibrated shock pump is needed for a mountain bike's suspension.

WORKSPACE

Get started by setting aside a space – in a garage, shed, or a spare room – for your bike and tools. An organized and tidy workspace will save time and make maintenance jobs much easier. In space too limited for a tool chest, a grid of wire mesh can be used to hang tools on a wall.

An adjustable workstand can double as a stand for storing the bike. Good workstands, such as those made by Park Tools, have a broad base for stability, adjustable height and a clamp that can be rotated. It's a worthwhile precaution to clamp your bicycle by the seatpost so as not to accidentally crush the frame's thin tubes. Exercise extra care clamping carbon-fiber tubes and seatposts.

A tray close to the stand can be used for keeping cogs, bolts and bits and pieces safe while you work on the bike. Better still, buy a magnetic metal dish. The floor area around the stand should be covered to protect it from greasy marks and various fluid drips and spills – use a plastic sheet. A mechanic's apron protects clothing from oil and dirt, and the pockets can be used for holding tools.

Below
Mini-pump for carrying on the bike.

Below
A bike stand is a
good investment for
the home mechanic.

SPARES

With a range of spares at
hand, you can complete
many jobs without an
extra trip to your local bike
shop. Brake pads are the
parts that wear out most
regularly; keep a spare
pair in your toolbox. Some
spare connector pins or
a Powerlink and several
extra links can keep a chain
going. Cables for gears and

brakes (they're different)
need to be replaced
infrequently. If you plan
to maintain your own hubs
and pedals, you might
also want to keep correctly
sized bearings.

Below
Keep nuts and bolts in
a dish when working.

TIPS

- Always use the correct size of Allen (hex) key or
  wrench; too large or too small and you will round
  off or damage the bolt.

- Wipe threads with a rag before installing them. In
  most cases, a dab of grease will prevent them from
  seizing. Some bolts benefit from a dab of thread-locking
  adhesive, such as Loctite, to prevent them from undoing.

MAINTENANCE

BASIC RULES: CLEANING & LUBING

Cleanliness is next to godliness for bicycle owners. Nothing ensures a bicycle will work smoothly and efficiently so well as keeping it clean and lubricated. A regularly cleaned bike will last longer, require less maintenance and also be cheaper to use. But it's important to do it correctly.

DRIVETRAIN

This is the most important part of the bike to keep clean and lubed. Grit sticks to dirty chains and will wear away the moving metal parts. You can clean the chain by hand, using a toothbrush (or stiff-bristled brush) and a degreaser or cleaner, such as those sold by Finish Line.

Alternatively, use a chain bath, through which a dirty chain is rotated, coming out sparkling. Regularly removing the chain to clean it (one technique is to put it into an empty soft-drink bottle and give it a shake with a degreaser) may weaken the chain; it's better to clean it on the bike. A toothbrush can be used to clean derailleur jockey wheels, cogs and chainrings – but don't let the degreaser come into contact with grease-laden components, such as hubs, headsets, pedals and bottom brackets.

Rinse off the drivetrain and give it a light spray with a water dispersant, such as WD-40 or GT-85. Wipe this off and wait for the chain to dry. Now the chain is ready to be lubed.

Above
A chain bath cleans bike chains.

Far left
Lube the chain regularly. Ensure lubricants are kept away from brake pads and braking surfaces (rims or rotors).

Left
A degreasing cleaner will speed the job up.

LUBRICATION

A bicycle-specific lubricant adds to the chain's lifespan. There are two choices: a wet lube, best suited to wet conditions because it clings to the chain, and a wax-based, dry lube. Dry lubes need to be reapplied more frequently; when dirt touches the chain, specks of the dry lube fall off with the dirt. In the case of both lubes, apply with a nozzle along the whole length of the chain, wipe off the excess and allow to dry – it's better to clean and lube a bike after rather than before a ride. Sprays such as WD-40 are not suitable as lubricants because they act as a degreaser on moving parts as large as a chain's links.

THE FRAME

Use soapy water to give the frame a wash, then rinse thoroughly. A bucket and soft brush (not the same brush used for the drivetrain) does the best job. Avoid using a powerwash or pressured hose around the bearings and seals.

Finally, dry the bike with a rag. Don't allow water to sit around headsets or bottom brackets; always wipe a rag around the seals. Apply fresh handlebar tape occasionally as a finishing touch.

Above right
Use a mild detergent to clean the bike but keep the degreaser away from bearings in hubs and headsets.

Left
Cables collect grime.

TIPS

- Keep the bike upright or water will seep into the headset.

- Don't use hot water, which melts grease; cold water and a mild soap are fine.

- Keep greasy and non-greasy brushes separate.

- Soften dried-on dirt by dampening it before washing.

- Rinse carefully and thoroughly.

DIAGNOSING PROBLEMS: WEAR & TEAR

Deducing what's wrong with a bike is often a matter of listening as much as looking. The full range of squeaks, rattles, clicks and clunks all have a cause; it's just a question of working out what each means before you can do anything about it. How your bike feels when you're riding it may also help with the diagnosis of a problem.

A skilled bike whisperer works by a process of deduction, ruling out possibilities until the source of a sound can only be one thing. Work out whether the sound occurs when you're pedaling or when you're not; whether it's when you're in or out of the saddle. Try swapping out different components – borrow someone else's wheel, change your pedals – to narrow down the possibilities. The following are some of the most common culprits and will give you an idea of what certain sounds may mean, but there's no substitute for developing your own detective skills.

Above
Wipe grime and grit off wheel rims to stop squeaking brake pads.

Left
Lightly grease metal seatposts to stop them from sticking.

Left
Worn and new
disc-brake pads.

SQUEAKS

The 'eek-eek-eek' of an unlubed jockey wheel is one of the most annoying sounds known to mankind. A simple drop of lube will make it go away. The rub of a metal cleat against the pedal can also squeak.

CREAKS

Often caused by movement between metal parts. Check:

- The rails under the saddle and adjust or tighten if necessary; where the rails enter the saddle is often a cause of creaking, a squirt of lube can remedy this.

- The seat collar and the frame; remove the collar, clean and dab some thread-locking adhesive on the inside where it slides over the seat tube.

- The seat post in the seat tube; remove, lightly grease the post if metal (not if carbon fiber).

- Where the handlebars are secured in the stem; undo and then re-tighten with a dab of grease on the threads of the bolts.

- That both pedals are tight; the drive side is tightened normally (clockwise) and the non-drive side is tightened counter-clockwise.

- All the crank and crankset bolts, as a loose bolt will allow movement.

- The dropouts where they meet the quick release; administer a clean and a dab of grease – some frames flex under power, so factor this into your investigation.

- Suspension pivots, as these are a notorious source of creaks on mountain bikes, but if tightening the bolt or a full bearing service doesn't solve it, there may be little you can do.

- The bottom bracket; this is less commonly a cause of creaks than the pedals and cleats. It doesn't help that both are used for pedaling making it harder to identify the source; try new cleats before investigating the bottom bracket; worn cleats, with shiny edges, are the most likely culprit.

If all these fail, check the frame for cracks by looking for imperfections in the paint finish.

SHRIEKS

Brake pads can squeal against the rim if there's dirt or grit embedded in the pad or as a result of the angle at which they meet the rim. Clean the rim of grime with a solvent and check the pads for wear and tear. Many modern brakes have pads that don't need to be toed-in (angled slightly inward at the front, *see p. 321*), but you may need to tinker with those that do so that you find the right position.

Disc brakes can squeal in the wet. Try dabbing some grease between the metal back of the pad and the piston. A warped rotor can also cause squealing, although this should be visible to the eye.

Below
Worn caliper
brake pads.

DIAGNOSING PROBLEMS: WEAR & TEAR

CLICKS

Worn ball bearings are a common cause of ticking sounds and, like a ticking alarm clock, are trying to tell you something: replace me before it's too late!

You can replace the bearings in certain types of hub (Shimano's cup and cone hubs) and pedals. Worn bearings appear pitted, but even if that's only one or two, change them all at the same time.

New wheels can click and tick as the spokes start to bed in. Older wheels may also produce sounds as the spokes rub against each other.

Check that the ends of the derailleur gear cables aren't interfering with the chain; secure them properly out of the way if they are.

A clicking or cracking sound coming from the cranks could be a loose crank arm, whether it's a square-taper or splined system (see Cranks box, p. 325). Refasten, with a dab of thread-locking adhesive.

RATTLES

At the front of the bike, check whether the headset is loose by pulling on the front brake and rocking the bike backward and forward. To tighten, loosen the stem bolts, tighten the top cap and then retighten the stem bolts.

There may be more innocuous causes, such as a loose reflector on a wheel.

Above
Regreasing hub bearings can prolong their life.

CLUNKS

Deeper, thudding bumps are easier to diagnose. A rhythmic 'whump' is often a tire rubbing against the frame, either because the wheel is slightly buckled (it will need truing with a spoke wrench), the wheel has not been replaced in the dropouts correctly or, less likely, the frame is misaligned or twisted. A tire or wheel that's too large may also rub. Check the paint; a rubbing tire will wear away a patch on the stays.

Very loose headsets will clonk rather than rattle. Again, test by holding the front brake on and pushing the handlebars forward and backward.

Bikes with suspension may clunk when air pressure has been lost and the inner components of the shock or fork are banging against the outer casing.

WEAR & TEAR

The moving parts of a bicycle suffer from wear and tear, even if they are carefully maintained. The drivetrain is the most problematic area, as the cassette, chainrings and chain are constantly in use.

The lifespan of the crankset (in mileage) will depend what it is made from — steel chainrings last longer than aluminum — and the quality of manufacture. Worn chainrings become shaped like shark's teeth as the chain "stretches." At the rear, the dips between the cassette's teeth flatten out and the whole chain may slip on the cassette.

Wheels too may suffer, as rims gradually grow thinner and ball bearings in hubs get pitted. Tires lose tread and develop splits, while the valves of old inner tubes may fail. But, in all cases, regular cleaning and lubing is guaranteed to make your bike's parts live longer.

Right
Frayed gear cables need to be replaced.

Right
Cables can rub holes in frames; protect the area with clear tape.

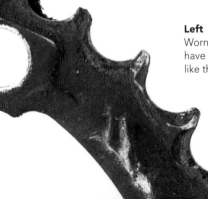

Left
Worn chainrings have curved teeth like those of a shark.

BEFORE YOU START: BASICS

Modern bicycles make life easy for their owners, for the most part. But, for new cyclists, a few fundamental features may be perplexing and are worth understanding before you set out on your maiden voyage.

WHEELS

Once the quick release is open, undo it and remove the wheel by giving the nut on the other side of the axle a couple of turns to get it past the tabs around the edge of the dropout. (These tabs are sometimes known as 'lawyer tabs' and are intended to hold the wheel in the dropouts should the quick release come undone. Hopefully you won't ever need to confirm whether they work or not.)

Before you do this, you may need to undo your brakes so the tire can pass between the brake pads.

On the caliper brakes of a road bike, a tiny lever moves the pads apart; on V-brakes and cantilevers you may need to unhook the cable (*see* middle picture, p. 318).

Above and right
When doing up a quick release, ensure the lever is flush alongside the frame or fork.

QUICK RELEASES

The quick release is an innovation that allows you to remove wheels and seatposts without any tools. It's a lever that operates a cam, clamping a hub into dropouts (the cut-out slots in the fork and at the rear of the bike frame) or gripping a seatpost in the seat tube. To undo a quick release, pull the lever out from its position against the wheel or seat tube.

Right
Use the lever to move brake pads apart before removing the wheel.

Left
Some mountain-bike forks have bolt-through axles for extra strength and stiffness.

TIRES

To replace the wheel, slide it back into the dropouts. To remove and then replace the rear wheel of a bicycle with a derailleur, you will have to guide the cassette's cogs under the top of the chain. Tighten the nut to finger tightness and then close the quick release – a moderate amount of resistance is required. It's customary to angle the quick release up, alongside the fork, or backward to prevent it being flicked out by a branch as you ride – although whether this has ever actually happened is another matter. Most importantly, don't forget to reattach the brake cable!

The next most important procedure to understand is pumping up a tire. The rubber inner tube, enclosed in the tire, will have a valve protruding from the inside of the rim. A short fat valve is a Schrader type, as used on car tires; a tall, thin valve is a Presta type, and by far the most common style.

Most bicycle pumps are compatible with both types (although you may need to flip an adaptor). With a Presta valve, undo the tiny tip of the valve then push the pump on to the end of the valve. You may need to lock the pump in place with a lever. Then inflate. Most tires have a recommended psi printed on the sidewall.

Left
Track pumps make it easy to inflate a tire.

AXLE NUTS

Not all bicycles have quick releases on the wheels. Older bikes will have wheels secured by nuts – 15mm is the usual size – that need to be undone with a spanner. When refitting the wheel, make sure that it is correctly aligned in the dropouts and rotating freely.

MAINTENANCE

REPAIRS: ON THE ROAD

Flat tires are a fact of life for every cyclist, so learning to repair a puncture is a necessity. Broken down into eight steps, it's a simple job and will save you money rather than paying a repair shop.

FIXING A FLAT TIRE

Above
Undoing a Presta valve top. Schrader valves are short and fat.

1. Ensure the tire is fully deflated by opening the valve fully and squeezing the remaining air out by hand.
2. Remove one side of the tire from the rim, by prying the flat end of a tire lever under the tire's bead until it comes away from the rim.
3. Lever the tire away from the rim, and use the hooked end to attach the tire lever to a spoke while you wedge a second lever under the bead. Working it up and down, edge the second lever around the rim, pulling the beading out over the edge of the rim as you go. Some tires can fit very tightly on to the wheel, so watch out for fingers.
4. When one side of the tire is free, pull the inner tube out and partially inflate it. This will help you find where the puncture is: listen carefully for hissing air, or run the tube past your cheek so you can feel the air escaping.

Tools required:
- 2 x tire levers
- Patch kit of vulcanizing fluid, crayon, chalk, sandpaper
- Patches and a pump

TIPS FOR AVOIDING PUNCTURES

- Ensure tires are properly inflated to avoid 'pinch' flats, where the tube is pinched against the rim.

- Use puncture-proof tires to minimize the risk of punctures from glass and debris in cities.

- Avoid cycling in the gutter and through potholes.

5. In addition to vulcanizing fluid and patches, a puncture repair kit will often include a crayon, a piece of sandpaper and a piece of chalk. With the crayon, mark the hole on the tube and slightly roughen the area with the sandpaper. Smear a small quantity of 'glue' around the hole, wait for it to dry and then apply the patch. Press it firmly and it should adhere. Once the patch is in place, you may grate a dusting of chalk on it to absorb excess stickiness.

Below
Changing an inner tube on the move.

6. Before replacing the patched tube, check around the inside of the tire for the culprit; you'll know roughly where to look from the position of the hole in the inner tube. Carefully remove any thorns, grit or shards of glass – or you'll soon have another hole to fix.

7. Fit the tube under the tire and, using your thumbs instead of levers as far as possible, reseat the tire onto the rim.

8. Inflate again.

TRICKS AND SHORTCUTS

- Most of the time, a puncture can be repaired without removing the wheel.

- If the hole is hard to find, you may have to submerge the inflated tube in water.

- Carry a spare inner tube and simply replace the punctured tube, which can be patched later in the comfort of your own home.

- CO_2 canisters rapidly inflate tires without having to pump.

- If you have a puncture on a ride but don't have a spare tube or repair kit, try tying a tight knot in the inner tube where the puncture is, or isolating it by using two tight zip ties either side of it.

THE COCKPIT: STEMS, HANDLEBARS, GRIPS & SADDLES

Setting up your bicycle's cockpit is the key to comfortable cycling. It's all highly adjustable.

STEM

The stem connects the handlebars to the bike via the fork's steerer tube and the headset. While the headset is a relatively complex part of the bike and will typically be installed by the manufacturer or your bike shop, the stem can easily be replaced at home. Many modern stems clamp around the fork's steerer tube and are secured by a pair of bolts. (An old-fashioned quill stem slips down inside the steerer tube and is secured by a wedge.) The headset's top cap fits on top of the stem, secured by a hex bolt, but remains a couple of millimeters above the top of the steerer tube.

The stem can be raised in increments of around half a inch by adding spacers (small rings) beneath it. Some stems can also be flipped so that they are angled upward or downwards.

In most cases, handlebars are held between a faceplate and the stem by two or more hex bolts. Where the faceplate is secured by four bolts, remember to tighten the bolts in a diagonal sequence so the handlebar remains straight.

Above top
Take care tightening bolts holding the handlebars in place.

Above
Check that the stem bolts are tight.

Left
Move spacers above or below the stem to raise or lower handlebars.

FITTING HANDLEBAR TAPE

1. Layer the bar tape.

2. Use a second piece around the brake levers.

3. Tape the ends tightly.

4. Bar plugs finish the job.

BARS

Handlebars, whether they're flat, dropped or raised, are an important part of finding the perfect fit. Look at width, rotation and the grips when fine-tuning the cockpit. Installing mountain-bike grips can be a headache; there are several tricks to ensuring they don't move around the bar, but the best guarantee is using lock-on grips, which are secured by a tiny hex bolt. Changing the handlebar tape of a road bike, a surefire way of freshening up a much-used machine,

is an art. There are two techniques: starting from the top or starting from the bottom. Ensure there's an overlap of at least one third of the tape's width all the way along the bar. The cables will typically be hidden away under the tape, in a groove along the handlebars. Finish the job by cutting the end of the tape at an angle and taping over the end with electrical tape. Bar plugs should be wedged in the open ends of the bars.

Below
Brake levers should be in line with the wrist.

SADDLES AND SEATPOSTS

Saddles can be moved backward and forward on rails before being fixed in place with one or usually two hex bolts. They can also be tilted up and down using these bolts. A level saddle is best for most cyclists; with the nose down, too much of your weight will rest on your hands. Ideally, your sit bones should bear most of your weight rather than the front of the saddle.

With the saddle attached to the seatpost, you can insert the post into the seat tube. Obey the minimum inset mark on posts when adjusting the height. The most important thing is to use

the right size seatpost; they're available in several different sizes separated by only a millimeter or two. Prevention is better than cure, and a dab of grease smeared around the post will prevent it from becoming stuck inside the seat tube. Should you find the post stuck inside your frame, you'll need to take emergency action. Clamp the post in a workstand and allow penetrating oil or a lubricant to seep around it. Then, try twisting the frame and post if you can't move it up or down. A sharp tap from a plastic mallet may free the post from rust (steel) or corrosion (aluminum).

Left
Seatposts go up and down, saddles backward and forward.

MAINTENANCE

BRAKES: CALIPER, DISC & V-BRAKES

Stopping a bicycle is the job of the brake. Most bikes have a brake per wheel (although BMXs often have just one), and over the years brakes have evolved from inefficient hub brakes to powerful disc brakes. There are three main types of brake today: calipers and V-brakes for road and hybrid bikes and disc brakes for off-road use. Save yourself some scary moments by setting up each type correctly.

CALIPER BRAKES

Caliper brakes are found on racing bikes and pivot around one point.

V-BRAKES

V-brakes are found on town and basic mountain bikes, and each arm pivots.

DISC BRAKES

Disc brakes are found on mountain bikes and use hydraulic fluid and pistons to push pads against the rotor.

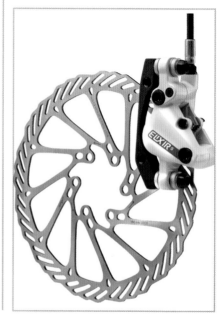

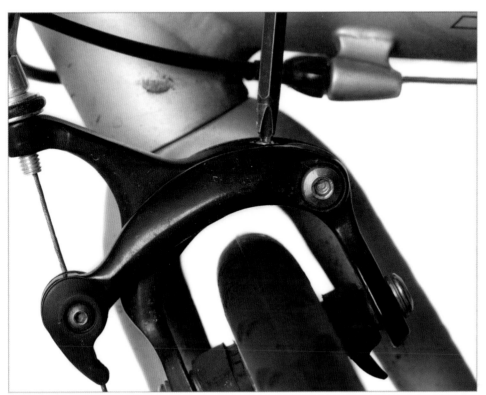

Left
Adjusting the
width of the arms.

CALIPERS

Road-racing bikes have
streamlined caliper brakes
that are attached to the
frame by a single bolt
through the center of the
fork crown or seat stays.
Most modern caliper
brakes' arms pivot around
two points (dual pivot):
the center and the side
opposite the cable stop.

Older designs can pivot
around just one point. The
drawback of caliper brakes
is that the compact design
is no use at all in muddy
conditions or with wider
tires, so their use is limited
to road bikes.

Right
Using an Allen
(hex) key to
secure the
brake pads.

Right
Tuning the
brake cable's
tension using
the barrel
adjuster.

BRAKES: CALIPER, DISC & V-BRAKES

SETTING UP AND TUNING CALIPER BRAKES

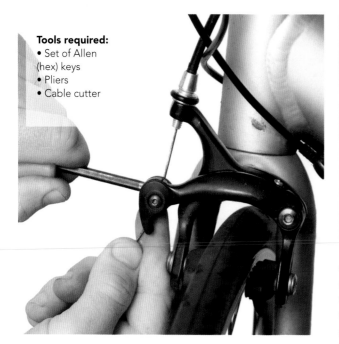

Tools required:
• Set of Allen (hex) keys
• Pliers
• Cable cutter

With caliper brakes, a cable runs from the lever, through a housing (a protective plastic tube) and down one side of the brake unit. Most brakes will be installed by a manufacturer or bike-shop mechanic. When you pull the brake lever, the brake should be fully on before the lever reaches the handlebars. If it is not, the cable can be tensioned by giving a couple of turns to the barrel adjuster where the cable exits the brake lever unit. If that doesn't

take up enough slack, you may need to pull some more cable through the clamp on the caliper itself. Pinch the calipers together, undo the clamping bolt and use pliers to pull a little more cable through, then retighten. Ideally, the brake's power will increase the harder you pull the lever.

The cables are held in place inside the lever unit by an anchor at one end. To change a cable, clip off the end cap at the other

end of the cable, undo the clamp at the caliper, and pull the cable back up through the lever. Ensure the barrel adjuster at the lever is fully tightened. Many new brake cables come pre-greased, but if not, then use a small amount of lube to coat the cable before pulling the lever closed, feeding the cable into the lever unit, down the housing and through the caliper's clamp. Squeeze the brake pads against the rim, pull the cable tight and secure the clamp. Now, loosen the barrel adjuster a couple of turns to move the pads away from the rim; you want a couple of millimeters of clearance on each side.

Left and above
Undo the retaining bolt and, while holding the pads together, pull through the cable before clamping it in place.

Below
An internal view of a road brake and gear lever.

Left
Pads for caliper brakes
are sometimes held
in the brake shoe
by a bolt.

V-BRAKES AND CANTILEVERS

Brake pads will need to be changed more frequently than cables. Examine the grooves along most types of pad; when the pads are almost smooth and the grooves have all but disappeared, it's time for a new pair. Pads are either held directly in the caliper with an Allen bolt, or secured in a shoe, also by an Allen bolt. Simply undo the old pads, slide in new pads and line them up with the rim – they can be moved down the arm and rotated. Older brakes benefit from having the pads 'toed-in' – slightly angled towards the rim at the front of the pad. This isn't necessary with some modern caliper brakes. The pad should make full contact with the rim but not touch the tire, or it will wear a groove in the rubber and damage the tire. If one side is closer to the rim than the other, use the small adjuster bolt on the brake arm to change the spring tension and the degree of pivot.

On non-racing road bikes, the standard brake is now a V-brake or cantilever. Unlike on the caliper brake, V-brake and cantilever arms are bolted directly on to brake bosses on either side of the forks or seat stays. Pulling the cable brings both arms closer together. It's a very simple, easy-to-maintain design that is also found on low- to mid-range mountain bikes, offering greater clearance than a caliper brake can. Cantilever brakes are operated by a center-pull, while modern V-brakes use a single cable that runs between both arms, using a noodle (a curved tube of metal). To release the cable (to remove a wheel for example), unhook the arm at one side and pull the cable through. Don't forget to reattach the cable before starting again.

The principles of changing pads and cables remain the same as for caliper brakes.

Left
Unhooking
the cable of
a V brake.

Left
Brake cables
are anchored
in place in
the lever.

SETTING UP LEVERS

Levers mounted on flat bars (rather than drop bars) should be angled slightly downward, so that when your hand rests on them it is in line with the rest of your arm as it comes down from your shoulder. Having the levers set up horizontally means that your wrist will be bent back slightly to operate the brakes. Forty five degrees is the rule of thumb for the starting position.

MAINTENANCE

BRAKES: CALIPER, DISC & V-BRAKES

Above
Disc-brake rotors are secured by Torx bolts.

Right
Pistons can be pushed back in place with a flat-head screwdriver.

DISC BRAKES

Disc brakes are used predominantly on mountain bikes (and, since 2010, cyclo-cross bikes). Offering greater stopping power and compatibility with wide tires and suspension systems, while performing reliably in the wet, they're an excellent upgrade option. However, they're also significantly more complex than V-brakes and require special mounts (IS or post mount); not all mountain bikes can take discs.

They work in the same way as a motorcycle brake: hydraulic fluid is pushed along a closed system to activate pistons that press two pads against a hub-mounted metal rotor. The larger the rotor, the greater the stopping power. Measured in millimeters, rotors of 160mm to 180mm are suitable for cross-country riding, while rotors of 200mm and above are generally used for downhilling. Torque is

CHANGING WORN BRAKE PADS

unleashed by disc brakes, so mounts, hubs and forks all have to be stronger than they need to be for rim brakes. There's even a case for saying that front disc brakes should be paired with bolt-through axles. Currently, mountain-bike forks are rated up to a certain disc size.

The handlebar unit of a disc brake includes a reservoir filled with hydraulic fluid: Dot 4 or 5.1 in the case of manufacturers Hope and Avid; mineral oil for Shimano and Royal Blood brake fluid for Magura brakes. Each manufacturer has its own design, but symptoms indicate similar problems for each. A spongy lever, that can be pulled all the way to the handlebar, indicates that there is air in the hydraulic system. The solution is to bleed the brakes – emptying and replacing the hydraulic fluid – which is a potentially messy job best done by a bike shop.

Worn brake pads also cause spongy brakes. Unlike rim-brake pads, disc-brake pads are formed from a hard compound that wears out. Each manufacturer's caliper is different, but in most cases the pads are accessible when the wheel is removed and are held in place by a retaining pin and circlip. Remove the pin (sometimes a bolt) and pull the pads out. They will be enclosed in a springy metal frame. Worn pads will be almost level with the metal backing. Replace old pads with new ones, a pair at a time. Before re-inserting, push the pistons inside the caliper back into place with a flathead screwdriver (or tire lever). Guide the pin or bolt through the pads and secure. While changing the pads, check for wear and tear – scoring and gouges – on the rotor, which can accelerate brake pad wear. Also check that the rotor is not warped and that all the bolts are tight. Do not touch the rotors with your fingers (or dirty rags); the oils on your skin will impair the brakes' performance.

Above top
Taking out the retaining pin.

Above
Removing disc-brake pads.

MAINTENANCE

PEDALS, CRANKS & BOTTOM BRACKET

The site of the transfer of power from the legs to the bike – the bottom bracket, cranks and pedals – is a crucial part of the drivetrain. With two sets of bearings and exposure to mud and moisture, there's plenty to maintain.

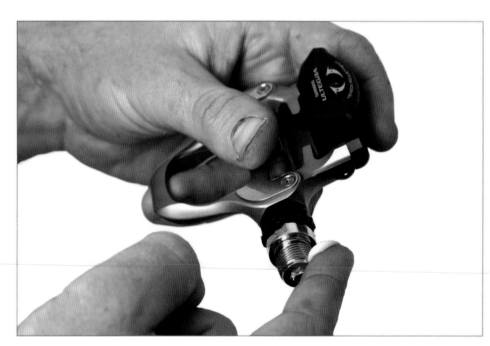

PEDALS

There must be more than a dozen types of pedal, from basic plastic flat pedals to finely engineered clipless pedals that cost more than some bikes. However, all rotate around a set of bearings that will undergo much wear and tear. Generally, the more expensive the pedal, the better and more long-lasting the bearings. You can gauge the health of the pedals' bearings by seeing if there is any play in the pedal, whether it spins smoothly or whether it makes any sounds when you're pedaling.

Pedals can be removed with a pedal wrench, which has an extra-long handle to keep your arm away from the crackset's sharp teeth and give greater leverage. A normal metric wrench will work fine. A few types of pedal need to be undone with an Allen (hex) key. The golden rule when it comes to removing and installing pedals is that the non-drive side (the left as you sit on the bike) has a reverse thread, so you turn it clockwise to loosen and counter-clockwise to tighten. The drive-side pedal has a normal thread, so works the opposite way. If your pedals are stuck in the cranks, drop a little penetrating oil or light lube around the join. Try using a longer wrench or giving it a sharp tap with a hammer.

Many pedals have L (left) and R (right) marked on the spindle. Before installing, dab some grease on the thread to prevent its becoming stuck again.

Above
Grease pedal threads to ensure they don't get stuck.

CRANKS

Cranks connect the pedal to the crankset. Many modern cranks, used with an external bottom bracket, can be removed with just an Allen (hex) key, while others require a special tool, a crank puller, that screws into the threads beneath the bottom bracket's dust cap.

REMOVING CRANKS

Above
1. Undo bolts.
2. Flip out divider.
3. Tap sharply with a mallet if they're stuck.

BOTTOM BRACKET

Despite its cryptic name, the bottom bracket is nothing to be afraid of: it's an axle sitting inside a bearing race. The whole assembly lives in the bottom bracket shell, which usually has a width of 68mm or 73mm. The design has evolved from square taper (the cranks fit on to a square-ended axle) to the current industry standard of an external bottom bracket where the bearings sit outside the bottom bracket shell, allowing a large-diameter bearing race.

External bottom brackets should be fitted by a bike shop, as the surface of the shell may need to be faced (to present a smooth, even surface) for a flush fit with the bottom bracket. Water infiltrating the bearings will quickly ruin the part.

Above top
Use a wrench or Allen (hex) key to undo pedals.

Above
Removing cranks.

MAINTENANCE

THE DRIVETRAIN

DERAILLEURS

The derailleur, invented by Paul de Vivie at the start of the 20th century, 'derails' the chain from one ring to another. The rear derailleur is a parallelogram incorporating two jockey wheels. As the derailleur moves the chain to smaller sprockets, the cage extends to take up the chain's slack. The range of the rear derailleur's movement, as it goes from large to small sprockets, is limited by two screws, usually above each other on the derailleur's body: on many derailleurs these screws are marked H (high) and L (low). The high gear screw ensures the derailleur doesn't move beyond the smallest cog (i.e. outward, so that it doesn't jam between the frame and cassette). The low gear screw ensures the derailleur doesn't move beyond the largest cog and into the wheel's spokes. When the high gear (H) screw is tightened it will move the derailleur inward. When the low gear (L) screw is tightened it will move the derailleur away from the spokes. When adjusting the high gear screw, the chain should be on the largest front chainring and when adjusting the low gear screw it should be on the smallest chainring at the front.

Cassette and chain

Hub and quick release

Derailleur bolt

Derailleur swing-arm

Cable barrel adjuster and clamp

High and low gear adjuster screws

Jockey wheel

Left
Threading a chain through the cage and around the jockey wheels.

CHANGING A GEAR CABLE

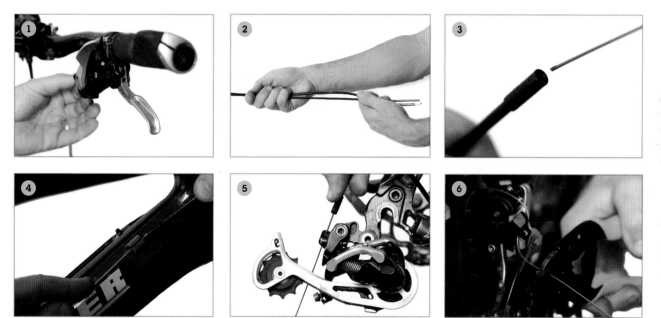

If the rear derailleur is damaged on a ride, or some links of the chain are damaged, a geared bicycle can be turned into a singlespeed. Break the chain, unthread it from the rear derailleur and remove enough links for it to be run around one of the rear cogs and a front chainring (not the largest if there are any hills on the way home). Reconnect the shortened chain and use a ziptie or cable tie to hold the derailleur out of the way or remove it entirely, if possible.

The front derailleur is a relatively crude piece of engineering, being a cage that shunts the chain from one ring to the next. It is fastened around the seat tube with the cable either approaching from underneath or above the unit. The same system of stop screws is used by the front derailleur.

Replacing a cable and tuning the gear shifts is the most likely form of maintenance to be required. With the shifter set to the lowest (easiest) gear, for front derailleur cable changes and in the highest gear for rear derailleur cable changes, thread the cable through the lever and the housing (apply a light lube if you can) along the frame and into the derailleur, where it should be clamped tight. When the limiting screws are correctly set, use the barrel adjuster at the shift lever to tune the gear changes by altering the cable's tension. Listen for when the chain is firmly seated on a cog and when it is rubbing against another or against the derailleur mechanism itself.

Above
1. Remove old cable.
2. Cut length of new cable.
3. Insert new cable in outer casing.
4. Thread through cable guides.
5. Secure in clamp.
6. Trim excess cable and fit cable end.

THE DRIVETRAIN

CASSETTES

The rear cassette – a collection of eight, nine or ten sprockets – sits on the body of the rear wheel's hub. A common system is Shimano's freehub, where the cassette lines up with grooves (known as splines) in the hub's shaft. It's a highly successful design, but as the chain ages it will wear out the cassette, and if you replace one, you have to replace the other. Wear in the freehub itself causes the cassette to slip under load. To change a cassette, remove the wheel and the quick release axle. Using the chainwhip to stop the cassette rotating (wrap it around the second largest sprocket), undo the lockring using the lockring tool. The cassette should slide off the freehub. Give the freehub a wipe before installing the new cassette and then replacing the lockring.

Town bikes, and even some mountain bikes, will sometimes have a hub with internal gears (from three to seven speeds). Since they're less exposed to grit and grime, the maintenance required for these hub gears is minimal, although they will need special attention when they do falter.

Above
An old cassette.

Right
A new cassette.

Tools required:
- Chainwhip
- Lockring remover
- Wrench to fit the lockring

REPLACING A CASSETTE

Left
1. Use a chain whip to undo the cassette.
2. Remove the lockring.
3 & 4. Clean the free-hub body.
5. Line up the grooves when sliding on a new cassette.

CRANKSET

The crankset is one of the more expensive bike parts, so it pays to keep it clean. Cranksets include one, two or three chainrings, in ascending order from the easiest gear (sometimes known as the granny ring) to the largest ring. The combination of the number of teeth on the front ring and the number of teeth on the rear sprocket gives you the size of your gear: 53 x 12, for example, is a very big gear.

Town bikes may have just one ring at the front, while road-racing bikes traditionally have a double crankset. A standard double crankset will have rings with 52 or 53 teeth and often a smaller 39-toothed ring. The new breed of compact cranksets makes mountains more manageable, with 50- and 34-tooth chainrings. You can also find triple on road bikes, with a 52/39/30 combination being a popular choice. However, most triple cranksets are found on mountain bikes, usually with 44/34/22-tooth combinations.

When cranksets wear out, their teeth become curved like shark's teeth, and the shifting deteriorates; the chain may jump off more regularly or slip. You can replace individual rings (steel is heavier but more durable than aluminum) by undoing the hex bolts, or you can replace the entire crankset.

TIP

A good bike shop will be able to advise on a compatible size and style of crankset.

WHEELS

The terminology of bicycle wheels – dishing, truing and lacing – might be intimidating, but as the part of the bike in contact with the ground and all its bumps, they deserve special attention.

Most wheels, whether they're mountain-bike wheels, robust enough to withstand a 20-foot drop, or featherweight road-racing wheels, consist of a hub suspended in the center of a rim by a number of spokes. Modern technology has seen carbon fiber enter the high-end wheel market, but the majority of wheels have an aluminum rim and hub with steel spokes. Day-to-day maintenance need be no more difficult than checking that the wheel is true: spin it in the bike's frame to see if it is warped. Does the rim swerve close to the brake pads or rub against them at any point? Pluck the spokes. Do any

make a lower pitched note than the others? Do they move?

Most well-made wheels will not need any adjustment. If the spokes are of varying tension or the wheel is out of true (not aligned in the dropouts), it is usually the result of a major impact that has dented the rim or bent a spoke. This may need a full rebuild with a new rim. In many ways wheel rebuilding is harder than building a wheel from scratch.

The strongest wheels tend to be handbuilt by experts using high-end hubs (such as those by Phil Woods, and Shimano also make excellent hubs), double or triple-butted stainless steel spokes and good quality rims. The more spokes a wheel has, the stronger it will be (depending on its intended use).

Above right
Using a spoke key to tune a wheel.

Left
A professional wheel-building jig.

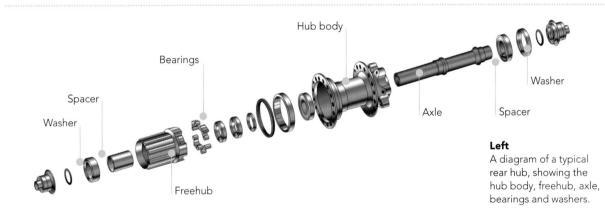

Hub body

Bearings

Spacer

Washer

Freehub

Axle

Washer

Spacer

Left
A diagram of a typical rear hub, showing the hub body, freehub, axle, bearings and washers.

The rear wheel needs to be stronger than the front, since it has to bear more weight and will be dished (meaning that, viewed from behind, the rear wheel looks like a dish – curved on the left and straight on the right to accommodate the gears). Dishing is necessary for the rear wheel, since the cassette is on one side of the hub yet the rim still needs to be centered in the frame; so the spokes on the right side of the hub are tighter than those on the rider's left, pulling the wheel's rim to the right.

Certain factory-built wheels, such as Mavic's racing wheels for road and mountain bikes, will need to be sent back to the manufacturer for servicing, but in most cases a slightly buckled wheel – one that rubs against the brake pads or wobbles slightly when spun – can be cured at home, although using a local wheel-builder is the foolproof option.

TRUING A WHEEL

To true your own wheels, you'll need a spoke key, which is a small wrench with a slot that fits around the spoke nipple where it protrudes from the rim.

Turn the bike upside down (unless you have your own truing stand in which the wheel can be placed) and remove the tire and inner tube so you can see clearly what's happening to the rim. Where the wheel is out of true, the spokes on the opposite side of the wheel need to be tightened, a quarter turn at a time.

If you are unsure, the best advice is to take the wheel to be repaired at a shop as an inexperienced person is likely to make things worse rather than better.

Tools required:
- Spoke key
- Small flathead screwdriver or spoke nipple driver if building your own wheels
- Rim tape and masking tape
- Truing stand (a bike turned upside down will suffice)

Right
A sealed cartridge bearing.

SUSPENSION

Suspension is a standard feature on modern mountain bikes, with even budget bikes getting a suspension fork at the front. Bikes further up the price scale may have rear suspension too, in its various incarnations. But this technology is no more than extra weight if it is not set up for each rider or carefully maintained for optimum performance.

Bicycle suspension works in the same way a motorbike's does: a metal coil or air-filled shock absorber dampens the force of jolts from the ground. Coil-sprung units tend to weigh more than air shocks but typically offer a plusher ride. The adjustability of modern technology means that suspension on a mountain bike can be made firmer or softer just by adding or losing air from the shock, or by using a spring of a different weight.

Front and rear suspension can be locked out with the flick of a lever when you don't want the shock to move at all, and the rebound rate, the speed at which the fork or rear shock bounces back to its original position after an impact, can be sped up or slowed down. Preload is the amount of force applied to the suspension before you sit on it; increasing preload will stiffen the suspension.

Compression damping is where a valve is used to control the rate at which the shock compresses. These adjustments can often be made using a dial on top of the fork, under its leg or on a rear shock, but they are dependent on the correct sag being set for the shock.

When servicing a suspension fork, each manufacturer will specify the appropriate weight and volume of oil required for each model in the user manual. If you are unsure, take the fork to a bike shop who will do the job. Servicing regimes, which vary in frequency according to the model, may include checking and replacing the seals, damper and spring as well as replacing the oil.

Tools required for servicing a fork include:
- Allen (hex) keys (often 1.5mm, 2mm, 2.5mm and 5mm)
- Wrenches (10mm for removing the fork legs)
- A plastic mallet and length of wood dowel
- Pliers
- Appropriate suspension oil and grease

Right
A Rock Shox suspension fork.

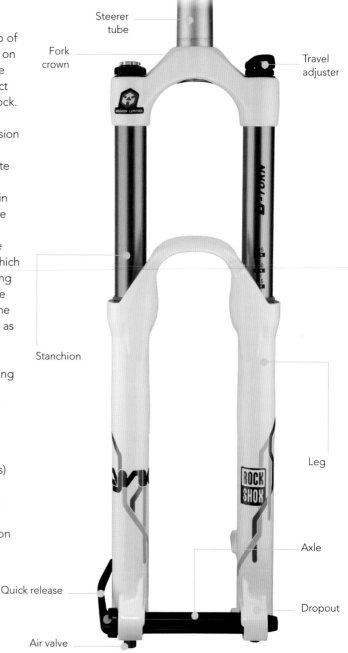

Steerer tube

Fork crown

Travel adjuster

Stanchion

Leg

Quick release

Axle

Dropout

Air valve

Below bottom
Air pressure affects your fork's performance. Lighter riders will use lower pressures than heavier riders, who will need a higher pressure in the air chamber to control the fork's travel.

Below
Use a zip tie to measure sag.

SETTING SAG

Sag is the amount a shock sinks into its travel when you're sitting still on the bike. Think of it as your default setting when riding along. Too much sag, and not only will you be inefficient but your shock will bottom out (hit the maximum extent of its travel); too little and you'll be underusing the fork's suspension travel and missing its full potential. You may also be bouncing around a bit more than necessary.

To set sag, you'll need a tape measure or ruler, a shock pump and a zip tie. Sag is reduced by adding air to the fork's air chamber. To increase sag, you need to let air out – shock pumps have a button you press to let out a few psi at a time. The valve is under one of the fork legs. Many manufacturers will have a recommended sag level for their product, depending on rider weight ranges (often printed on the fork or in the manual).

However, these can be inaccurate (typically allowing too little sag) and there is no substitute for working it out yourself.

Dial out all preload and compression damping from the fork. Note the maximum length of the travel (measured by the manufacturer in millimeters).

Tie a zip tie around the base of the stanchion where it meets the seal. Gently lower yourself on to the bike (wearing and carrying all the gear you would normally).

As the fork compresses, it will move the zip tie up the fork's stanchion. Get off the bike, and where the zip tie has stopped is the current sag. The same process works for setting the sag of a rear suspension unit.

MAINTENANCE

SUSPENSION

REAR SUSPENSION

There are numerous competing designs for rear suspension, and it can be a very confusing marketplace, with different manufacturers all claiming their system is the best. What is true today is that most rear suspension is pretty good, certainly from the middle of the market up. Ultimately, the choice should come down to what system performs best for you on a test ride. At a very basic level, the greatest distinction is probably between single-pivot designs, where the suspension pivots around a single point, and multi-link designs, such as

Specialized's patented four-bar Horst link design. Single pivot designs tend to be less sophisticated and have fewer moving parts (sometimes just a swing arm) so there is less to go wrong.

Multi-linkage designs are often better at tracking the ground and are less inclined to suffer from rider-induced bob (bounce). However, technology is moving so fast, with virtual pivot points and compression damping in the shock itself, that the moment you identify the best or the worst systems at the time, the situation has already moved on.

Right
A Rock Shox
coil rear shock.

Compression adjuster

Eyelet

Shock body

Reservoir

Spring

Rebound adjuster

Eyelet

TIP

Do not lubricate sticking fork stanchions or shock with grease or a spray like WD-40. It will ruin them. Likewise, don't wash forks or shocks with detergent or degreaser; it will strip the lubricating oil and ruin the unit. Instead, it may be time to service the fork or shock or check the oil levels inside, topping up with the manufacturer-approved fork oil in order not to void the warranty.

MAINTENANCE

The servicing routine of each type of suspension unit will be outlined in the user manual; some are more demanding than others, so if you're not inclined toward tinkering with oil and damping mechanisms, select one of the less delicate forks or shocks. As a basic routine, be sure to wipe the stanchions and shaft after each ride to stop water or dirt working its way under the seal.

Depending on the model of fork, you can pry the seals up and wipe thoroughly underneath. A foam ring beneath the seals should be soaked in special oil (each manufacturer will sell its own), ensuring that the stanchions are lubed. You can remove the fork's lowers by undoing the bolts at the foot of the fork legs, although you'll need to refer to each manufacturer's user manual.

To check for wear, listen for unusual sounds: a knocking sound suggests worn bushings. Hold the brake on and rock the bike – if there's a knocking sound but no movement in the headset it may be the fork bushings. To replace bushings and seals follow the manufacturer's instructions for the specific model of fork or shock.

GUIDE TO JOBS

Bicycle maintenance is a learning process involving trial and error. But following the manufacturer's own instructions and using the correct tools will cut out many unecessary mistakes. Jobs can be categorized according to complexity, with the most complex requiring special tools and a degree of confidence. If you have a good relationship with your local bike shop, don't be afraid to telephone them for advice mid-job.

Basic:
• Repairing a puncture
• Changing brake pads
• Changing brake cables
• Replacing a chain

Intermediate:
• Replacing gear cables
• Replacing a cassette
• Installing a front or rear derailleur
• Truing a wheel
• Servicing a hub
• Servicing a pedal
• Bleeding a disc brake

Complex:
• Installing and replacing the bottom bracket
• Installing or replacing a headset
• Building a wheel
• Servicing suspension units

Above
A four-bar linkage design.

TIP

Wear and tear on the shock or the fork is revealed by scratches on the fork's stanchions and the shock's shaft. Oil inside a fork should be checked, topped up or changed according to the manufacturer's requirements.

GLOSSARY

Cycling has its own vocabulary and terminology, some of which are used in other sporting activities and some of which are purely cycling specific. Here is an A to Z of some useful terms:

Aerobic
Oxygen demands by the body that can be met during sustained exercise. Anaerobic exercise pushes the body to demand more oxygen than can be provided by respiration

Air
Getting both wheels off the ground when mountain biking

Allen key (also Hex key)
A hexagonal wrench that slots inside a matching bolt

Apex
The middle of a curve or corner, on the road or on an off-road trail

Audax
A long, organized group ride ridden at a steady pace, meeting checkpoints. Also known as a randonnée in France

Barrel adjuster
A cylindrical, threaded cable stop, located at the lever, that tensions or slackens brake or gear cables

Bead
The wire or plastic edge of a tire that tucks inside the rim

Berm
Banked corner you can ride up, enabling you to maintain speed through the bend

Bonk (also to blow up)
When a rider's body runs out of fuel, resulting in a sudden loss of energy, a feeling of weakness in the legs, and a failure to keep pace

Bottom bracket
A watertight housing in the frame, through which the spindle connecting the cranks is allowed to rotate as the rider pedals

Boss
Small posts on the rear stays and front forks around which caliper and V-brake arms pivot

Braze-ons
Features, such as bottle mounts and rack mounts, brazed on to a metal bicycle frame

Break
A group of racing cyclists that has escaped the main peloton

Bunch (also Peloton)
Collective name for a pack of racing cyclists

Cadence
Pedal revolutions per minute

Carbs
Carbohydrates, a cyclist's key source of energy

Cassette
Part of the drivetrain, located on the rear wheel, comprising an assortment of cogs of increasing size, over which the chain runs

Century
A 100-mile bike ride

Chain suck
Afflicting mountain bikers more than road riders, when the chain becomes wedged between the chain stay and the chainring

Chain stay
Part of the bike frame, it is the tube that connects the rear dropout to the bottom bracket, to which the chain runs parallel

Clean
To ride a section of trail without putting a foot down (dabbing)

Cleat
The small metal or plastic attachment to the sole of a cycling shoe that slots into a clipless pedal

Clipless pedals
Pedals with an internal mechanism rather than clips and straps, allowing the rider to lock into the pedals by way of a cleat on the sole of the cycling shoe

Clips and straps
A method of securing the foot to the pedal without the necessity of specially adapted shoes

Components
All the parts attached to the bicycle frame, such as the handlebars, wheels and brakes

Crank
The arm that connects the pedals to the bottom bracket and axle

Damping (see also Rebound damping)
The way in which vibration is reduced, either by using suspension units, polymer inserts or bumpers

Derailleur
A front derailleur 'derails' the chain from one chainring and guides it to a larger or smaller chainring. A rear derailleur shifts the chain from cog to cog along the cassette

DH
Common abbreviation of downhill, referring to a type of mountain bike or mountain bike race

Discs
Typically, hydraulic-powered brakes for mountain bikes, which use brake fluid to close pistons and brake pads on either side of a rotor

Draft
To ride close behind another rider to save energy

Dropout
The n-shaped slot in the frame into which the wheel's axle is located

Drop
A very steep incline (of any length or height) down which mountain bikers can ride or jump off

Drops
The lower portion of a racing bike's curved handlebars

Fixie
A fixed-wheel bike on which the rear wheel has no freewheel, so freewheeling is impossible; as the wheel turns so must your legs

Flat
A puncture

Flex
When the frame bends or twists very slightly as maximum power is applied

Forks
Two legs either side of the front wheel, which hold the wheel in place and connect it, through the frame, to the handlebars – can be rigid on a road bike or with suspension on a mountain bike

Freeride, freerider
An extreme branch of mountain biking featuring man-made stunts and big air (see Air)

Freewheel, Freehub (noun)
The system by which a cassette sits on a hub and can spin freely in one direction, while engaging to transfer power from the pedal to the wheel, via the chain, in the other

Freewheel (verb)
To coast along without pedaling

Friction shifting
An old-fashioned, pre-indexing gear-changing system

FS
Common abbreviation of full (or dual) suspension, referring to a mountain bike that has suspension for the front and rear wheels

Gnarly
Semi-ironic description of a technically difficult trail section

Gradient
The steepness of a slope

Grand Tours
The three most important stage races in the calendar: the Tour de France, the Vuelta a España and the Giro d'Italia

Granny gear/ring
The smallest, easiest-to-turn front chainring, used for climbs

Hack bike (also beater)
An inexpensive and expendable bike used for errands or winter rides

Hardtail
A mountain bike without rear suspension

Headset
The bearing assembly at the top and base of the head tube, through which the forks connect to the handlebars, allowing the forks to rotate within the frame

Hike-a-bike
Sections of impassable trail along which a mountain bike has to be pushed or carried

Hub
The core of the wheel, from which spokes suspend the rim

Hybrid
A practical bike that shares features of road bikes (such as smooth tires) and mountain bikes (such as flat handlebars)

Indexed
When changing gears, each gear is located with a 'click', making shifting more accurate

Knobby
The protruding tread on tires for extra grip off road

Line
The preferred route through a section of off-road trail

Loop
A ride that starts and finishes at the same point

Moto-style
Having the front brake lever on the right and rear brake lever on the left, as is usual in the UK but the opposite of the USA

Mountain bike (MTB)
Accepted term for an off-road bike known as VTT in France (vélo tout terrain, literally all-terrain bike)

Off camber
A piece of trail or road, often curving as it follows the contour of a hill, that slopes to the side, away from the direction in which you wish to go – the opposite of a berm

Panniers
Luggage-carrying bags supported by a bicycle rack

Pedals
Platforms for the feet, which are available in numerous styles but all with one thing in common: the left pedal (non-drive side) screws into the crank with a reverse thread

Peloton (also Bunch)
A large, tightly-packed group of racing cyclists

Pinch flat
A puncture caused by pinching the inner tube between the rim and a hard object, usually resembling a snake bite, with two parallel holes

PSI
Pounds per square inch – a measure of pressure useful when inflating a tire or adjusting a shock absorber

QR
Common abbreviation for a quick release, a lever that allows wheels and seatposts to be removed speedily

Ratio
The number of teeth on a front chainring multiplied by the number of teeth on one of the rear cogs, e.g. 53 x 11

Rebound damping
A crucial part of suspension technology controlling the time it takes for the suspension to reset between hits

Rim
The outer hoop of a wheel

Saddle
On which a cyclist sits – can cause saddle soreness

Sealed bearings
Bearings housed in a sealed cartridge, which need to be replaced as a unit rather than individually

Slicks
Smooth tires

SPDs (sometimes referred to as 'spuds')
Stands for Shimano Pedaling Dynamics – a clipless pedal design

Spin
To turn the pedals rapidly rather than pushing hard

Stays
The rear triangle of a bike frame

Technical
A difficult and challenging section of trail to negotiate

Teeth
The raised notches around the edge a chainring or cog that catch and locate in the chain, the number of which determines the size of the gear

UCI
The Union Cycliste Internationale (UCI) is the governing body for a number of professional races, including the World Championships in all disciplines, but it doesn't control many of the largest, including the Olympics and the Grand Tours. Points accrued at UCI-sanctioned events go toward end-of-year rankings; however, many of the best known pro riders focus on their own or their team's targets, which usually include the Grand Tours. Many countries, and indeed individual states, also stage national or state championships

Valve
Two types of inner tube are available: Presta, tall and thin, and Schrader, short and fat. Most bikes these days have Presta valves

Wheel suck
A cyclist that rides in the slipstream of another but doesn't take a turn on the front

Zone
The desired state in which to be when riding – 'in the zone'

THE CYCLING BIBLE

LINKS

CHAPTER 1
THE BIKE

www.specialized.com
Comprehensive line of bicycles
and gear

www.ifbikes.com
Custom builder of road and
mountain bikes

www.nicolai.com
German-made mountain bikes

www.pegoretticicli.com
Italian handbuilder

www.brooksengland.com
British saddle maker

www.sram.com
Component manufacturer

www.shimano.com
Clipless pedal and component
manufacturer

www.brompton.co.uk
Folding bikes

www.pashley.co.uk
British-style town bikes

www.velorbis.com
Danish-style town bikes

www.islabikes.co.uk
Children's bikes specialist

www.likeabike.co.uk
Balance bikes for children

www.burley.com
Bike trailers for children

www.wethepeoplebmx.de
BMX specialists

www.larryvsharry.com
Danish cargo bikes

www.thorncycles.co.uk
Touring bike and tandem bikes

www.condorcycles.com
London-based shop with
own-brand performance road
bikes

www.kryptonitelock.com
Secure locks for bikes

CHAPTER 2
THE GEAR

www.assos.com
Road biking racewear

www.rapha.cc
High-end cyclewear

www.sugoi.com
Mountain biking clothing,
especially good for women

www.gorebikewear.com
Bikewear, including
waterproof gear

www.finisterreuk.com
Merino wool base layers

www.giro.com
Bike helmets

www.oakley.com
Eyewear for cyclists

www.deuter.com
Backpacks and hydration packs
for cyclists

www.crumpler.com
Cycle bags for commuters

www.dainese.com
Body armor for mountain
bikers

www.knog.com.au
Bike lights for commuters

www.lupine.de
Bike lights for mountain bikers

www.garmin.com
GPS navigation specialists also
making bike computers

CHAPTER 3
TECHNIQUES
& SAFETY

www.bikeability.org.uk
UK-based cycle instruction

www.lcc.org.uk
London Cycle Campaign,
the British capital's influential
advocacy group

www.bikenewyork.org
New York advocacy group

www.bikeleague.org
League of American Bicyclists

www.bv.com.au
Bicycle Victoria, Australian
advocacy group

www.bicyclensw.org.au
Bicycle New South Wales,
Australian advocacy group

www.imba.com
International Mountain
Bicycling Association, a non-
profit organization looking after
trail access and management
– 'bringing out the best in
mountain biking'

CHAPTER 4
FITNESS & NUTRITION

www.clifbar.com
US-made energy bars and gels

www.scienceinsport.com
British-made energy drinks, gels and bars

www.oobafit.com
Custom fitness programs online

www.trainright.com
Cycle-specific training from Lance Armstrong's coach

CHAPTER 5
RACING

www.letour.fr
Tour de France official website

www.lavuelta.com
Vuelta a España official website

www.uciprotour.com
Information on the road season's major race series

www.uci.ch
Governing body of world cycle sport, and organizer of events in all disciplines, including the Mountain Bike World Cup and World Championships

CHAPTER 6
DESTINATIONS

www.sustrans.org.uk
British organization creating national cycle routes

www.ctc.org.uk
National cyclists' organization in the UK

www.adventurecycling.org
Adventure Cycling Association plots routes across America

http://nzbybike.com
Information on Cycleways, Great Rides, Rail Trails and mountain bike rides across New Zealand

www.paradise-press.co.nz
Pedallers' Paradise – source of all knowledge when it comes to cycle touring in New Zealand

www.aevv-egwa.org
European Greenways Association, listing all greenways in Europe

www.ecf.com
The European Cycling Federation, home of the EuroVelo mapping project

www.blackburndesign.com
Sturdy racks for touring

www.ortlieb.de
German-designed waterproof panniers

CHAPTER 7
MAINTENANCE

www.pedros.com
Lubes and tools

www.parktool.com
Manufacturer of all cycle-specific tools, the website also contains a useful instructional section

www.rockshox.com
Leading manufacturer of suspension shocks and forks with user manuals online

www.sheldonbrown.com
US bicycle mechanic guru

THE CYCLING BIBLE

LINKS

FURTHER READING

The Yellow Jersey Companion to the Tour de France
Edited by Les Woodland,
Yellow Jersey Press

Presented alphabetically, from Djamolidine Abdoujaparov, a Russian sprinter nicknamed 'The Tashkent Terror' because of his fearless maneuvers in a 50-mph bunch sprint, to Joop Zoetemelk, a solid Dutch rider who had the misfortune to have been competing during Eddy Merkx's reign, a more accessible and enjoyable companion to the Tour cannot be imagined. As well as the riders, their lives fleshed out with personal anecdotes, the book explains details such as who wears the maillot jaune and who carries the lanterne rouge.

The Rider
Tim Krabbé,
Bloomsbury Publishing

The Rider is the story of one race, the 1977 edition of the Tour de Mont Aigoual, a 137-km (85-mile) dash through the Cévennes, for amateurs. It captures perfectly the stillness and introspection that are inescapable when grinding out the miles. Written by the Dutch author of The Vanishing, The Rider is the best piece of fiction writing about cycling.

The Escape Artist
Matt Seaton,
Fourth Estate

Seaton's moving account of his amateur racing career set against his wife's battle against cancer is an insight into what drives enthusiasts to get up at 6 a.m. for a three-hour bike ride in the cold and rain.

Rough Ride
Paul Kimmage,
Yellow Jersey Press

Now a sports journalist, Kimmage's first-hand account of the hard life of a domestique in the pro peloton includes candid accounts of doping.

The Great Road Climbs of the Southern Alps and The Great Road Climbs of the Pyrénées
Graeme Fife,
Rapha Racing

These collectable guides to the Tour de France's most famous climbs feature evocative photography alongside Graeme Fife's expert writing. Plenty of historical detail is included in these authoritative texts.

Road Bike Maintenance and Mountain Bike Maintenance
Guy Andrews,
FalconGuides

Comprehensive maintenance guides for both road and mountain bikes.

MAGAZINES & WEBSITES

www.bicycling.com
US print and online cycling magazine

www.cyclingweekly.co.uk
British print and online cycling magazine

www.cyclingnews.com
Race results and features

http://english.gazzetta.it
Online English version of Italian sports newspaper *La Gazzetta dello Sport*

www.velonews.com
Journal of competitive cycling

www.singletrackworld.com
British mountain biking magazine and website

www.quickrelease.tv
Cycle advocacy and news

www.copenhagenize.com
Danish cycle culture website

www.theridejournal.com
An occasional, much sought-after cycling journal, published in Britain

www.bicyclingaustralia.com
Australian road and mountain biking magazines.

www.australiancyclist.com.au
Australian cycling magazine

www.bikeradar.com
Online home of several British cycling magazines

www.nzmtbr.co.nz
New Zealand's leading mountain biking magazine

www.nsmb.com
Freeride mountain biking online magazine from Canada

www.dirtragmag.com
Off-beat magazine about offroad riding

INDEX

THE CYCLING BIBLE

INDEX

INDEX

THE CYCLING BIBLE

INDEX